Cultivating Citizens

APPLICATIONS OF POLITICAL THEORY

Series Editors: Harvey Mansfield, Harvard University, and Daniel J. Mahoney, Assumption College

This series encourages analysis of the applications of political theory to various domains of thought and action. Such analysis will include works on political thought and literature, statesmanship, American political thought, and contemporary political theory. The editors also anticipate and welcome examinations of the place of religion in public life and commentary on classic works of political philosophy.

Cultivating Citizens

Soulcraft and Citizenship in Contemporary America

Edited by
Dwight D. Allman and Michael D. Beaty

LEXINGTON BOOKS
Lanham • Boulder • New York • Oxford

LEXINGTON BOOKS

Published in the United States of America
by Lexington Books
A Member of the Rowman & Littlefield Publishing Group
4720 Boston Way, Lanham, Maryland 20706

PO Box 317
Oxford
OX2 9RU, UK

British Library Cataloguing in Publication Information Available

Library of Congress Cataloging-in-Publication Data

Cultivating citizens : soulcraft and citizenship in contemporary America / edited by
Dwight D. Allman and Michael D. Beaty.
     p. cm.—(Applications of political theory)
   Includes bibliographical references and index.
   ISBN 0-7391-0452-7 (hc : alk. paper)—ISBN 0-7391-0453-5 (paper : alk. paper)
   1. Citizenship. 2. Ethics. 3. Civics. 4. Democracy—United States.
5. Theological virtues. 6. Epicureans (Greek philosophy) 7. Political science—
Philosophy. I. Allman, Dwight D., 1957– II. Beaty, Michael D. III. Series.

JK1759 .C85 2002
323.6—dc21   2002009874

Printed in the United States of America

♾™ The paper used in this publication meets the minimum requirements of
American National Standard for Information Sciences—Permanence of Paper
for Printed Library Materials, ANSI/NISO Z39.48-1992.

Contents

Acknowledgments

This volume is an outgrowth of the 1999 Pruit Memorial Symposium at Baylor University. The editors would especially like to thank Mr. and Mrs. Lev H. Prichard and to pay tribute to the late Mrs. Helen Pruit Matthews. Their generous support of Baylor University has made possible this annual event that honors Helen Pruit Matthews and her brothers, Lee Tinkle Pruit and William Wall Pruit. We would also like to thank Dr. Herbert H. Reynolds, chancellor and president emeritus of Baylor University, for his gracious assistance and Dr. and Mrs. Howard Dudgeon for a munificent contribution that enabled us to bring to the Pruit Symposium an unprecedented gathering of prominent scholars. President Robert B. Sloan and Provost Donald D. Schmeltekopf are likewise due an offering of thanks for their unflagging support of our ambition to stage such a conference. A number of individuals have provided their essential skills and hard work in readying this manuscript for publication. We are obliged to recognize, in particular, John Basie and Sara Harper, interns for the Institute of Faith and Learning, and Jenice Langston, administrative assistant in the Department of Political Science, whose many labors and cheerful assistance have made this collection a much better book. Dustin Stewart, an M.A. candidate in the Department of English, prepared the index. For the remaining defects, we alone take responsibility.

Introduction

Citizenship and Soulcraft in Contemporary America

Dwight D. Allman

Entangled in the American tradition of popular government are two prevalent ways of thinking about the matter of citizenship. The one, identified with modern liberalism, concerns itself with rights and liberties, especially with respect to claims on private property, which government is meant to secure for each citizen. The other, usually identified with classical republicanism, treats as primary the problem of forming citizens suited to the demands of freedom and self-governance, addressing the other questions of our common political life always with an eye to this highest priority.

With his famous argument in *Federalist* 10, which takes "the first object of government" to be "the protection of different and unequal faculties of acquiring property," James Madison gives expression to the former conception.[1] Jefferson's quarrel with Hamilton and those who urged a rapid industrialization of the young nation exemplifies the latter. Jefferson defended his preference for an agrarian order largely in terms of the civic character of the new republic, fearing that an economy based principally on manufacturing would desolate the rural seedbed of civic virtue: "Cultivators of the earth are the most valuable citizens. They are the most vigorous, the most independent, the most virtuous, and they are tied to their country and wedded to its liberty and interests by the most lasting bands."[2]

In the course of America's experiment with self-government, the tendency to conceive of citizenship as a collection of publicly guaranteed rights and freedoms—often reformulated in recent history into a language of entitlements—in support of the individual's private pursuit of a material well-being has generally prevailed. Even the quest for a morally substantive, deontological theory of justice—a dominant concern of liberal political philosophy for much of the last half-century—has generally sought to define the just state in structural and procedural terms, which translate citizenship into an finite equation of institutionally embedded rights and liberties. For John Rawls in *A Theory of Justice*, citizenship thus entails no specific duties. The individual owes duties either to all persons qua persons or to none at all. Acts of benevolence, heroism, or self-sacrifice may be vital to civic life, but the condition of citizenship generates as such no obligation to perform them.[3]

Recently, however, the age-old problem of cultivating citizens has attained new prominence. Contemporary political theory has increasingly focused attention on the qualities and capacities that the exercise of self-government, not to mention the practice of justice, necessarily presumes. In the past decade, what some call "citizenship theory" has emerged out of a roaring debate between the partisans of a rights-based, self-directing individualism and the partisans of a civic existence grounded in the formative experience of community. These rivals nevertheless share a common presupposition: "What the state needs from the citizenry cannot be secured by coercion, but only [through] cooperation and self-restraint in the exercise of private power."[4] At the same time, social scientists from many disciplines find themselves increasingly preoccupied with questions about current levels of civic engagement and the vitality of contemporary civil society. "Bowling Alone," a now-famous article published in 1995 by Harvard political scientist Robert Putnam, provided the catalyst for a debate that has consumed the social sciences. Also important to the rehabilitation of the question of citizenship, especially as a question of broad, public interest, has been a palpable sense among many Americans that the "moral fabric" of society is in evident disrepair.[5] The 1990s, moreover, saw the creation of multiple public forums, commissions, councils and other organizations to address a perceived deficit of citizenship in American public life.[6]

A nationwide outpouring of patriotic sentiment in reaction to events of September 11 raises the prospect of latent reserves of civic spiritedness and commitment that belie the portrait of a society in which citizenship has lost its moral valence. For the present, however, it remains at best unclear whether this reaction amounts to a freshly aroused civic identity and revitalized civic energies or merely an opportunity (albeit unparalleled) for channeling deeply felt and collectively experienced emotions into a reconstructed ethic of public life. The poignancy of such an experience, however broadly felt, is no guarantee that relevant civic and social practices will result. As William Galston has observed, "The terrible events of September 11, and their aftermath, have created a surge of patriotism and a new sense of connection between young Americans and their public institutions. For many, it is their first experience of public service as meaningful; of national leaders, local leaders, police officers, firemen, and their fellow citizens as virtuous, even heroic. But no civic invisible hand guarantees that these effects will endure."[7] This much at least seems clear: The issues of civic virtue, public service, personal sacrifice, and responsibility have become vital questions for Americans again. Suddenly it appears, moreover, that certain capacities—courage, for example—might be prerequisite for everyday existence. At the same time, the idea of broad obligations and duties, tying one to relations, neighbors, and fellow citizens and deriving from one's participation in and interconnection to a neighborhood, a community, and a nation seems to be enjoying new currency. The stirring examples of heroism and sacrifice by police and firefighters "in the line of duty," or by regular citizens, who as passengers on an airplane appear to have taken up readily the fight against the perpetrators of terror, have made it almost impossible to hold in focus that peculiarly modern conception, given seminal expression by Hobbes, of society as merely a constellation of individual pursuits, desires, and ambitions with no claims on one's allegiance or support beyond the tight horizons of a calculable, material self-interest.

This volume brings together a set of diverse essays that reflect variously and in multiply connected ways on the matter of citizenship, some approaching their topic primarily as a historical inquiry and others essentially as a contemporary reflection on our present day. The volume has therefore been divided into two broad categories, "Cultivating Citizens as a Historical Problem" and "Cultivating Citizens as a Contemporary Problem." However, those contributors who approach this question through the lens of history do so always with one eye on the present, while those who take up the matter as a contemporary issue do not thereby foreswear historical reflection or analysis. In brief, all of them take the question of cultivating democratic citizens as a guiding concern that the present moment calls forcefully to our attention. The extraordinary events that have occurred since this volume and its essays were first conceived would seem, if anything, to cast a more timely, perhaps even urgent, light on its subject matter. If the tragedy of 9/11 has somehow raised the question of the meaning and import of citizenship in contemporary America with new and singular force, if among the human devastation and ruin an opportunity for fresh reflection on the civic order suddenly beckons us, the rich conversation about citizenship that arises from these pages should recommend itself all the more compellingly. It is a primary task of this introduction to trace the outlines and mark the significant intersections of the conversation contained within.

CULTIVATING CITIZENS AS A HISTORICAL PROBLEM

Walter Nicgorski, in the first of four chronologically ordered essays concerned with the history of the question of cultivating citizens, frames his weighty reflection on Cicero's vigorous engagement with Epicureanism at the end of Rome's republican era with an account of Thomas Jefferson's considerable admiration for Epicureanism and the corresponding antipathy he directed toward Cicero. Through Jefferson, Nicgorski brings to bear on contemporary America questions about the civic influence and implications of Epicureanism first posed by Cicero (106–43 B.C.) to his fellow Romans. Jefferson found in Epicureanism's identification of the *supreme good* with "ease of body and tranquility of mind" the enlightened conception of a far-sighted self-interest upon which he believed an improved, modern species of politics should properly rest. He viewed the atomistic and materialistic cosmology by which the Epicureans defined the natural order as the most consistent of the ancient accounts with the superior science of modernity. Jefferson, however, determined that the resources of Epicureanism, while constituting the greatest contribution of the Greeks to moral philosophy, were inadequate to the needs of republican government. As Nicgorski explains, Jefferson doubted that the elevated hedonism modeled by Epicurus would ultimately direct the practice of Epicureanism when translated into a public philosophy. Jefferson thus sought to temper the powerful attraction of bodily comforts and pleasures, which he feared the Epicurean conception of happiness as a strictly material phenomenon would only reinforce, with a teaching drawn at least partly from the Christian Gospels about the obligation to others that each person bears.

   Jefferson's enthusiasm for Epicureanism led him to dismiss Cicero as a commentator on, and critic of, that school of philosophy, which Cicero knew first hand, even though Jefferson's own qualms about the operation of the Epicurean teaching on a republican polity and citizenry paralleled in significant ways the very critique advanced by Cicero. Nicgorski emphasizes that the question of citizenship arises most prominently for Cicero in relation to his critical engagement with Epicureanism, whose doctrines were championed by a distinguished and increasingly large following in Cicero's Rome. With his intricate account, Nicgorski catalogues two classes of criticism that structure Cicero's critique of Epicureanism: one *descriptive,* the other *normative.* On the descriptive level, Nicgorski finds in Cicero the objection that Epicureanism as a moral doctrine cannot in important ways account for the practice of many of its most celebrated adherents, especially those who have distinguished themselves through service to and sacrifice for their community. Cicero fears, moreover, that as a normative teaching Epicureanism will dampen the natural appeal of vital goods and virtues not associated with bodily pleasure and diminish the cultural standing of exemplary lives and deeds whose significance cannot be given by an Epicurean calculus. On the same plane, Cicero worries that the importance assigned to the state of tranquility (an emphasis that serves to differentiate from common hedonism the Epicurean conception of a life organized around bodily satisfactions) will likely deflect or deflate the energy and spirit that might otherwise be invested in civic affairs and the active life of politics. Nicgorski traces this objection directly to Cicero's own involvements with capable men such as his lifelong friend Atticus, who as a good Epicurean chose to live outside the arena of public life, thereby depriving his city and fellow citizens of exceptional talents and potential leadership. In sum, Nicgorski stresses that it was the social and civic deficiencies rather than the ultimate truth-value of Epicureanism that primarily engendered Cicero's opposition—though Nicgorski explores, before he is through, Cicero's nuanced and somewhat provisional case against the truth-content of Epicureanism as well.

In his conclusion, Nicgorski contemplates once more Jefferson's unease with Epicureanism and, in particular, with the Epicurean cast of the public philosophy Jefferson saw taking root in the young republic. To the temptations endemic in this public philosophy—an exaggerated confidence in the manifold power of self-interest to provide for the common good, the self-satisfaction that so readily attaches to our economic, technological, and military prowess, and the self-absorbtion with individual pleasures and material comforts—Nicgorski draws special attention, suggesting that perhaps herein lies our own "Epicurean temptation," a condition, in his words, "which allows us to look past, or not to search deeply into, the causes of the diminishing quality of citizenship and of the seemingly diminishing fund of true leaders." Nicgorski thus finds in Cicero's political-philosophical engagement with Epicureanism a valuable means of revisiting and perhaps rekindling what we might identify as old-fashioned "Jeffersonian concerns" for our contemporary civic life. The aftermath of 9/11 prompts one to wonder whether it could be precisely here that the enduring significance of those events will finally reside, as an opening to a common, concentrated reflection on just such concerns.

Nicgorski notes that Jefferson, whose sectarian faith in modern science and secular progress led him to imagine that Unitarianism would turn out to be the American religion, nevertheless located in the Christian Gospels indispensable resources for nourishing a public culture capable of holding self-sacrifice and an ethic of other-regarding service within the circumference of a "self-interest rightly understood." In his essay, John von Heyking looks to Augustine (354–430) for assistance in thinking about the place of religion in the equation of contemporary citizenship. Swimming against traditional currents of interpretation concerning Augustine's teaching on politics, von Heyking draws from the bishop of Hippo Christian arguments for reconceiving civic life as "a source of moral rejuvenation." On von Heyking's account, liberal democracy has long depended on other institutions and extraneous resources to supplement its achievement of liberty with investments of purpose and meaning. This predicament leaves liberalism vulnerable to the mistaken charge that its public life is devoid of purpose and meaning. In Augustine, von Heyking finds a teaching that links the Christian admonition to love God and neighbor to a valorization of political engagement and of a politics that facilitates, even presumes, such engagement. Cast in this light the cultivation of citizens looks to be a shared responsibility in which both churches and the state necessarily have a vital stake and play intertwined roles.

Two broad ambitions direct von Heyking's thoughtful exposition of Augustine here. On the one hand, he seeks to identify and expound the ways in which Augustine affirms an engagement with political life, by identifying it as the temporal plane of moral formation. As von Heyking explains it, "Politics is that area where a multiplicity of human beings engages in a multiplicity of relations that form their persons as images of God and help to bring about their various perfections." On the other hand, von Heyking sets forth a case for an Augustinian construction of the relationship between church and state according to which each discovers its necessary complement, if not completion, in the other. As citizens, Christians find that their religious commitments imbue limited and concrete civic engagements with a transcendent meaning attuned to innate longings fixed on eternity. Civic life thus assumes profound significance as it proves able to address the full height of our human yearning. As disciples, in turn, they exercise most universally and productively those qualities that demarcate the Christian life within the realm of civic association and political contestation. In the public arena the Christian virtues of faith, hope, and love find occasion for their broadest manifestation. In sum, "political life and life in the church serve as *exempla* for each other."

Cary J. Nederman next takes up the history of the idea of citizenship and pursues his innovative account of its evolution into the late Middle Ages. Nederman notes that the contemporary framework for thinking about the question of citizenship is typically constructed around a dichotomy between an active, participatory, and self-directing citizen, on the one hand, and a passive, politically inert, and externally directed subject, on the other. While he concedes the historical significance and influence of these rival conceptions, especially for the Latin Middle Ages, Nederman argues that a third conception looks to be the more historically important and theoretically promising for our contemporary reflection on the task of cultivating citizens. He traces to Sir John Fortescue (c. 1395–c. 1477) in fifteenth-century England the synthetic formulation of *dominium regale et politicum* ("royal and political rule"), which amounts to a grounding of the idea of citizenship on the material interests, as opposed to the spiritual welfare or moral vitality, of each individual "citizen-subject."

Taking the originally Aristotlean categories of "royal rule" and "political rule," at least as these had been translated into the context of medieval Europe, Fortescue forged the basis for a new, proto-constitutional understanding of monarchy. Royal rule, conceived as a pastoral office and charged ultimately with the salvation of souls, thus comes to be replaced by a notion of governance rooted in popular consent, based on the rule of law and sustained by a calculation of the material benefit accruing both to king and subjects from *dominium regale et politicum*. Nederman points to the recognizably modern cast of Fortescue's political calculus: Material self-interest undergirds a regime in which each individual's stake in the common welfare is chiefly defined in economic terms. At the same time, however, Nederman emphasizes that Fortescue does not simply reduce citizenship to isolated calculations of the individual material advantages that derive from this particular order of association. Fortescue insists rather on the collective priority of "equity"—that is, on a common life conceived as a just and politically negotiated allocation of burdens and benefits. Citizens, then, must assume the role of evaluating government on such terms, for citizenship thus centers around the public task of assessing what is equitable in the distributive equation of material well-being. Nederman adopts Richard Flathman's nomenclature to describe Fortescue's formulation as a "chastened" citizenship in which "extramaterial considerations" are excluded from its conceptualization. But in locating the calculus of material interest within a distributive ethics based on the priority of equity, Fortescue recapitulates, interestingly enough, Aristotle's classic description of a genuinely political existence as consisting in a community of citizens who deliberate on the matter of the just and the unjust.[8]

Nederman's exposition of Fortescue makes plain that the prominent fifteenth-century jurist anticipates to a remarkable extent the definitively modern and liberal politics that would come of age only in the seventeenth century. A final historical essay, Nathan Tarcov's disquisition on John Locke (1632–1704), focuses on the concerns that exercised this most celebrated of the fathers of modern liberalism with respect to the problem of cultivating citizens for a liberal polity. Tarcov dispels a common misunderstanding, even among students of social and political theory, that Locke's formulation of a liberal politics essentially ignores—or at best addresses only minimally—the problem of fashioning citizens suited to such a regime. His elucidation of Lockean liberalism carefully traces the boundaries within which Locke organizes what he plainly recognized as the vital soulcraft presupposed by liberal statecraft.

To be sure, Locke excludes the pursuit of salvific or moral virtue from the political or public realm, designating a private sphere of life as the appropriate space for these endeavors. This limit on the authority of liberal government and the exercise of its powers derives from two fundamental considerations. First, Locke posits as the natural condition of human beings a state of freedom and equality, upon which he bases his justification of political power and authority. Accordingly, government is properly conceived of as an arrangement of collective powers for the practical end of securing these (originally natural) conditions. Second, he holds that essential differences, which demarcate the goods of the body from those of the soul, make possible only structures that facilitate and protect the pursuit of bodily goods. Because an individual's pursuit of salvation and/or perfection "neither interferes with their pursuit by others, nor can be interfered with by the violence of others," liberal government properly confines itself to policing the realm of our material well-being. It should be noted, however, that Locke readily acknowledges the need in a liberal state for citizens who exhibit what Tarcov denominates *civil* and *liberal* virtues, as well as the need to propogate certain civil and liberal doctrines that must be generally shared by its citizenry. While the expressly limited ends of liberty and equality preclude the involvement of liberal government in the quest to save or to perfect souls, liberalism nevertheless presupposes certain qualities, dispositions, capacities, and even convictions that it necessarily seeks to inculcate in its citizens. Tarcov catalogues, in fact, a lengthy list of these qualities, drawn from Locke's treatise on education. Liberalism does have a stake in cultivating certain human types, but any such undertaking is strictly defined by, and limited to, the moral and intellectual requirements of a liberal order.

But this tidy picture is complicated by the fact that the case for liberalism as an order of society (not to mention as a mode of existence) must ultimately rest on specific claims about the best life for human beings and, thus, about the nature of salvific and moral virtue. Even Locke finds himself traversing paths first blazed by Socrates, Plato, and Aristotle. As Tarcov notes, "It is never sufficient to consider the cultivation of good citizens without also considering the cultivation of good human beings." The contest with those (e.g., Sir Robert Filmer) who champion other formulations of the state compels Locke ultimately to defend liberalism as the political framework implied by that conception of life to which human beings are naturally suited and inherently drawn. Locke's portrait of the liberal citizen—an independent, self-directing individual who grounds his life on the authority of his own rational judgment—thus arises as if from the palimpsest of what he calls "the state of nature," for it is the political imaging of Locke's natural man.

Tarcov compellingly states Locke's case for a liberal order of society, illustrating how powerfully Locke invokes our proud sense of ourselves as independently capable beings to whom liberty and equality are universally due. Locke's forceful expression of this sense of our human dignity, which he ties to our common rational nature, is among his greatest contributions to modern politics. But Tarcov likewise suggests that this achievement is a kind of recovery (in the wake of Machiavelli and Hobbes) of something of the elevated conception of politics that antedates modernity, underscoring the perpetual relevance of historical engagement with the premodern tradition of political thought, from which Locke, too, took guidance and inspiration.

CULTIVATING CITIZENS AS A CONTEMPORARY PROBLEM

Tarcov's exegesis of Locke illuminates a certain paradox of Lockean liberalism that is at the same time present in the American tradition of democratic government. Locke's formulation of the grounds of political legitimacy limits government to the task of securing basic rights—the preconditions of a politics ordered around the naturally prescribed ends of freedom and equality. Locke, therefore, does not represent politics as a formative enterprise, one that aims at the cultivation of a particular kind of human being. On the contrary, liberal government properly concerns itself only with the material interests, not the spiritual or moral formation, of the individual. But it is nevertheless the case, as Tarcov makes clear, that liberal society as conceived by Locke requires a citizenry characterized by the possession of "particular virtues or dispositions," and this society must therefore concern itself with "the development of particular capacities," as well as with "the propagation of particular truths or doctrines." Locke thus devotes a significant number of pages to the matter of cultivating citizens who possess both the "generic civic virtues" and the "specific liberal virtues" that his liberal polity presumes. While liberal society does not thereby foreswear the possibility of using even force to promote liberal or civic virtue, it is compelled by its fundamental commitment to a limited, liberal kind of politics to rely largely on certain "civil agencies" to foster the beliefs, capacities, and virtues that a liberal order assumes. These agencies consist, first and foremost, of institutions like the family and the church, both of which Locke consigns to the nonpolitical realm of private pursuits and influence, and of a program of education manned by educators attuned to the needs and committed to the ends of a liberal politics.

It is, in turn, with these civil institutions and associations that the essays comprising the second half of this volume are mostly concerned. On the basis of what we here learn of the tensions between the ends and requirements of liberal politics as outlined by Locke, we might expect his liberal regime to exhibit a genetic susceptibility to certain disorders. For example, given Locke's account of political life as simply a practical means of securing the freedom and equality that define the natural condition of human beings, a politics rooted in this conception of the boundaries of political life might well be tempted not only to proscribe any official program of salvation or moral perfection and insist on a formal separation of church and state but also to banish all moral and religious argument from public or political discourse. It is precisely this attempt at a strictly procedural politics, commanding us to bracket every attachment to particular conceptions of the good, that Michael Sandel, in his concluding essay on "Liberalism, Consumerism, and Citizenship," describes as the "public philosophy" of contemporary America. Sandel argues that this public philosophy impoverishes civic life by placing off limits the vital resources we require in order to cultivate a genuinely self-governing citizenry, especially in the face of ubiquitous economic forces that seek to fashion us individually and collectively into creatures designed to fulfill market imperatives of production and consumption.

Alexander Astin echoes this concern in his reflection on the deficiencies of higher education in contemporary America in light of its historical commitment to democratic citizenship and leadership. As Astin observes, "promoting 'good citizenship' and 'developing future leaders' are two of the most commonly stated values in the mission statements of colleges and universities." Astin conceives of citizenship as anchored in an understanding of the political system, its functions and institutions, and in the possession of core values and beliefs that sustain those institutions and motivate democratic participation. Astin likewise contends that America's institutions of higher learning are uniquely equipped to cultivate citizens suited to a liberal-democratic politics: "Democratic *behavior* is most likely to occur when the person has acquired certain knowledge, understanding, beliefs, and values. These 'internal' qualities are precisely the kinds of qualities that educational institutions are in an ideal position to foster."

For a variety of reasons, however, a curriculum directed by the civic priorities articulated in most mission statements is not generally found in American colleges and universities. Among policy makers and the general public, prevailing conceptions of higher education represent the academy as primarily a system of occupational training guided by market demands and operated as a kind of consumer-service industry. At the same time, relentless competition for institutional prestige and material resources drives the agendas of administrators, while faculty members are largely absorbed in the quest for individual and professional advancement. These conditions all conspire against the civic ideals that dominate most mission statements. Astin argues, however, that contemporary higher education *ought* to conceive of itself as something of a workshop for democratic citizenship, ensuring that students not only obtain a textbook knowledge of the American system of government but also take part in service-learning projects that emphasize and encourage the qualities and capacities that our participatory politics assume. He goes yet further, arguing that faculty members ought consciously to model the virtues of good citizenship, particularly in their dealings with students and colleagues. Colleges and universities, moreover, should structure themselves around an institutional commitment to America's democratic ideals and practices. Astin's case for *why* American higher education should, and *how* it might, contribute to the task of fashioning the citizens and the civic qualities that our political life and institutions require thus parallels Sandel's advocacy of a public philosophy that affirms the priority of citizenship for self-government, and that therefore recognizes the indispensable role of a (mostly private) civic realm rich in moral ties, formative associations, and informal involvements that actively promote democratic citizenship as an integral part—or at least an indispensable condition—of the best life for human beings to lead.

In his exploration of issues confronting specifically Christian colleges and universities, Michael Beaty begins by noting that "education for citizenship" continues to be "an expressed goal" of many religiously identified colleges and universities, especially those with a Protestant heritage. Beaty's critique of Martha Nussbaum's program of reform for contemporary liberal education grows out of his professedly sectarian commitments to a Christian life and mode of higher education. He believes Christians must ultimately reject Nussbaum's ideal of cultivating "citizens of the world," a term she borrows from the ancient Stoics in constructing a civic ideal to inform the task of imparting liberal values to, and fostering liberal virtues in, a generation coming of age in an increasingly diverse America and interdependent world. Beaty's protest against Nussbaum's program of liberal education turns on the fact that it amounts to a form of soulcraft aiming at the cultivation of a particular type of human being, one characterized by qualities and commitments that Beaty insists are fundamentally at odds with a life of Christian discipleship. He notes that Nussbaum distinguishes her multicultural version of liberal education from its traditionalist rival on the grounds that it alone is capable of liberating the individual from provincial horizons, habits, and customs to a life in which one exercises full sovereignty over one's thoughts, speech, and self. In this way, Nussbaum acknowledges (at least implicitly) that a liberal politics cannot ultimately be neutral, as contemporary liberalism has often aspired to be, with respect to the choice of the best life for its citizens. At the same time, Nussbaum's case in favor of one and against another version of liberal education, both of which she nevertheless believes "fit citizens for freedom," necessarily calls attention to the question of just what resources are best suited to cultivating citizens for contemporary democracy. Beaty sees a fundamental tension between Nussbaum's formulation of liberal education, which aims "to form autonomous individuals who are first and foremost maximally independent and self-directed, and for whom an individual's own choices about moral ends and practices are the ultimate authority," and an education devoted to the end of fashioning individuals "who think, will and behave Christianly." Moreover, Beaty contends that Nussbaum's thinking about an education that equips citizens for contemporary democracy is blind to the historical contribution of America's churches in nurturing democratic citizenship. Protestant churches, in particular, have traditionally played a vital civic role, analyzed so compellingly by Tocqueville, that stems not from a common, underlying commitment to the liberal ideal of individual autonomy but from the guiding beliefs and defining practices of these (essentially illiberal) institutions.

Beaty's argument with Nussbaum usefully illustrates Tarcov's contention in relation to Locke that liberalism cannot ultimately avoid the question of how best to order social and political life, and that soulcraft constitutes therefore an integral part of liberal politics. It may be opposed or neglected; it cannot be dispensed with. A successful liberal politics, moreover, must give judicious attention to certain issues of the soul—to moral and intellectual formation that places liberal commitments to individual liberty and

equality in conspicuous relation to the highest human possibilities. This re-
alization, in turn, casts a complex light on the relation of church and state.
America's tradition of liberalism prescribes a politics that, insofar as it is
based on the separation of religion from the public sphere in order to limit
the exercise of collective power to bodily relations and material interests,
appears nevertheless to look to the church to sanction its ends and fundamental institutions as well as to help in shaping its citizens and directing its
leaders. Such a conception of the manifold, intricate, and almost symbiotic
connections between church and liberal state informs Jean Bethke Elshtain's Christian reflection on our contemporary condition. She explores how
religious convictions "give form and texture to a way of being and knowing
that imbeds strong norms for action."

Elshtain concentrates on *hope,* a defining Christian virtue, which unlike
optimism does not presume a world where all problems have solutions and
perfect contentment is ever within reach. Elshtain suggests, in fact, that
Christian hope represents a vital moral and civic resource capable of sustaining a sometimes fruitless and often dispiriting engagement with political
and civic life. In this way, she underscores how sectarian commitments
might, in fact, prove essential to the equation of a healthy democratic order,
implicitly confirming Sandel's view that the quest to segregate religiously
based convictions and motivations from public action and discourse has
succeeded only in impoverishing and enfeebling our democratic politics.[9]
Elshtain calls on America's churches to "play a critical role as interpreters of
the culture to the culture." It is again the quality of hope, rooted in religious
faith, that she relies on to steer such engagements around the shoals of condemnation and despair. In and through their churches, Christian citizens
might "live out an alternative" to the current "abortion regime" by display-
ing a hands-on concern for the life of every child, born and unborn, with
provisions and programs for serving and nurturing children of all back-
grounds. She also calls on Christians to engage popular entertainment, not
simply as critics or censors but as participants in the broader society who
are able, as such, to discover the ways in which mass-cultural events like the
film *Titanic* might through the lens of hope be usefully read as expressions
of a spiritual hunger for the rich experience of redemptive community. Like
John von Heyking, Elshtain finds in Augustine a teaching pertinent to the
contemporary concern with civic life and identity. She follows Augustine in
tracing a large-hearted openness to the world and engagement with fellow
citizens to qualities of soul nourished in sectarian communion and ordered
around the theological virtues of faith, hope, and love. For an America in
which the word "cynical" is too often mistaken for a compliment, she observes: "Delight and wonder are part and parcel of hope and trust; for, as
Augustine would say, without hope and trust, our hearts are locked away.
He was right."

With his inquiry into whether Americans have lost their virtue, Alan Wolfe does not so much oppose the introduction of moral or religious argument into the public square as question the possibility of consolidating any moral teaching as a public philosophy for an age devoted to "moral freedom." Wolfe observes that there is "a widespread feeling in the land, akin to the Great Awakenings of America's past, that something has gone profoundly wrong with the country's moral character." He identifies this feeling, first and foremost, with right-wing social critics like Robert Bork and William Bennett, as well as with conservative Christians. These standard-bearers of the American right contend that the primary source of morality is religion, that the present age is dominated by "secular humanism," and therefore, that America must be reawakened to its religious faith if the country is to be saved from its moral and social degradation. He reviews, at the same time, certain social critics on the left, where he finds that while the culprit changes, the final diagnosis is remarkably similar: "For liberals and leftists, racism is a moral vice fully as corrosive as hedonism is for conservatives." Wolfe, however, insists that reports on the degenerate state of contemporary America are altogether misguided. These jeremiads all fail to consider properly the singular accomplishment that marks present-day liberal society as unique in human history. Americans today are intent on exercising the same prerogatives within the sphere of morality that they have long exercised in politics and economics. According to Wolf, ours is the age of "moral freedom"; individuals now fully assume for themselves the authority to decide what duties they owe to self and others. But the assertion of moral freedom represents much more than the universal extension of freedom to yet another realm of human endeavor. It stands as the ultimate freedom, for "moral freedom involves freedom over the things that matter most." In contemporary America, there are consequently "no questions the answers to which must be found outside the purview of freely choosing people."

Wolfe considers this achievement to be so novel and so radical that the idea of moral freedom is nowhere to be found among the reflections of the great moral thinkers in our Western tradition (though he elsewhere observes that "a concern with excess moral freedom has been a consistent theme of western social and political commentary"). Even for Kant, who prizes our capacity for autonomy, morality is conceived as "the exact opposite of a do-as-you-please affair."[10] Likewise, the tradition of church-state separation and religious toleration inaugurated by Locke presumes, in each case, a higher power to whom is owed ultimate obedience. As Wolfe explains: "The idea of religious freedom [championed by the American Founders] stakes out a position independent of the state's authority only to clear the way for God's authority." In short, Wolfe emphasizes that both Kantian ethics and Lockean toleration "assumed the existence of a prior moral world," while contemporary moral freedom "assumes that the individual is in charge of his own destiny." Since the 1960s, Americans in large numbers have assumed for themselves the one freedom that had always been forbidden—the freedom, as Wolfe puts it, "to choose all the arenas in which to be free." A new brand of individualism thus emerged, based on the assertion of a radical autonomy from every claim or authority that one has not chosen for oneself. (Walter Nicgorski's study of the dangers of Epicureanism—both as perceived by Jefferson in eighteenth-century America and by Cicero in first-century Rome—provides helpful historical perspective on this rather grand claim.)

Wolfe recognizes that such an assertion entails risks, for "society would be impossible if each person simply decided to follow his/her own inclinations in everything he/she did." But he also believes that the advent of moral freedom marks a permanent change in the moral landscape of American society. Critics point with alarm at catalogues of unsettling developments—such as trends in contemporary marriage and family life by which unmarried cohabitation increased almost 1,000 percent between 1960 and 1998; divorce rates have soared since a generation ago; and the percentage of children under eighteen living in single-parent homes has reached historical levels—yet a moral consensus on fundamental issues largely eludes contemporary society. (As Wolfe later reveals, however, "Americans continue to believe, with respect to the family, that two-parent families are the best way to raise children.") Empirical studies may forge the boundaries of broad agreement about the nature, direction, and even perhaps the consequences of social change, but statistics will never produce substantive agreement "on the issues so many care most about, such as whether our conduct makes us sinners in the eyes of God." In sum, Wolfe finds no reason to believe that Americans are prepared to relinquish their hard-won freedom to choose individually and for themselves the moral terms on which to base their lives. He therefore concludes that critiques of contemporary social and civic life necessarily miss the mark insofar as they require Americans to embrace a common morality in working together for a common good.

Michael Sandel takes direct aim at these conclusions with his reflection on the problem of contemporary citizenship. He suggests that the portrait Wolfe paints of present-day America significantly misconstrues the reality. Wolfe depicts a contemporary society predicated on individual choice and moral freedom, which stands over against a traditional society—the inspiration of much nostalgia on the part of right-wing social critics like Bork and Bennett—that demanded conformity to common norms and acceptance of common ideals. Wolfe implies, moreover, that a public commitment to character formation and the cultivation of citizens is neither feasible nor desirable in the age of moral freedom. Sandel, however, contends that under the guise of choice and freedom, contemporary liberalism conspires with free-market capitalism to shape a society of consumers in ways that are often inimical to the preconditions of free government. Wolfe holds up the sovereign ability to choose as the ground of individual and moral freedom, but Sandel counters that this very conception of "the freely-choosing, individual self, unencumbered by antecedent moral ties," in which freedom ultimately rests in the selecting of one's ends for oneself, expresses the public philosophy of contemporary liberalism. As such, it necessarily exerts an influence on political life and promotes the formation of *a certain kind* of individual. Wolfe's polemic against the possibility of tailoring individuals into citizens of prescribed dimensions, in fact, traces the outlines of a contemporary public philosophy with its attendant, if often covert, soulcraft.

Sandel, in turn, thinks that cultural conservatives have rightly perceived that the issues of civic virtue and character formation are vital to our national politics. Where this right-wing politics of virtue falls short, however, is in its failure to recognize or to contest "the corrosive power of an unfettered market economy." Conservatives justifiably point to popular culture as having a coarsening influence on civic life and moral character. Sandel, however, pursues this insight to its implicit conclusion with an analysis of the market forces and economic imperatives that underlie and, increasingly, configure popular culture—and, by extension, civil society as a whole. And yet, not only has private enterprise come to represent and to justify itself in the voluntarist language of the unencumbered choosing agent—the prevailing liberal ideal—but public agencies and services also now commonly conceive of themselves in consumerist terms that have been valorized by the wholesale identification of the marketplace with this conception of a fully self-directing, sovereign self. Sandel highlights the difficulty that this potentially solipsistic conception of political life has in recognizing, not to mention defending, a public realm where a common civic identity might be forged and molded. As a consequence, it invites and sanctions an increasing commercialization of public life—Sandel explores in particular the now-widespread practice of state lotteries—transforming government in the process into the purveyor of a degraded and perverse mode of civic education. Contra Wolfe, Sandel thus insists: "This culture does not reject soulcraft, but exerts an implicit, de facto soulcraft. In the name of the voluntarist conception of freedom, it shapes persons who think of themselves more as consumers with choices and less as citizens with duties and obligations."

With his critique of contemporary liberalism, Sandel consciously points back (at least as far as Aristotle) to a republican conception of government that gives priority to the problem of fostering citizens capable of free government. In the end, however, he also points us toward a future in which the prospects for self-government appear to hinge on the exercise of a novel kind of civic virtue—a capacity, in the face of the historically unique complex of overlapping and often conflicting obligations that today claims us, to adjudicate these irreducible if divergent claims so as to preserve, in each case, their integrity. Choices will certainly have to be made, but only if these are made from a consciousness of what Sandel usefully describes as the "multiply encumbered self" can we hope to navigate successfully between the "two corruptions" that demarcate the moral horizon of our age—the Scylla of fundamentalism and the Charybdis of a storyless self. It follows, moreover, that the exercise of such an encumbered agency must be embraced as the noble aim of a formative politics that will necessarily understand and explain itself as an argument for the best human life. The thought that this volume, as the final event of a symposium by the same name, might contribute at least to the prologue of such an argument has inspired these labors.

NOTES

1. Compare John Locke's very similar statement in his "Second Treatise": "The great and chief end therefore, of Men's uniting into Commonwealths, and putting themselves under Government, is the Preservation of their Property." John Locke, *Two Treatises of Government,* ed. Peter Laslett (Cambridge: Cambridge University Press, 1991), 350–51.

2. From the letter to John Jay, Aug. 23, 1785 in *The Portable Thomas Jefferson,* ed. Merrill D. Peterson (New York: Penguin Books, 1975), 384.

3. See John Rawls, *A Theory of Justice* (Cambridge, MA: Harvard University Press, 1971), 114–17. See also Michael Sandel's discussion of "Kantian liberalism" in *Democracy's Discontent* (Cambridge, MA: Harvard University Press, 1996), 13–17.

4. Will Kymlicka, *Contemporary Political Philosophy: An Introduction* (Oxford: Oxford University Press, 2001), 285.

5. Polls conducted by the Gallup Organization and others over the past several decades indicate a pattern of steady growth in the number of Americans who seem to believe that the moral condition of the nation is a serious problem. In 1996 (March 20–22) and again in 1998 (September 13–15), 90 percent of those polled responded either that "a moral crisis" or "major problems," existed with respect to "the condition of morals in the country today." When asked about their feelings concerning "moral and ethical standards in our country," only 23 percent in a 1999 (February 4–8) poll chose "optimistic." See www.gallup.com/poll/indicators/indmoral.asp. See also Alan Wolfe's brief history of the jeremiads that have shaped the public discourse of recent years in his essay, "Have Americans Lost Their Virtue?," contained in the second part of this volume.

6. Several prominent examples are the Council on Civil Society and the National Commission on Civil Renewal. See Wolfe below at pp. 129–31. Having single-handedly provoked a major debate in the social sciences concerning the vitality of American civil society, Robert Putnam has now organized the most extensive study ever conducted of civic engagement in America in conjunction with his Saguaro Seminar at Harvard's Kennedy School of Government. The study involves a partnership with nearly three dozen community foundations and organizations that concern themselves with civic life and engagement. The guiding aim of this seminar, as expressed in its mission statement,

is to "develop a handful of far-reaching, actionable ideas to significantly increase Americans' connectedness to one another and to community institutions over the next five years." See www.ksg.harvard.edu/saguaro.

7. William Galston, "Can Patriotism Be Turned into Civic Engagement?" *The Chronicle of Higher Education,* Nov. 16, 2001, B16–17.

8. See Aristotle, *Politics,* I: 2, 1253a.2–18.

9. In his recent book, Robert Putnam observes: "Churches provide an important incubator for civic skills, civic norms, community interests, and civic recruitment. . . . [Moreover,] churchgoers are substantially more likely to be involved in secular organizations, to vote and participate politically in other ways, and to have deeper informal social connections." Suggesting a profoundly formative link between religious activity and citizenship, Putnam likewise notes: "In one survey of twenty-two different types of voluntary associations, from hobby groups to professional associations to veterans groups to self-help groups to sports clubs to service clubs, it was membership in religious groups that was the most closely associated with other forms of civic involvement, like voting, jury service, community projects, talking with neighbors and giving to charity." Robert D. Putnam, *Bowling Alone: The Collapse and Revival of American Community* (New York: Simon and Schuster, 2000), 66–67. See also Steven A. Peterson, "Church Participation and Political Participation: The Spillover Effect," *American Politics Quarterly* 20 (Jan. 1992): 123–39.

10. Wolfe's own characterization of Kantian ethics as self-consciously opposed to the equation of morality with the license to do whatever one freely chooses appears to constitute an implicit acknowledgment that Kant does not, in fact, fail to recognize the existence or the exercise of what Wolfe describes as "moral freedom." Kantians would likely take issue with Wolfe here, contending that what separates Kant and Wolf is not that the latter is able to conceive of a possibility to which the former was altogether blind but that the former rejected the identification of moral freedom with the act of choice as such. For Kant's treatment of the question of freedom in relation to the problem of moral action, see Book II, "Dialectic of Pure Practical Reason," of his *Critique of Practical Reason.*

Part I

CULTIVATING CITIZENS AS A HISTORICAL PROBLEM

1

Cicero, Citizenship, and the Epicurean Temptation

Walter Nicgorski

"I too am an Epicurean," wrote Thomas Jefferson in 1819.[1] Jefferson followed this confession with an explanation. "I consider the genuine (not the imputed) doctrines of Epicurus as containing everything rational in moral philosophy which Greece and Rome have left us." Singling out Epictetus as a source for what was good in the Stoics, Jefferson then noted that the Stoics' "great crime" consisted in "their calumnies of Epicurus and misrepresentations of his doctrines; in which we lament to see the candid character of Cicero engaging as an accomplice." Jefferson was not the first to take offense at what he regarded as Cicero's misrepresentations of Epicurus and Epicureanism. Cicero indicates that the charge appeared, at least in one respect, in his own lifetime,[2] and Jefferson stood in the stream of a revival of Epicureanism over the previous three centuries.

Jefferson was certainly not the last to raise up Cicero's critique of the Epicureans as an obstacle to taking Cicero seriously as a philosopher. He immediately followed his lament over Cicero's accomplice role by characterizing Cicero as "diffuse, vapid, rhetorical, but enchanting."[3] Though recent years have witnessed a renewed interest in and appreciation for Cicero as a thinker, there remains a widely shared conviction that Cicero has unfairly maligned Epicureanism, and this apparent unfairness or incompetence can loom as an obstacle for those who might otherwise look to Cicero for moral-political understanding. Carl Richard, who tells us much about Jefferson's turn to and struggle with Epicureanism in his lucid and useful 1994 work *The Founders and the Classics*, also reports on James Wilson's admiration for Cicero. Richard writes, "Like most of the founders, Wilson was completely persuaded by Cicero's misrepresentation of Epicureanism."[4] Richard continues by complaining of Cicero's misrepresentation of Epicurus on the gods, of

Epicurus on human nature, and of Wilson's destroying with Cicero's help "his Epicurean straw man." That Richard feels no need to provide any evidence for the claim that Epicureanism is being misrepresented is simply a reflection of a strong strain of support, especially in academic discourse, for the view that Cicero got the Epicureans wrong.

In what follows, I propose to take a good, if necessarily limited, look at the evidence for this charge of misrepresentation. I do this primarily by exploring what Cicero says in his philosophical writings about Epicurus and the Epicureans and by setting this in the context of the overall character and method of his moral and political philosophy. This would seem to be a first and important step in testing specific claims that his treatment is unfair and inadequate. I do not enter far at this point into the rich recent scholarship on Epicurus but seek to provide the kind of sympathetic reading of the extensive writings of Cicero that has characterized recent work on the much more limited sources we have for Epicurus and Epicureans.[5]

What is at stake in this inquiry is not simply fair-minded access to Cicero, and specifically to Cicero on citizenship, for it is in his struggle against Epicureanism that Cicero comes to speak most about citizenship—which I understand to be significant and sustained participation, inclusive of leadership where appropriate, in one's political community. What is also at stake may be our ability to face ourselves as the children of Jefferson and the citizens of the Republic and way of life he was so influential in fashioning. Perhaps the postmodern sensitivity to predispositions that color and shape all endeavors, even that of the inquiring intellect, allows us to ask whether our resistance to Cicero's critique of Epicureanism reflects our discomfort with the exposure of the political implications, not of a crude hedonism but of a sober and seemingly virtuous, calculated pursuit of self-interest, that which is often considered self-interest rightly understood, and that which is particularly and intentionally turned loose in modern free societies. Lest I seem to jump too readily from a particular dispute about Cicero among scholars of Hellenistic philosophy and others to a large critical issue for citizenship in modern societies, it is important to sketch more of what Jefferson's preference for Epicurus and resistance to Cicero's critique entailed for him and others of the Founding generation before turning to Cicero proper and a sampling of his recent critics.

Jefferson expected an ever-wider victory for Epicureanism in America, though his expectations were colored more by worry than by any triumphalism. For him Epicureanism was a compelling philosophy, superior when set against any classical alternative. Richard has concluded that Epicurus was overall Jefferson's "favorite philosopher."[6] Jefferson sought to get Epicurus right, and in doing so he prepared as early as 1800 a "Syllabus of the doctrines of Epicurus" wherein he summarized the position of Epicurus as "Happiness the aim of life. Virtue the foundation of happiness. Utility the test of virtue. The *summum bonum* is to be not pained in body, nor troubled in mind."[7] Jefferson went far in identifying with Epicurus. In a later letter in his own name, he wrote that "nature has constituted *utility* to man, the standard and the test of virtue."[8] Jean Yarbrough, in her recent book on Jefferson and American character, tells of a Jefferson ever more attracted to Epicureanism after leaving the "prison" of public affairs and then writing to various friends about "ease of body and tranquillity of mind" being the supreme good.[9] Jefferson thought Epicureanism destined to triumph as long as people were free to think for themselves; it was superior not merely in its moral philosophy but also in its compatibility with the advances of physical science and with what Jefferson regarded as sensible thinking about divine beings.[10] On the matter of divinity, Jefferson predicted that Unitarianism, with its distant Epicurean-like divinity, was the wave of the American future. With his characteristic occasional hyperbole, he wrote in 1822, "I trust there is not a young man now living in the United States who will not die an Unitarian."[11]

Jefferson, however, also thought that Epicureanism exemplified a deficiency of all of classical moral philosophy, in that it was overly self-centered and feeble in teaching regard for others.[12] However moderate and even austere the way of Epicurus in pursuing the avoidance of pain, Jefferson understandably doubted that this would be the way Epicureanism would manifest itself as a popular teaching. He anticipated Tocqueville's later finding in the democratic people of America—a characteristic emphasis on the pursuit of material comforts and gratifications. Like his sometime adversary John Adams, Jefferson foresaw the opportunities for a diffusive prosperity in this free nation as a threat to the kind of aware and engaged citizenship he considered critical to freedom.[13] He foresaw with lament a time when Americans generally would lose themselves in the pursuit of wealth. He seems to have shared entirely Adams's view when the latter wrote, "The disposition to luxury is so strong in all men, and in all nations, that it can be restrained, where it has the means of gratification, only by education, discipline, or law."[14] Adams seems to have been comfortable in anchoring his perspective on the human condition in Cicero's moral teaching, citing with approval Cicero's reminder to his son and others that we are not born simply for ourselves.[15] Jefferson's response to the deficiency was to supplement Epicureanism, first with a teaching about an inherent moral sense that directs us in responsibilities to others, and then with selections from the Christian Gospels. Thus he sought to create a mix that would represent a sound philosophy for republican citizenship and life.[16]

However compelling the apparent truth of Epicureanism, Jefferson was clearly troubled as to whether it could be an effective public philosophy for the new Republic. He seemed to sense what Eva Brann in her retrospect on Jefferson and republican education called, following Tocqueville, a "debilitating alliance"—an alliance formed by the joining of "the vigorous intellectual materialism" that was part "of the founding philosophy of this Republic" with "democratic tastes."[17] No doubt mindful of partisan advantage, Alexander Hamilton interpreted Jefferson's inner struggle as simply a masking of Jefferson's Epicurean soul. Writing about Jefferson in 1792 in the public press, Hamilton observes, "But there is always a first time, when characters studious of artful disguises are unveiled; when the vizor of stoicism is plucked from the brow of the Epicurean; when the plain garb of Quaker simplicity is stripped from the concealed voluptuary."[18] The same elements of Jefferson's struggle are evident in Tocqueville's own entertainment of the possibility that rational self-interest, self-interest rightly understood, might be the emerging basis for a new citizenship in the democratic age.[19] Tocqueville entertains this possibility even as he acknowledges that traditional Christianity has shown itself to be the basis for American democracy and a check on various dangerous democratic tendencies. Is it not the same struggle on Washington's mind when—in that justly acclaimed section of his Farewell Address where the first president proclaims religion and morality as "indispensable supports" to political prosperity—he concludes by observing, "Whatever may be conceded to the influence of refined education on minds of peculiar structure, reason and experience both forbid us to expect that national morality can prevail in exclusion of religious principle"?[20] For Washington, then, there can be no effective Epicurean morality supportive of the Republic.

"One must ultimately wonder," muses Paul Rahe, "whether, within a republic, a system of morals grounded solely in enlightened self-interest can really suffice." Rahe makes this statement as he begins the penultimate chapter both of his massive study of republican government and of his volume on republican government in America.[21] Similar doubts, states Rahe, were widespread in America of the 1780s. Rahe brings forward the testimony of an anonymous writer in the Virginia press of the period: "While mankind consider the obligations to the exercise of virtue as derived from no higher source than the advantages accruing therefrom to society, it is no difficult matter for every individual to satisfy himself, that, provided he can persuade others to the disinterested practice, his dispensing with it in his own case will be a thing of little moment." So the writer concludes that "declamations on the advantages and necessity of public and private virtue fall from the lips of every one, while their lives are stained with the most sordid and selfish practices." Paul Rahe notes that these concerns—concerns, I might add, reflected in Jefferson's personal struggle, Washington's critical farewell observation, and in the interventions in public prints of ordinary citizens—were addressed by Cicero when in a well-known passage in the *De Legibus* he argued, in Rahe's words, that "the civility required for the maintenance of civil society can hardly be sustained on a foundation of calculation alone."[22]

CICERO AND EPICUREANISM

To return to the case of Cicero: The passage from the *De Legibus* and most other passages in his philosophical writings where Cicero discusses the moral requisites of republican government are aimed either directly or indirectly at the Epicureans. If Cicero got the Epicureans wrong, as Jefferson and others have said, his teaching on citizenship is at best badly skewed by having a wrong target; at worst it is simply worthless, because it misses a viable basis for effective citizenship. If Cicero has the Epicureans essentially right, and if we can reasonably assume that Epicureanism has broadly triumphed in modernity, as Jefferson anticipated, there is reason to believe that we might not only learn from Cicero about the requisites of a public philosophy supportive of sustained and meaningful citizenship but that we might also learn in ways especially attuned to our distinctive modern condition. What then has Cicero said about Epicurus and the Epicureans?

Cicero's life (106–43) spanned a large part of the Roman Republic's last century, a deeply troubled, faction-ridden period that yielded ultimately to what Cicero regarded as the tyranny of Caesar and then to the line of emperors. The political struggles of Cicero's life amidst shifting triumvirates and the demagogic, class-driven politics of the time, which was filled with almost daily drama and much intrigue, is an oft-told story finding its place in our literary as well as our historical canon. It is a focal point too for political theorists who would ponder the institutional devices that the Roman political community had developed to bring about "mixed" government as a way to stabilize and strengthen the Republic, a way then tested by the democratic appeal of an apparently more responsive and more centralized government under Caesar. It was in this time, and in Italy in particular, that Epicureanism, a doctrine for living developed by Epicurus some two hundred years earlier, had a widely noted revival. It became the dominant philosophical school during the years Cicero lived.[23] Later Montesquieu would claim that this doctrine, in the vulgar form it frequently took, was a cause of the Republic's demise.[24] One wonders, however, if the degree of political and social turmoil in the wealthy and extended Roman state did not feed the growth of a doctrine that invited withdrawal into the sweet delights of personal gardens,[25] to paraphrase a formulation of Montaigne, a later discriminating admirer of Epicurus. Perhaps Epicureanism grew in some form of counterpoint or mutual interaction with the Republic's demise, each strengthening the other.

Cicero thought that Epicureanism was clearly an obstacle to saving the Republic even if it was not a primary cause for its decline. His critical outlook on Epicureanism could not on the surface be plausibly considered ill informed or self-serving. Before his thirtieth year he had attended in Athens lectures of Zeno of Sidon, worldwide head of the Epicurean school, and earlier at Rome he had listened to Phaedrus, "an earnest expositor of that widespread doctrine."[26] In those youthful years his friend of a lifetime, Atticus, embraced the doctrine of the Garden and remained a faithful Epicurean thereafter through the years of extensive correspondence and friendship with Cicero.[27] In his correspondence Cicero discusses the conversion to Epicureanism of Cassius, the co-conspirator against Caesar, as well as the conversion of the lesser-known Trebatius.[28] Also in his correspondence he admires the poetic genius of Lucretius, one of the great Roman literary expositors of Epicureanism who shared the Republic's last century with Cicero.[29] Cicero would have found much comfort and support had he joined the Epicurean *geist* sweeping across Rome and the Roman-dominated world. Rather, he became history's most prominent critic of Epicureanism.

Though a keen student of philosophy from his earliest years and exposed to Epicureanism in those years, it is only relatively late in life—after years consumed in public service at the bar, in the forum, and political ascent through the *cursus honorum* to Rome's highest office—that Cicero launches a written assault on the doctrine of the Garden. The incoherences and dangers of Epicureanism become one of the great themes of his philosophical writings. The theme surfaces already in the 50s, when he writes his most manifestly political/philosophical works, *De Re Publica, De Legibus,* and *De Oratore.* It also shows in certain speeches of this time and in a letter to Atticus late in 50.[30] In the next decade of the 40s, before Caesar's execution in 43 followed by the Republic's decisive fall and Cicero's own execution, Cicero undertakes a quite systematic critique of Epicureanism in the *De Finibus Bonorum et Malorum, De Natura Deorum,* and *Tusculanae Disputationes,* this last being a work that Jefferson seemed to ponder carefully as a young man. Though each of these dialogues is of a distinctive character, the voice of Cicero, at least regarding Epicureanism, is not difficult to discern.

A more significant dimension of that literary form, with respect to the issue of this inquiry, is that Cicero is called on as author to represent the Epicurean position. The first two books of the *De Finibus* report a conversation in which Epicureanism is examined and challenged by Cicero himself as a character in the exchange; the conversation's dramatic setting is but five years earlier (the year 50), and the exposition and defense of the Epicurean position is given to Lucius Manlius Torquatus, a political leader of a respected family who was afterward killed fighting for Pompey's cause.[31] Torquatus and Cicero have their exchange in the company of a young man, also since fallen in battle, who is inclined to be critical of Epicureanism but is cast as a judge of the encounter and likely intended to be seen as a potential convert to Epicureanism. In the disputation on the gods, *De Natura Deorum (ND),* the exposition and defense of the Epicurean view is assigned to Gaius Velleius, whom Cicero reports was a Roman senator regarded as the Epicurean leader among Romans.[32] In the disputations at Tusculan, the views of Epicurus, his pupil Metrodorus, and Zeno—the head of the school, whom Cicero had heard—are frequently paraphrased or directly quoted from Cicero's sources.[33]

The *Tusculans* also provide explicit internal evidence (written into the text by Cicero) that certain of Cicero's interpretations of Epicurus and Epicureanism were disputed by the advocates of that school.[34] This work and the *De Finibus* seem to provide formal textual evidence of a very active debate Cicero is having with the Epicureans through the 50s and 40s as he is forcibly pushed from political life and, according to one historian, is tempted to sanctify the retreat and delights of the Garden by embracing its views.[35] There are, then, in the situation in which Cicero finds himself (a vital contemporary Epicurean community inclusive of many of his friends, common sources, and texts, such as notes on Zeno and writings of Epicurus, and immediate descendants of historical personae whom he has made Epicurean representatives in his work) constraints that would likely check any tendency to consciously and significantly distort or caricature the Epicurean view. His challenges to his interpretation of Epicureanism further draws one to believe that despite Cicero's firm and rhetorically powerful opposition to the Garden, Cicero is being true to his Academic philosophical method in having an Epicurean voice make the case for that doctrine, though Cicero is here, as often, exercising that method in a rhetorical mode.[36]

Those three philosophical works—*Fin., ND, Tusc.*—in which that opposition is so potently expressed, were all written in the middle months of 45. This seems to be a period of Cicero's coming to terms with Epicureanism, systematically and quite comprehensively, after some years of interchange with friends and others about the Epicurean way of life. Approximately a year and a half later, now after Caesar's assassination, Cicero pens what will be his last philosophical work, *De Officiis,* a treatise on duties, in the form of an extended letter to his son, studying in Athens. Here the grounds on which Cicero worked out his opposition to Epicureanism in the previous year are clearly in evidence, yet Cicero is going beyond opposition to Epicureanism to an appropriation of the concept of utility, into an ethics marked by realistic attentiveness to human inclinations and desires and the need for the requisite level of participation and leadership to provide for effective political community. In his attention to utility, with its strong Epicurean associations, Cicero eschews the seemingly disembodied understanding of man and the anti- or apolitical tendencies associated with pure Stoicism. He works out a synthesis of right *(honestas)* and expediency *(utilitas)* following directly from the efforts of Panaetius of Rhodes, who embraced a form of modified Stoicism. Cicero again is exercising his Academic-Socratic method in forging a position that draws from the mainline schools of philosophy without simply embracing the entire system of a school—an eclectic approach that is often wrongly derided for being of this character.

There is no surprise, given Cicero's earlier work, in the nature of this synthesis built around the immediate responsibilities of human life. The elements in this position, including firm opposition to the fundamental principle of Epicureanism, were evident earlier. Though earlier Cicero had explored in *Natura Deorum* the Epicurean cosmology and understanding of the divinities and, in the first part of *Fin,* had initially ranged through the standard divisions of philosophy—looking at the adequacy of Epicureanism with respect to physics and logic—Cicero's dominant concern with and chief objection to the Garden was to its moral philosophy and the ethical-political implications of that philosophy.[37]

Where Cicero wished above all to engage, and did engage, the Epicureans is, not surprisingly, where he has been challenged, by Jefferson and others, about the accuracy of his rendering of Epicureanism. To follow the argument and seek the ground of Cicero's critique of Epicureanism promises even more than simply informing ourselves better on how Cicero made his case, and hence what might be the difficulties with Epicureanism in modern as well as ancient garb. Examining his encounter with the Epicureans allows us to see how the great rhetorical power of Cicero is bound up with, and in service to, subtlety of understanding and a Socratic devotion to truth. Examining his encounter provides a possible opening to an appreciation of the distinctive philosophical method of Cicero and its relationship to the practical horizon of citizenship and leadership.

CICERO'S QUARREL WITH EPICUREANISM

Certain understandings of the human end *(finis/telos)* of happiness, claims Cicero in *Officiis,* undermine any meaningful sense of duty *(officiium).*[38] The Epicurean understanding was most on Cicero's mind, perhaps solely on his mind, when he wrote this. Except for that of the Epicureans, the teachings of all major schools on the nature of the ultimate good or happiness can be supportive of duty and hence of a notion of right that stands, at least to some degree, independent of calculated expediency. Thus Cicero looks toward Stoicism and the Peripatetic teaching, in their various forms and possible mixtures, for a philosophical approach on which to build an ethics, some rules for the duties of daily life.[39] From his stance as a moderate skeptic of the Academic school, Cicero sees himself able to appropriate what makes sense of the teachings of those schools that does not undermine the very idea of duty.

The location and manner of his treatment of the Epicureans in *Fin.* illustrate his broad judgment of the ethical incapacity of this teaching, for the Epicurean position is treated first, as it is in *Natura Deorum,* and is firmly challenged and opposed. The remainder of the dialogue, however, leaves the reader less clear about where Cicero stands on the claims of the other major schools. Contestations involving the views of these schools, in this work and elsewhere in Cicero's writings, seem more exploratory, though not necessarily abandoning the basic adversarial mode that the Academic school welcomes as a way of illumination and therefore as a method for choosing the probably true position. Epicureanism seems, then, to be treated first, perhaps, partially in acknowledgment of its widespread popularity but also, it seems, in a spirit of "let's get it out of the way, so serious philosophical discussion can begin."[40] As Robert Denoon Cumming observed thirty years ago in defending Cicero's procedure against charges such as "random eclecticism" and *"bricolage,"* Cicero's "arrivals at solutions to political problems regularly take the philosophical form of reconciling other oppositions between philosophical positions by anchoring them all to their common opposition to Epicureanism."[41]

It is interesting to note now, and then to keep in mind for its bearing on steps ahead, that the point at which Cicero finds the critical error of Epicureanism, its understanding of the ultimate good, is where Cicero places the crucial issue for philosophy. Reviewing his philosophical writings in *De Divinatione,* a sequel to *Natura Deorum,* Cicero writes, "the foundation *(fundamentum)* of philosophy has come to be seen in the supreme good and the worst evil. . . . [A]ll of philosophy is illuminated to the greatest degree by the recognition that virtue suffices for living happily."[42] One might be inclined to say that this shocking claim that philosophy is somehow grounded in an answer to the critical question of moral philosophy is not surprising coming from Cicero, for Cicero after all actually expects philosophy to nourish virtue and understands virtue in a way that makes it an end in itself.[43]

Yet his statement about the foundation of philosophy and the way all philosophy is illuminated can also be read as related to how one gets some firm ground for those judgments of what is probably true about all dimensions of reality, judgments that are the fruit of inquiry for the Socratic Academic philosopher Cicero professes to be. This suggests that philosophy is grounded in a given moral horizon or intuition that is expressed initially in a systematic way in the determination of what constitutes the supreme good for human beings. It suggests that a mistake at the foundational level, such as the Epicureans make, will work to deny the very possibility of philosophy, and for Cicero this would be the deepest explanation of why the Epicureans tend to become a cult of dogmatists, not careful with definitions or particularly interested in logic, more focused on the sayings of their master than in being a community of Socratic inquirers.[44] It is hard to understand how Cicero might fairly pin Epicureans in such a corner unless one is reminded of the tension between Cicero's brand of skepticism and the assurance Epicureans have in sense experience and their reasoning from that basis.[45] It is not that Cicero abstracts from ordinary reliance on sense experience. It is rather that he and other skeptics of the Academic Socratic sort challenge the comprehensive metaphysical, cosmological, and psychological explanations spun out by the Epicureans from their primary sense experiences.[46]

Against such an assured comprehensive Epicurean materialism, Cicero privileges moral experience as the critical factor in larger explanations of the human condition that can, after all, only be more or less assured. In Cicero's view then, the Epicurean view that pleasure is the supreme or ultimate good cuts off at the root the sense of duty and right as independent of and noninstrumental to pleasure. In thus cutting off the core of moral experience as ground, as fundamental, it excludes a critical factor in the basis for philosophical judgments. But what can one do with the pleasure principle itself as a basis? Perhaps the Epicurean conviction about the nature of happiness is the critical determinant in their own assurance in their larger explanation of the whole. Some have even suggested that the larger view is more a therapy to gain peace of mind than a serious scientific explanation or dialectical inquiry.[47] In this vein, Cicero, the skeptic about larger structures built from any principle but especially from this principle, which ignores the distinctively human, expects that the pleasure principle would sink operationally to its ground of greatest assurance—that is, the immediate sensual pleasures commonly experienced by humans and animals. The test of these pleasures are those individually felt. The inherent uncertainty of all larger propositions would recurrently pull all human enterprises back to one solid ground, the pleasure the self feels, along with the calculated instruments to that pleasure.[48] In this kind of world, there is little point to philosophy as Cicero understands it.

Cicero traces the emphasis on pleasure to Epicurus himself, saying that he offers an allegedly sophisticated, but in the end a less consistent, version of Aristippus's earlier ethical teaching, founded on pursuit of sensual pleasure.[49] Much of Cicero's engagement of Epicurus, especially in *Finibus,* takes the form of trying to get straight just what Epicurus and the Epicureans mean by this "pleasure" that they make the supreme good. Is it simply "freedom from pain"? Or must not pleasure involve some kind of satisfaction or titillation that carries beyond that apparently neutral state of "freedom from pain"? There are other questions and probes that Cicero puts to the Epicurean teaching, and these have been explored closely in recent scholarship on *Finibus.*[50] While any school of thought that persists more than a generation or two is likely to develop divergent understandings and at least seeming confusions in points of their teaching, Cicero suggests the problems in the Epicurean tradition are considerable and arise at crucial points; he hints that a form of moral embarrassment plays a part in the Epicureans' trying to moderate or mask the crudeness and danger of their moral theory.[51] Cicero does report that Epicurus holds that it is nature's voice that through sense experience draws us toward pleasure *(voluptas)* and away from pain *(dolor).* This basic reality is underneath our every action and choice. There is to be no argument on this; it is a fact of our sense experience.[52] Nature seems, then, to speak differently to Epicurus and Cicero.[53]

Though acknowledging that there are disputes in his time and among Epicureans themselves as to just what Epicurus held on the primacy of bodily pleasure, among various types of pleasure, Cicero has Torquatus in *Fin.* clearly concede that he thinks a true Epicurean will reduce all pleasures in the end to bodily pleasures.[54] Mental pleasures are pleasures insofar as they are anticipations or assurances of bodily pleasures. Those more ethereal pleasures must be able to "cash out" in this form, or the very foundation of Epicureanism is upset. The beginning and the end of the pleasure principle, Epicurus is said to have taught, is in the bodily or sense experience of pleasure. There is less controversy in the tradition about the status of virtue and the virtues. Epicureans see them as instrumental to pleasure. Epicurus once suggested that they were a necessary means to pleasure, and that observation can surely suggest that they are so implicated with the end or goal of the truly faithful Epicurean that they might appear to be the end itself.[55] Both Epicurus and Cicero, however, seem to be insisting that pleasure is one thing and virtue is another, and Cicero describes Epicurus's view in a way that would seem acceptable to Epicurus, namely, that the virtues are habitual practices instrumental to pleasure.

These practices or Epicurean virtues are developed from what I would call the "calculative injunction," which is more commonly referred to as "the hedonistic calculus." In Epicurean ethics, this calculative injunction is second in importance only to the supreme end itself, pleasure. Near the end of *Tusc.* Cicero gives expression to this injunction: The Epicurean "wise man will use a kind of balancing [*compensatio*—literally, balancing of account books— we would say, "looking to the bottom line"] so that he will flee pleasure if it is likely to bring greater pain, and he will embrace pain if such promises greater pleasure."[56] One can see in the calculative injunction an opening to forms of social contract thinking, to one kind of basis for patriotism and, in sum, to all actions, habits, and institutions that might take their bearings chiefly from the dominant way of construing "self-interest rightly understood," namely, as maximizing pleasure in the long run.

It is important to notice Cicero's recognition of the virtuous—even ascetically virtuous—way of life of Epicurus as well as of the overall laudable, decent lives of his own Epicurean acquaintances and friends, such as Atticus. It is important because a common error is to suppose that the philosophical hedonism that is Epicureanism is one and the same with crass or vulgar hedonism, which expresses itself in excessive and usually self-destructive indulgence in one or another or various sensual pleasures. It seems that at least some of those who think Cicero "gets Epicurus wrong" believe that Cicero committed this common error. However, this is patently not the case, though

Cicero has an argument of another kind that connects vulgar hedonism to philosophical hedonism. That argument emerges best against a closer view of the testimony Cicero gives to the virtuous practices of Epicureans and how he explains such nobility in Epicureans.

Epicurus, writes Cicero, was a "good" and "kindly" and "humane" man *(bonus et comis et humanus)*, a kind and attentive friend, who expressed many noble opinions. His virtue, according to Cicero, was even severe judged against the moderate indulgence in sense pleasures that custom generally allows. He never intended licentiousness in his teachings. The issue is not, insists Cicero repeatedly, his character; it is, rather, a deficiency in intellect with a resulting unsoundness in the doctrine he shaped.[57] The doctrine is not worthy of philosophy; it is the mask of philosophy—plebian philosophy at best.[58] The doctrine does not warrant the kind of life that was exemplified by Epicurus and certain others of the Epicurean persuasion. Such people, says Cicero, live better than their theory, and he explains this as natural goodness overcoming the strictly logical and ethical implications of a certain view of the supreme good, with its implied self-understanding.[59] In his prologue to the *De Re Publica,* Cicero quite pointedly notes that concerns for security of self and pleasure have not, over the years, kept leading men from rising to the defense and service of the political community. Apparently even Epicureanism's rise and its elemental appeal at all times have not worked to overcome nature's call to genuine virtue. Cicero clearly understands that many Epicureans and others would come to practice a calculated or pseudo-virtue. Restraint and moderation as Epicurean strategies for pleasure are, after all, basic to Epicurean doctrine. Yet Cicero does exonerate certain Epicureans, finding in them at least the inclination and first vintage of genuine virtue; these are the individuals who, he says, live better than their theory. Cicero acknowledges their virtue while condemning the doctrine they hold.

In the light of this acknowledgment, Cicero's objection to Epicureanism can be seen as having a descriptive as well as a normative dimension. In finding people who live better than their professed Epicureanism, Cicero is testifying to significant instances where Epicureanism does not constitute an adequate description or explanation. To most, this failure in description would not seem notably threatening or dangerous; rather, it appears of mere academic interest, a matter of getting the psychology of motivation just right, one effort in building up the science of human affairs. Cicero, however, does appear concerned with a dangerous result of the descriptive inadequacy of Epicureanism. His concern seems best expressed as a form of the claim that we tend to become as we describe ourselves. In other words, along with those cases (perhaps exceptional cases) where persons live better than their theories, there are other instances where the theories or descriptions pull into their mold those who embrace them. How would this happen? Cicero is concerned that the simple call or appeal of virtue in itself, the attractiveness of goods other than pleasure, and the examples of self-giving ancestors and patriots (such as those called up before Torquatus by Cicero in *De Finibus*) would lose their purchase on our attention and culture in the face of an Epicurean explanation of self.[60] Thus nature's resistance to Epicureanism would be increasingly disarmed, and there would be experienced ever more widely the overtly dangerous consequences of Epicureanism as a normative doctrine.

THE CIVIC CHARACTER OF CICERO'S
OPPOSITION TO EPICUREANISM

One of these consequences of Epicureanism as a normative doctrine brings into view the tie, in Cicero's eyes, between philosophical hedonism and vulgar hedonism. The doctrine that pleasure is the supreme good and the entailed injunctions to avoid pain and pursue pleasure constitute collectively an invitation to many to do with sanction what they are very much inclined to do; the doctrine opens the door to indulgence and emphasis on self. There are shocking cases of indulgence run to scandalous extremes, such as that of Piso, denounced by Cicero for his congenial embrace of the doctrine of the Garden;[61] there is also the less spectacular, one assumes more guarded, indulgence that Cicero associates with the growing popularity of Epicureanism in his time.[62] That popularity is accounted for, in Cicero's view, by its appeal to what was always there in human nature and is evident, or even more evident, in those of the basest behavior.[63]

Cicero is aware that vulgar hedonism in both its shocking and more ordinary forms is not the intent of Epicurus; and he knows that such vulgar indulgence is not the way of those good Epicureans who either live more faithfully than most to the full calculus, including that of the "virtues" of Epicurus, or live better than the doctrine of Epicureanism. These more refined Epicureans do, however, manifest the second dangerous consequence of Epicureanism as a normative doctrine. Their emphasis is on tranquility *(ataraxia)*, and that very emphasis signals the special resistance in their Epicureanism to vulgar hedonism and their own special pull to the "virtues" so exemplified by the revered founder of the school. That emphasis on attaining and maintaining tranquility means that even as they resist vulgar hedonism, they are likely to emphasize avoidance of active participation and leadership in political life.[64] That tendency, that part of Epicureanism, remained powerful in the very Epicureans Cicero was most inclined to admire, but for him it represented a critical deficiency and a great threat to the security of the Republic and to all the other goods that might come from political life.[65] In drawing those who were, in a sense, by nature the best of the Epicureans (hence among the best of men)[66] away from political life, the doctrine tended to deprive the political community of the leadership it would need not only for all the usual reasons but also for containing the effects of the vulgar hedonism that would increasingly draw politics toward self-interested faction and intrigue. Atticus chose largely to stand aside in the struggles for the Republic that marked Cicero's life. Cicero feared this would be the way of other potential leaders drawn to the Epicurean teaching.

The human and political consequences of Epicureanism were, according to Cicero, disastrous. Cicero does not regard these consequences as simply settling the matter of the possible truth of Epicureanism. It is as if Cicero can hear modern voices, such as the existentialist cry of the essential incongruity and tragedy of human existence, and as if he had already internalized (as one might expect of a Socratic) Leo Strauss's warnings that truth is one thing, utility another, and that philosophy cannot be edification.[67] Three times in his dialogues *De Legibus* and *De Oratore*, at points where he dismisses the Epicurean position as inappropriate to the question at hand, he also explicitly indicates that such a dismissal is not in itself a statement determinative of the truth of Epicureanism.[68] Could the doctrine of the Garden be true but morally and socially destructive? Space allows here an examination of one of these instances, and it can serve to draw together Cicero's essential judgment of Epicureanism and reveal further his own philosophical method.

In the *De Legibus,* Cicero's professed interest is in teaching *rationem recte vivendi,* the way of right living, through a speech *(oratio)* intended to strengthen republics, to stabilize cities, and to bring people to reason.[69] As the discussion of this rhetorical dialogue approaches that key question of the natural foundation of justice, Cicero observes that what he is laying out is not consistent with the teachings of all philosophical schools. It is significant that the aspects of those teachings that he then reviews are those concerning the supreme good. Though the dialogue portrays him at this point as speaking with his Epicurean friend Atticus, Cicero is remarkably harsh on the school of Epicurus—making, however, two interesting concessions to the school's followers.

The Epicureans are dismissed from contributing to what Cicero is seeking to build, because of their conception of the supreme good as essentially physical pleasure. Cicero orders them to keep their talk to their gardens and requests them to abstain "for now" *(paulisper)* from every bond of political community, no part of which do they understand, nor have they ever wished to *(ab omni societate rei publicae, cujus partem nec norunt ullam neque umquam nosse voluerunt).* The first concession can be seen in the fact that the Epicureans are only banned at this time; it is a time of founding, or refounding, in speech. The concession is specifically in the suggestion that Epicureans might be tolerable in stable, settled regimes; perhaps the kind of "virtue" certain Epicureans exemplify can go a long way in some regimes. Self-interest, rightly understood, has, after all, some stability, at least in the right mix of circumstances.

This passage also reminds us of Cicero's focus on the intellectual failure of Epicureanism. The Epicureans are said not to understand anything about political community; nor do they care about it sufficiently to remedy their deficiency. It should be noted that in this same part of the text, where Cicero orders *(jubeamus)* Epicurean talk to be confined to their gardens, he strongly endeavors to persuade *(exoremus)* the skeptical New Academy to be silent. The Socratic academicians with whom Cicero most often identifies are not banned from hearing the discourse at hand, for Cicero wishes to win them over to what he will say about legal foundations *(quam quidem ego placare cupio, summovere non audeo).*[70] Thus, Cicero indicates again his inability to respect the Epicureans as a philosophical community, a community of inquirers.

That disrespect is not, however, a claim that the principle of the Garden's teaching has been philosophically proved wrong or that Cicero is about to do that here. In the course of this passage, in which Cicero both describes the Epicurean position on the supreme good and seeks to isolate the school, he remarks that this exile to their gardens and away from civil community is invoked—and here is the second concession—even if they speak the truth about the end of human action *(etiamsi vera dicunt),* for this is not the time or place to dispute such matters *(nihil enum opus est hoc loco litibus).*[71] What could Cicero possibly mean by saying that the Epicureans may be speaking the truth about this matter but yet must be ostracized? This, like the often troubling observation in the *De Oratore* that philosophies are not tested here with a view to which is truest but to which would be most befitting and useful to the orator or statesman, can be seen as revealing Cicero's understanding of the limitations of his own argument from public consequences.

In conceding that the Epicureans may be speaking the truth, Cicero seems to be facing up to the fact that the basic incongruity between the Epicurean conception of happiness and a commonly felt need for moral foundations may be where we are finally left. Although Cicero does not think that the incongruity he highlights is in itself a decisive argument against the truth of this view, or that that kind of knowledge is attainable that would allow an absolute and certain dismissal of the Epicurean view as wrong, the identification of incongruity is in keeping with the character of many of his arguments as he seeks what is probably true among the teachings of the schools. Given the widely perceived need for moral restraints and for a legal and political order based on such restraints, drawing out the implications of the Epicurean teaching on happiness renders it a less credible, a less probable, view.

In saying that this is not the time or place for determining the truth of this teaching, Cicero appears to be admitting that much more can and should be said on the credibility of this view than simply noting, as he does here when writing primarily of legal foundations, that this teaching cannot be reconciled with a public order grounded in norms of nature.[72] The incongruity he highlights turns out to be but the surface of a deeper incongruity between the Epicurean teaching and human nature. The arguments establishing this deeper problem, and hence the improbability of the Epicurean view, are concentrated in those first two books of *Fin*. There one finds not only more arguments of the kind made in this key passage in *De Legibus* and arguments about apparent inconsistencies and obscurities in the Epicurean teaching but also a testing of the reading of nature—the entire setting of the human being in nature—that is used to support the critical teaching on the supreme good. A series of arguments and considerations, constituting what Cicero appears to regard as "reasons of a broad sort," lead him to as clear and sure a view as is attainable on the important questions of philosophy entailed in his rejection of Epicureanism.[73] At the heart of those reasons—or more precisely, what makes them work as reasons for Cicero and others—is what I would call his "effective criterion" of truth: namely, what makes one position more probably true than another. That effective criterion appears to be an inherent sense of the good that carries with it an alternative (in contrast to Epicureanism) reading of nature. The Epicurean understanding of the supreme good and the public consequences of that view play, then, an important part, the most important part for Cicero, in an assessment of the likely truth of the Epicurean philosophy.

Has Cicero misread Epicureanism and Epicurus, as Jefferson came to believe and as Richard, our contemporary, holds with sufficient assurance that he gives no document or argumentation? We do not know enough about the specific focus of Jefferson's complaint to determine if it is centered on the same concern over Cicero's understanding of Epicurean pleasure that had surfaced in Cicero's own lifetime. We have little more from Richard than from Jefferson, but we have enough to notice that Richard's sense of Cicero's misrepresentation extends beyond the moral philosophy of Epicurus to the latter's understanding of the gods.[74] Contemporary and recent scholarship that is critical of Cicero's understanding of Epicurus shows various points of focus, some apparently continuous with those of earlier critics, but there are internal differences in this scholarship as to whether Cicero is a reliable source for Epicureanism and whether Cicero is essentially right about Epicurus.[75] That part of Cicero's critique of Epicureanism that seems to most exercise Richard is relatively little disputed in modern scholarship. I am referring to Cicero's passionate concern with the Epicurean doctrinal opposition to political participation and leadership—that is, with the apolitical and withdrawn nature of the Epicurean life. The fundamental individualism and denial of altruism at the root of Epicurean withdrawal are likewise rarely contested by the modern defenders of Epicurus and Epicureanism.[76]

CONCLUSION

Jefferson, even as he criticized Cicero for misrepresenting Epicurus, was struggling with the societal effects of Epicureanism that so concerned Cicero. Jefferson, as noted earlier, sought to supplement Epicureanism in ways that would make it more other-regarding and thus a more effective public philosophy. The Epicureanism that Jefferson predicted for us citizens of modern liberal democracies, the Epicureanism within us, may still make it difficult to hear the voice of Cicero. There is in our prosperity and our seeming enlightenment a sense of comfort in our ability to do reasonably well with the public tasks of the present and future, to find the right balance among competing interests, and to rely on our seemingly sound institutions to avoid calamities of the public order. Perhaps it is our Epicurean temptation that allows us to look past, or not search deeply into, the causes of the diminishing quality of citizenship and of the seemingly diminishing fund of true leaders. The temptation is our quiet confidence that enlightened self-interest has worked and can work.

Like the ancient Epicureans, we have, often for good reasons, a studied fear of religion and of any forms of prospective personal change that promise to nourish a less self-centered and a more public-oriented way of life. There are good reasons for caution in the face of prospects and promises of transforming human nature. Aristotle, for one, warned of political solutions that ignore our rooted concern with ourselves, but he sought to overcome excessive selfishness.[77] The experience of history, especially modern history, yields powerful warnings of the dangerous paths we would take if we followed those who aim too high and promise too much in pointing us to a new order of humankind. Caution too is called for because we live in times when it is not evident which communities—or which levels of community—represent those into which the self should fold. Cicero, so apparently Rome centered, had already pointed to the possibility of another kind of transnational citizenship.[78] This challenge to finding community on an appropriate human scale in the face of our larger, interdependent patterns of life is a great one for the political thought and leadership of the present and future.

Over the last generation, there has developed in academic circles more willingness to consider, as people of common sense always did, personal character as relevant to politics and to the kind of political communities we are and can become. We need to keep this focus and explore more deeply and carefully, from the resources of our tradition, what self-understandings foster good character in a free society. By doing so, we will be working on the same ground that gives the prospect of enriching our citizenship and leadership. Cicero once wrote his Epicurean friend Atticus complaining of the public impact of those who refer all matters to self-interest, reject any altruism, and avoid vice only for fear of its consequences.[79] Early in the Revolution, John Adams wrote Mercy Warren,

> Public Virtue cannot exist in a Nation without private, and public Virtue is the only Foundation of Republics. There must be a positive Passion for the public good, the public Interest, Honor, Power and Glory, established in the Minds of the People, or there can be no Republican Government, nor any real Liberty: and this public Passion must be Superiour to all private Passions. Men must be ready, they must pride themselves, and be happy to sacrifice their private Pleasures, Passions and Interests, nay, their private Friendships and dearest Connections, when they stand in Competition with the Rights of Society.[80]

Closer to our time, at the midpoint in the century we have just left, Walter Lippmann observed,

> The modern trouble is in a low capacity to believe in precepts which restrict and restrain private interests and desire. Conviction of the need of these restraints is difficult to restore once it has been radically impaired. Public principles can, of course, be imposed by a despotic government. But the public philosophy of a free society cannot be restored by fiat and by force.[81]

At the least then, what is called for today in this free society is a culture policy—perhaps largely implicit and touching on many public policies—that does not exclusively privilege our assured Epicureanism. Put positively, such a culture policy would attend to public and social space for the examination of self-understandings and for living out and perpetuating religious understandings consonant with an effective public philosophy.

NOTES

I thank Frederick Crosson, David Fott, Carlos Lévy, and Gretchen Reydams-Schils for their comments on earlier versions of this essay. I am grateful to the Earhart Foundation for support in preparing the original version of this essay for the Pruit Symposium at Baylor University, and to Baylor University for providing this occasion.

1. Letter to William Short (October 31, 1819). Short was a long-time friend of Jefferson and a fellow Virginian. A few years earlier, Jefferson in writing another friend praised "the doctrines of Epicurus . . . notwithstanding the calumnies of the Stoics, and caricatures of Cicero." Letter to Charles Thomson (January 9, 1816). *The Writings of Thomas Jefferson*, ed. Andrew Lipscomb and Albert Bergh (Washington, DC: Thomas Jefferson Memorial Association, 1905), 15: 219, 14: 386. Carl J. Richard provides information on Jefferson's life-long interest in Epicureanism in *The Founders and the Classics* (Cambridge, MA: Harvard University Press, 1994), 187 ff. Gilbert Chinard provides some evidence that the assessment of Cicero and other material in the letter to William Short were taken by Jefferson from a 1791 abridgement by Enfield of an earlier multivolume critical history of philosophy. "Jefferson among the Philosophers," *Ethics* 53 (1942–43): 264–65.

2. *Tusculanae Disputationes (Tusc.)* 3.37–38, 49–51.

3. Letter to William Short, 15: 219

4. Richard, 175–76.

5. Much of what we know about Epicurus's teaching we know indirectly through the texts of Cicero and Cicero's contemporaries Lucretius and Philodemus. Three letters of Epicurus and a summary of his teaching are preserved in Diogenes Laertius. There are fragments of his otherwise extensive writings to be found here and there. David Sedley estimates that we have less than 1 percent of what Epicurus wrote. *Lucretius and the Transformation of Greek Wisdom* (Cambridge: Cambridge University Press, 1998), 86 n. 108. Also, A. A. Long, *Hellenistic Philosophy* (London: Duckworth, 1986), 18. Certain of Cicero's accounts of Epicurus and Epicureanism as well as other primary sources are collected with commentary in A. A. Long and D. N. Sedley, eds., *The Hellenistic Philosophers* (Cambridge: Cambridge University Press, 1987), 1: 25–157.

6. Richard, 187.

7. Letter to William Short, 15: 223–24. Chinard (265) claims the Syllabus is taken directly and substantially from Enfield's abridgement, n. 1, above.

8. Letter to Thomas Law (June 13, 1814), Lipscomb and Bergh, 14: 143.

9. Jean M. Yarbrough, *American Virtues: Thomas Jefferson on the Character of a Free People* (Lawrence: University Press of Kansas, 1998), 162. Jefferson is here paraphrasing the very words of Epicurus.

10. Richard, 189; Yarbrough 154 ff., 160–65.

11. Richard, 189.

12. Yarbrough, 19–20; Richard, 187.

13. Yarbrough, 12, 74, 135.

14. John Adams, "A Defence of the Constitutions of Government of the United States of America," *The Works of John Adams* (Boston: Little, Brown, 1851), 6: 103–4.

15. *De Officiis [Off.]* 1.22. Adams's use of this in an 1811 letter is cited in Richard, 63. Cicero attributes the teaching to Plato both here in *Off.* and also in *De Finibus Bonorum et Malorum [Fin.]* 2.45–46.

16. Yarbrough is particularly helpful at exploring Jefferson's uneasiness with Epicureanism and his efforts to supplement it and modify it; see 24, 161, 164–65, and passim. Richard notes that Jefferson read the Gospels through an "Epicurean lens" and believed that both Jesus and Socrates were Epicureans; 189, 191–92. Jefferson's letter to Thomas Law (above, n. 8) is direct and eloquent in defending an independent and inherent moral sense that rebels against any tendency to act for our self-interest.

17. Eva T. H. Brann, *Paradoxes of Education in a Republic* (Chicago: University of Chicago Press, 1979), 95.

18. From the *Philadelphia Gazette of the United States,* as quoted in Richard, 93.

19. For example, see pp. 14–15, 235–36, 525 ff., as well as his referring to his expectation of a decent or virtuous "materialism" that will not so much corrupt as enervate the soul. Alexis de Tocqueville, *Democracy in America,* ed. J. P. Mayer (Garden City, NY: Doubleday, 1969).

20. "Farewell Address," *Messages and Papers of the Presidents,* ed. James D. Richardson (Washington, DC: Bureau of National Literature and Art, 1907), 1: 220.

21. Paul A. Rahe, *Republics Ancient and Modern,* vol. 3, *Inventions of Prudence: Constituting the American Regime* (Chapel Hill: University of North Carolina Press, 1994), 206.

22. Rahe directs readers to *De Legibus* [*Leg.*] 1.40–43.

23. *Fin.*1.13; *Tusc.* 4.6–7. That Cicero's anti-Epicureanism and his political opposition to Caesar were related and the extent of the tie of Epicureans to Caesar's cause are noted in Carlos Lévy, *Cicero Academicus* (Rome: École Française de Rome, Palais Farnèse, 1992), 402 n.84, 95 and n.157.

24. As noted and discussed in James H. Nichols, Jr., *Epicurean Political Philosophy* (Ithaca, NY: Cornell University Press, 1972), 190 ff.

25. Miriam Griffin argues that this explanation of the Epicurean revival is not sufficient and points to additional factors. "Philosophy, Politics and Politicians at Rome," *Philosophia Togata*, ed. Miriam Griffin and Jonathan Barnes (Oxford: Clarendon Press, 1989), 8–9.

26. E. G. Sihler, *Cicero of Arpinum* (New York: G. E. Stechert, 1933), 25. See *Fin.* 1.16; *Tusc.* 3.38; *Epistulae ad Familiares* [*Fam.*] 13.1.2. Griffin (6) thinks it likely that Cicero heard Phaedrus initially at Athens.

27. *Fin.* 1.16, where Cicero reports attending the lectures of Zeno and Phaedrus in the company of Atticus; also 5.3. The nature of the Epicureanism of Atticus is explored in Robert J. Leslie, *The Epicureanism of Titus Pomponius Atticus* (Philadelphia: College Offset Press, 1950), and in Cyril Bailey's review of Leslie's book, *Journal of Roman Studies* 41 (1951): 163–64; more recently in Miriam Griffin, "From Aristotle to Atticus: Cicero and Matius on Friendship," *Philosophia Togata II*, ed. Jonathan Barnes and Miriam Griffin (Oxford: Clarendon Press, 1997), 105 ff.

28. *Fam.* 7.12, 15.16.

29. *Epistulae ad Quintum Fratrem* 2.11.5. A more extensive discussion of his singular reference to Lucretius and the somewhat mysterious overall silence about him is found in my essay "Cicero and the Rebirth of Political Philosophy," *The Political Science Reviewer* 8 (Fall 1978), 89 and n.50. Also, see Sedley, 1 ff. At another point in his letters (*Fam.* 6.11.2), Cicero professes friendship with the Epicurean Siro, who was to be Virgil's teacher. Philodemus, also a contemporary of Cicero and a prominent Epicurean teacher and writer whose work is sometimes taken as a source for parts of Cicero's *De Natura Deorum*, is also treated with notable reticence in Cicero's extant work, being named specifically only once and on that occasion in company with Siro (*Fin.* 2. 119); without being directly named, he is, however, discussed at some length in *In Pisonem* [*Pis.*], 68 ff.

30. *Epistulae ad Atticum* [*Att.*] 7.2. Notable among the speeches are *Pis.* in 55 and *Pro Sestio* in 57.

31. On the reliability of Cicero's account of Epicureanism in *Fin.* see Phillip Mitsis, *Epicurus' Ethical Theory: The Pleasures of Invulnerability* (Ithaca, NY: Cornell University Press, 1988), 7–8, 73. Overall, there is much confidence in Cicero's account. See Michael C. Stokes, who finds in *Fin.* "the fullest consecutive account extant" of Epicureanism. He claims that Cicero does not "misrepresent" Epicureanism and believes it is "not yet proved" that Cicero failed to pay careful attention to the extant texts of Epicurus. "Cicero on Epicurean Pleasures," *Cicero the Philosopher*, ed. J. G. F. Powell (Oxford: Clarendon Press, 1995), 145, 150–53, and passim. Similar confidence in Cicero's account is found in Carlos Lévy, "La Dialectique de Cicéron dans les Livres II et IV du *De Finibus*," *Revue des Études Latines* 62 (1984): 111–17, and in his *Cicero Academicus*; Gisela Striker, "Epicurean Hedonism," *Essays on Hellenistic Epistemology and Ethics* (Cambridge: Cambridge University Press, 1996), 196–208;

Jacques Brunschwig, "The Cradle Argument in Epicureanism and Stoicism," *The Norms of Nature*, ed. Malcolm Schofield and Gisela Striker (Cambridge: Cambridge University Press, 1986), 113–44, esp. 127; Malte Hossenfelder, "Epicurus—hedonist malgré lui"; also in Schofield and Striker, 245–63. Hossenfelder finds Cicero overall reliable except in one instance (257). Not overall supportive of the adequacy and/or fairness of Cicero's account are Brad Inwood, "*Rhetorica Disputatio: The Strategy of* de Finibus II," *The Politics of Therapy: Hellenistic Ethics in Its Rhetorical and Literary Context*, ed. M. Nussbaum, *Apeiron* 23 (1990) 4: 143–64; and Long, 30.

32. *ND.* 1.15, 58. The dramatic date for *ND.* is 77–75.

33. The speaker who uses these quotations, comments on them, and usually argues with them is designated "M" in the text, probably standing for Marcus, Cicero's first name, or *magister* (teacher). Internal evidence in *Tusc.* makes clear that M, the major voice throughout the disputations, is Cicero himself. At times, however, M as Cicero *persona* speaks to counter and refine the student's or young man's *(adolescens)* opinion and may not necessarily reflect the view of Cicero the author. Apparently the "M" and "A" *(adolescens)* designations for the speakers in *Tusc.* are not found in the earliest manuscripts; see A. E. Douglas, "Introduction," *Tusculan Disputations* I (Warminster, England: Aris and Phillips, 1985), 16, n.48.

34. Above, n. 2.

35. Manfred Fuhrmann draws heavily on Cicero's correspondence through this time in making this suggestion. *Cicero and the Roman Republic* (Oxford: Blackwell, 1992), 151–52.

36. See especially *Fin.* 2.1–3 for Cicero's own recognition of that rhetorical mode and its limitations. Inwood denies that Cicero presents Epicureanism fairly in this mode but also sees the rhetorical approach as able to advance the truth in certain ways; see especially 152–63. Also see Philippa Smith, "How Not to Write Philosophy: Did Cicero Get It Right?" in Powell, esp. 311–12, 321.

37. *Fin.* 1.28–29, where the dialogue turns to focus on issues of moral philosophy.

38. *Off.* 1.5.

39. *Off.* 1.6.

40. Cicero seems to regard Epicureanism as "the philosophy" easiest to comprehend and easiest to dismiss. *Fin.* 1. 13, 27; 3. 1–3. *Tusc.* 2. 7; 4. 6–7; 5. 108. *Academica [Ac.]* 1. 5. Also, Inwood, 143–44.

41. This description, Cumming says, "at any rate" applies to Cicero's procedure in "political philosophy"; I assume that comment reflects an understanding of political philosophy inclusive of moral philosophy, for it is there that the critical engagement of Epicureanism takes place. *Human Nature and History* (Chicago: University of Chicago Press, 1969), 1: 236. See Lévy, *Cicero*, 539.

42. *Div.* 2.2.

43. See, e.g., *Tusc.* 1.119, 2.13, 5.5.

44. *Tusc.* 3.36; *Fin.* 3.40, 5.50; *ND.* 1.93 (on the Epicurean abuse of Socrates). Griffin ("Philosophy," 16), in treating Roman attitudes toward philosophy, notes the view, which Cicero shared, that the Epicureans were "the most dogmatic of all" philosophers. Yet Griffin ("From Aristotle," 104 ff.) suggests a considerable urbanity and flexibility in the Roman Epicureans with whom Cicero associated. On the character of Epicurean "philosophy" as well as the tradition of opposition between Epicureans and Academics before Cicero, see David K. O'Connor, "The Invulnerable

Pleasures of Epicurean Friendship," *Greek-Roman-and Byzantine Studies* 30 (Summer 1989) 2: 170–71; Paul A. Vander Waerdt, "Introduction," *The Socratic Movement* (Ithaca, NY: Cornell University Press, 1994), 7–8 and n.24; Harold Tarrant, *Scepticism or Platonism?* (Cambridge: Cambridge University Press, 1985), 126–27; Martha Nussbaum, "Therapeutic Arguments: Epicurus and Aristotle," in Schofield and Striker, 74; Nichols, 20 ff.; Lévy, "La Dialectique," 123; *Cicero,* 173, 398 ff.; A. A. Long, "Socrates in Hellenistic Philosophy," *Classical Quarterly* 38 (1988) 1: 155–56.

45. This tension is manifest within Lucretius, *De Rerum Naturam,* iv. 469–521. See the commentary of Sedley on this passage, *Lucretius,* 85–90. Note Jefferson's Epicureanism in this respect, as expressed in a letter to John Adams (August 15, 1820):

> Rejecting all organs of information therefore but my senses, I rid myself of the Pyrrhonisms with which an indulgence in speculations hyperphysical and antiphysical so uselessly occupy and disquiet the mind. A single sense may indeed be sometimes decieved [*sic*], but rarely: and never all our senses together, with their faculty of reasoning. They evidence realities; and there are enough of these for all the purposes of life, without plunging into the fathomless abyss of dreams and phantasms. I am satisfied, and sufficiently occupied with the things which are, without tormenting or troubling myself about those which may indeed be, but of which I have no evidence.

The Adams-Jefferson Letters, ed. Lester J. Cappon (Chapel Hill: University of North Carolina Press, 1959), 569.

46. In *ND,* as already noted above, the Epicurean view is stated and challenged first. Cicero gives the role of critic in the dialogue to Cotta, identified as an Academic skeptic. My argument here is that for Cicero the Epicurean position on the divinities and ultimate matters is implausible, chiefly because of its lack of congruity with the moral experience of human beings and the needs of that experience. Such an argument is possible in part because the skeptical inquiry of the likes of Cotta and Cicero himself undermines the assurance of "scientific" truth claimed for the Epicurean understanding of the whole, the Epicurean worldview.

47. Notable on this theme is Nussbaum in Schofield and Striker, 39 ff., 68, 73; also, *The Therapy of Desire* (Princeton, NJ: Princeton University Press, 1994), 124 ff., 492–93. See Sedley's concern that Nussbaum's contrast of therapeutic argument with other philosophical approaches may be exaggerated. "The Cure of Souls," *TLS* (June 24, 1994): 9–10. Also, Vander Waerdt's emphasis of the role of removing false opinions for reaching tranquillity with his resulting concern that Nussbaum goes too far in reducing the philosophical element in the Epicurean therapeutic strategy. "The Justice of the Epicurean Wise Man," *Classical Quarterly* 37 (1987): 2: 412.

48. *Tusc.* 3.41 ff., Hossenfelder, 251 ff., Stokes, 158, 162 f., 166, 170.

49. *Fin.* 1.23; 2.15, 35–36. *Tusc.* 2.17 ff., 5, 95–96.

50. See n. 31 above, especially the work of Stokes.

51. *Tusc.* 3.41; *De Oratore [De Or.]* 3.62.

52. *Fin.* 1.23, 30; 2.98. Notes 48 and 49 above.

53. On the depth of the difference between Epicurus and Cicero, see Lévy, *Cicero,* 362–64, 401–02, 433–34; O'Connor, 177–81.

54. *Fin.* 1.55; 2.21–22. On the controversy within the Epicurean tradition on this, *ND.,* 1.111 ff.; *Tusc.* 3.37.

55. *Fin.* 1.25, 45–46; 2.73; 5.74, 93. *Tusc.* 3.48–49; 5.93 ff. *Fam.* 15.19.2; *Off.* 3.118; Lévy, *Cicero,* 424 ff.

56. *Tusc.* 5.95.

57. See, e.g., *Fin.* 2.80. *Tusc.* 3.46; 5.26–31. In a similar assessment, Cicero confesses in a letter (to Memmius, June or July 51, *Fam.* 13.1.2) to have lost respect for Phaedrus, the Epicurean teacher of his youth, as a philosopher but to continue to hold him as "a good, amiable and dutiful man" *(bonus et suavis et officiosus).* Also, *Fam.* 15.19.3. Centuries ago Petrarch appeared to get this aspect of Cicero just right. He described "what Cicero feels about Epicurus: Cicero approves of his character in many passages, while he everywhere condemns his intellect and rejects his doctrine." "On His Own Ignorance and That of Many Others," trans. Hans Nachod, in *The Renaissance Philosophy of Man*, ed. Ernest Cassirer, Paul Oskar Kristeller, and John Herman Randall, Jr. (Chicago: University of Chicago Press, 1948), 55.

58. On Epicurus himself as philosopher, *Tusc.* 5.73, *Fin.*1.26. On popular Epicureanism of Cicero's time, *Ac.* 1.5, *Tusc.* 4.6–7, n. 44 above. Cicero actually uses the phrase and concept of plebian philosophy in reference to thinkers who deny the Socratic/Platonic claims for the immortality of the soul. *Tusc.* 1.55; *De Senectute* 85.

59. *Off.* 1.5; *Fin.* 2.28, 35, 80–81; *Ac.* 2.37 ff.; *Tusc.* 5.87 ff. One senses in Mitsis and others an uneasiness with this argument of Cicero and the suspicion that if Epicureans are thought to be living better than their theory, one may not understand their theory adequately.

60. On an Epicurean basis, the call to virtue is unrealistic: *Tusc.* 2.17 ff.; 3:32 ff.; 5:73–75, 88 ff. The allure of wealth will triumph: *Fin.* 2.84–85. The notion of pleasure must be kept at a distance: *Fin.* 2.117–18.

61. *Pis.* 68 ff.; *Post reditum in Senatum* 14–15; above, n. 30.

62. Theodor Mommsen, the formidable and formative nineteenth-century historian of Rome and overall no friend of Cicero, appears to have shared much of Cicero's view of Epicureanism. At one point Mommsen notes the spread of Epicureanism in the late Republic against the backdrop of a reaction to Stoicism: "It was principally antipathy towards the boastful and tiresome Roman Pharisees [the Stoa], coupled doubtless with the increasing disposition to take refuge from practical life in indolent apathy or empty irony, that occasioned during this epoch the extension of the system of Epicurus to a larger circle." Earlier in his *History* Mommsen assessed Epicurus and Epicureanism much as Cicero had: "But this Roman Epicureanism was not so much a philosophic system as a sort of philosophic mask, under which—very much against the design of its strictly moral founder—thoughtless sensual enjoyment disguised itself for good society." *The History of Rome*, trans. William P. Dickson (New York: Charles Scribner's Sons, 1905; reprinted Glencoe, Ill.: Free Press, 1957), 5:444; 4:201.

63. *Fin.* 1.25; *Tusc.* 3.50–51; 4.6–7. *Fam.* 15.19.2–3. It is interesting to note that the Stoic Epictetus, whom Jefferson singled out as one who misrepresents the Epicureans, thought that among the deficiencies of this philosophy was its inability to put up resistance to those "goods" that were already equipped with great persuasive power for most human beings. See "Arrian's Discourses of Epictetus" in *The Stoic and Epicurean Philosophers*, ed. Whitney J. Oates, trans. P. E. Matheson (New York: Random House, 1940), 356–57.

64. "Likely to" is used advisedly here. Leslie (13) has summarized the Epicurean tradition with respect to exceptions to the general rule—exceptions, however, that can be said to follow from the calculative injunction that gives rise to the general rule: "Prominent participation in affairs was permissible if the necessity of self-preservation

compelled, or if one were of such an inherently active disposition that only thus could he be happy."

65. In a letter to his Epicurean friend Paetus (*Fam.* 9.24.4) in the last year of his life, Cicero indicates his appreciation of the comradeship and philosophical discourse of the Epicureans and endeavors to make clear that the key objection for him is the lack of dedication to the Republic by Epicureans. Cicero indicates he is ready to give his life for this cause. Griffin discusses this letter and Cicero's self-affirmation as an indication that he has not converted to Epicureanism. "Philosophical Badinage in Cicero's Letters to His Friends," in Powell, 339; also on this and other correspondence with Epicureans, "From Aristotle," 108.

66. As suggested above (in the reference to the prologue of *Rep.* on p. 14), the claim that one might live better than his theory is also applicable in principle and hypothetically to an injunction to avoid politics in order to maintain a tranquil soul. It seems, however, that when Cicero draws on the notion of living better than the theory, he has in mind virtuous living such as that of Epicurus that contrasts with the expected tendency to vulgar hedonism and not political efforts that would contrast with the counsel to avoid politics. Griffin ("Philosophy," 12–13) notes that a number of Roman Epicureans were, for whatever reasons, involved in politics. Martha Nussbaum (*The Therapy*, 495–96) notices in certain Epicureans a concern with others and the world around them that goes beyond the official doctrine of the school.

67. In another context Cicero had explicitly entertained the notion, suggestive of latter-day existentialism, that nothing but nature is to blame for burying truth in darkness and thus putting the norms we seem to need beyond our reach. *Ac.* 1.44–45; 2.32. *Orator* 237–38. Leo Strauss, *Natural Right and History* (Chicago: University of Chicago Press, 1953), 6; "What Is Liberal Education?" *Liberalism: Ancient and Modern* (New York: Basic Books, 1968), 8.

68. *Leg.* 1.39; twice in *De Or.* 3.64.

69. *Leg.* 1.32, 37.

70. Woldemar Görler closely examines this passage in "Silencing the Troublemaker: *De Legibus* I. 39 and the Continuity of Cicero's Skepticism," Powell, 85–113. Görler persuasively rebuts those scholars who take this passage as an indication that Cicero is not at this time an Academic skeptic. In addition, see Lévy, *Cicero*, 515. Görler also notes (101) that such skeptics in Cicero's dialogues are not individuals who intend destructive moral and political effects from their inquiry and seem in many ways moral exemplars for Cicero. One might conclude that their philosophical methodology, like the Epicureans' specific dogma, did not necessarily predict the moral quality of their lives.

71. *Leg.* 1.38–39. At *Tusc.* 3.51, Cicero remarks that if the Epicureans hold the truth, it is not such as can be publicly stated in general or in politically responsible bodies, and it is not a truth that will win public acclaim when articulated by a potential leader or Epicurean wise man. See also *Fin.* 2.74, *Brutus*, 131.

72. Similarly regarding *De Or.* 3.64: the inappropriateness of a philosophy, in the light of the need for persuasion and public leadership, does not settle the question of its truth, but it becomes a factor in determining whether the philosophy is consistent with human nature. At *Tusc.* 5.82 Cicero is inclined to think those very courageous Stoic statements about the self-sufficiency of the virtuous life are also the truest; perhaps the utility of such statements in the public realm plays an important part in mak-

ing them appear true; see also *Paradoxa Stoicorum* 23, where what is truest is also found to be the most useful. Cicero does seem to be using something like overall congruence, or that which is fitting as the standard of truth, and to regard humankind as attuned by nature in a number of ways to this truth.

73. At *Ac.* 2.66 Cicero speaks of his own way of determining the probably true as one wherein broad understandings rather than minutely refined arguments play a greater part *(rationes has latiore specie, non ad tenue elimatas)*.

74. Above, p. 3–4.

75. All forms of critique of Cicero on Epicurus and our testing of them can benefit from an effort to understand Cicero's thought more completely and in its distinctive integrity, and, of course, such testing ultimately requires the equally careful engagement with the limited extant sources for Epicurus and the Epicureans that we have outside the texts of Cicero. Nevertheless, what has been sketched of Cicero's thought in this paper gives some basis for challenging the correctness with which some criticize Cicero while elevating Epicurus and Epicureanism. Paul MacKendrick, in his useful, compendious study entitled *The Philosophical Books of Cicero* (New York: St. Martin's Press, 1989),146, argues that Cicero was selective in what he chose to use and attack among the writings of Epicurus. Bruce Harris shares this view in his much earlier study, *Cicero as an Academic* (Auckland, NZ: University of Auckland, 1961), 17. What Cicero chose to overlook, claims MacKendrick, is the "nobility" of the Epicurean teaching—specifically "the quietude, the asceticism, . . . the social contract as the basis for justice, the warmth of the Epicurean concept of friendship." MacKendrick concludes, "In sum, Cicero is not a safe source for understanding Epicureanism, chiefly because he assumes a viciousness not inherent in the doctrine." Rather than assuming a "viciousness" in the doctrine, Cicero makes an argument about a defect in the doctrine that leads it to be a facilitator of the human inclination to sensual indulgence. Cicero does not so much ignore such aspects of Epicureanism as the emphasis on quietude and asceticism, etc., as he makes an argument about their unstable or dangerous character. Cicero's arguments may not be convincing to all, but we must not suppose that the "busy" Cicero makes no plausible arguments (also, n. 31 above). The tendency to be dismissive of aspects of Cicero's critique without sufficiently entering into his argument and the overall character of his thought is evident even in more mainstream and generally more compelling scholarship; this is scholarship, such as Brad Inwood's, that has some appreciation for Cicero. Inwood (151) points at Cicero's "mere prejudicial slanders against hedonism" in Book II of *Finibus*. Earlier Inwood (144) had made the revealing comment that "there is much in Cicero's treatment of Epicureanism which sympathetic modern students of the school find unfair." It is revealing in that it calls attention to the role an academic attraction to philosophical hedonism may be playing in the reading of Cicero, the Garden's great opponent. Inwood (153 ff.) goes on to, among other things in his piece, a serious engagement with the question of Cicero's grasp of "the subtleties of Epicurean pleasure." It is on this part of Cicero's understanding of Epicurus and the related status of Epicurean "virtue" that most concerns with Cicero's adequacy and fairness focus. Vander Waerdt ("The Justice," 408) writes of Cicero's "uncharitable interpretation of Epicurus' position" and a resulting "systematic misrepresentation of Epicurean doctrine." Conceding that what Vander Waerdt brings out may have been underrepresented in the post-Cicero tradition of criticism of Epicurus and Epicureans, I seek in this essay to call attention to Cicero's own understanding of the philosophical hedonism or

high-toned utilitarianism of Epicurus and his argument on the nonviability of this hedonism. The plea here is for a charitable interpretation of Cicero. Overall in his essay
Vander Waerdt is properly insistent on the pleasure/pain basis for all that Epicurus
teaches and discerningly notes that most critics of Epicureanism, including Cicero, are
not looking specifically at the Epicurean wise man but rather at Epicureanism as embraced by ordinary people.

76. Mitsis is an exception; see 97 and 102 n.7 for some explicit indication of his in-
terpreting Epicurus in such a way as to find altruism and aspects of a virtue-based justice rather than simply a contractual understanding of justice. Qualified support for
the interpretive direction of Mitsis is found in Julia Annas, *The Morality of Happiness*
(Oxford: Oxford University Press, 1993), 293, 448; Striker, "Greek Ethics and Moral
Theory," 177, and "Epicurean hedonism," 198 ff.; Nussbaum (with respect to friendship), *The Therapy*, 250; Griffin, "From Aristotle," 102. Opposing this interpretive direction are Inwood, 157 n.26; O'Connor, 167, 182; Vander Waerdt, "The Justice," 407
n.22, 416 n.56, 420–21. At 405 Vander Waerdt touches on the struggle over this matter within the Epicurean tradition; such differences are explored further by him in
"Hermarchus and the Epircurean Genealogy of Morals, *Transactions of the American
Philological Association* 118 (1988): esp. 102–3.

77. Especially, *Politics* 1263a40 to 1263b5. Tocqueville (448) writes of the impossibility of overcoming love of riches, but the possibility of making men honest in their
pursuit of wealth.

78. Explored in my "Nationalism and Transnationalism in Cicero," *History of European Ideas* 16 (January, 1993): 785–91.

79. *Att.* vii. 2; also *Fam.* 7.12.

80. Letter to Mercy Warren (April 16, 1776) in *Warren-Adams Letters, Being
Chiefly a Correspondence among John Adams, Samuel Adams, and James Warren*
(Boston: Massachusetts Historical Society, 1917; reprint, New York: AMS Press,
1972),1: 201–203.

81. Walter Lippmann, *The Public Philosophy* (New Brunswick, NJ: Transaction
Publishers, 1989), 114. Originally published as *Essays in the Public Philosophy* by Little, Brown, 1955.

2

Soulcraft, Citizenship, and Churchcraft: The View from Hippo

John von Heyking

In January 1996, Reverend Joe Wright of the Central Christian Church of Wichita, Kansas, opened a session of the Kansas State Senate with a prayer meant to solicit God's help in forming the souls of wayward legislators, and the citizens they led, for the good of the *polis* and for the city of God. His prayer included the following invocations:

> We have lost our spiritual equilibrium and inverted our values.
> We confess that we have ridiculed the absolute truth of your Word and called it moral pluralism.
> We have worshipped other gods and called it multiculturalism.
> We have exploited the poor and called it the lottery.
> We have killed our unborn children and called it choice.
> We have shot abortionists and called it justifiable.
> We have ridiculed the time-honored values of our forefathers and called it enlightenment.
> Guide and bless these men and women who have been sent here by the people of Kansas, and who have been ordained by you, to govern this great state.
> Grant them your wisdom to rule and may their decisions direct us to the center of your will.
> I ask it in the name of your son, the living savior, Jesus Christ.
> Amen.[1]

Reverend Wright's prayer was not the bland, politically correct platitude that citizens have come to expect from politically in-touch religious leaders. Rather, it reflects a growing anxiety that Enlightenment hallmarks such as instrumental rationality, autonomy, and the privatization of religion are corrupting society. It reflects the anxiety common to liberal de-

mocracy, as noticed by Alexis de Tocqueville, that individualism undermines morality. Tocqueville considered modern freedom a great achievement but also a problematic one, because, faced with unlimited possibility, "limitless independence" and the "perpetual agitation of all things
[that] makes them restive and fatigues them," people may soon hand
themselves over to a master.[2] Liberal democracies tend not to articulate
clearly the moral basis of freedom, and this lack of clarity can engender
despair, because although people acknowledge the existence of their
freedoms, those very freedoms prevent the forming of a dominant social
or political authority that explains *why* they enjoy those freedoms. The despair that results from the perceived meaninglessness of their freedoms
(expressed today as "instrumental reason," "technicism," "secularism,"
etc.) can lead people to seek meaning by throwing themselves into surro-
gates for religion, such as totalizing ideologies or closed subcultures that
purport to provide all of life's answers and to explain, and explain away,
the meaning of freedom. While many may have some sympathy with Reverend Wright's petitions, his outlook is problematic. He appears to reject
any possibility that the political can serve as a source of moral rejuvenation—all rejuvenation must come from without, from the saving grace of
Jesus Christ. No mention is made of statesmanship or the possibility that
non-Christians can practice virtue. His position reflects the inability of
modern human beings to negotiate properly their longings for temporal
happiness that can be realized in temporal arrangements, and their longing for eternal happiness, which is natural but that human beings often
and immoderately demand political life to satisfy. Such immoderation
consists in an attempt to harmonize the cities of man and of God.

By making this argument, he might be said to follow in the Christian tradition of Augustinianism, named after St. Augustine, who is supposed to
have taught that political life, as originating in sin, cannot be a source of
moral order and that any rejuvenation must come exclusively through the
channels of the Christian church.[3] Political Augustinianism has been criticized from many quarters, because either it merely aggravates modernity's
privatization of religion by creating closed subcultures of piety that withdraw
from the main political culture, or it makes political life subservient to the interests of the church at the expense of those outside the sacerdotal order.[4]
Both criticisms, the former modern and the latter medieval, are based on an
Augustinianism that sees politics as based on sin *(propter peccatum)*. This
essay offers the beginnings of a different account of Augustine's political
thought by examining what can be called his "moderated elevation" of politics, which speaks to our predicament.[5] While most modern interpreters
agree that politics, for Augustine, is *propter peccatum,* they usually do not
portray the moral possibilities of social life in terms as stark as just outlined.
Rather, scholars such as Jean Bethke Elshtain point to the ways that civil so-

ciety's institutions, such as the family and churches, can rejuvenate liberal society's moral order.[6] However, civil society is not the same as political life, and some have gone farther and noticed Augustine's recognition of the role of politics in cultivating virtue.[7] Politics, for Augustine, is a positive good that satisfies longings for togetherness in particular relations, but instead of being dominated by the church, it actually shares an interdependent, yet separate, relationship with the sacerdotal order, whose function is to fulfill man's longings for eternal happiness. This relationship is important to consider, because soulcraft is a responsibility shared both by the church(es) and by a political order whose purpose goes beyond simply that of peace and security (which is nevertheless a rare and important achievement). Any attempt to renew political life must inevitably deal with the issue of how religious authority relates to political authority. Augustine's understanding of the relationship between political life and the church provides a way of indirectly cultivating wayward souls that avoids the modern extremes of a pervasive secularism that engenders a sense of meaninglessness and its corresponding reactions in totalizing ideologies and closed subcultures.

AUGUSTINE AND POLITICAL SOULCRAFT

One of the obstacles to thinking about soulcraft and statecraft is that, since Hobbes, we have come to regard politics as instrumental and procedural—that is, not political in the classical sense. Attempts by Rousseau, Hegel, Marx, and others to save or transform modern liberalism from its shallowness have been destructive, generating and/or aggravating the kind of spiritual pathologies well documented by writers such as Jacob Talmon and Eric Voegelin.[8] Others, such as Yves Simon, advocate a moderated and elevated polity that allows for soulcraft and avoids ideological extremism. Simon contends that from the citizen's perspective, human existence must appear hopeless if the community is not recognizable as the highest attainment of nature, because it is "virtually unlimited with regard to diversity of perfections, and virtually immortal."[9] Voegelin makes a similar point when he writes that political society "is as a whole a little world, a *cosmion,* illuminated with meaning from within by the human beings who continuously create and bear it as the mode and condition of their self-realization."[10] In short, political life is made meaningful because it shapes human personality and cultivates virtues. The "virtual immortality" of political life, moreover, partially compensates for the brevity of mortal life. Can this view of politics be reconciled with an Augustinian eschatological hope and faith, according to which the status of earthly life, including political life, would appear to be radically diminished?

Augustine is often thought to have rejected this kind of understanding of politics and the perceived idealism of the ancient political philosophy that sustained it. For him, politics is *propter peccatum,* a consequence of original sin, and political life lays no claim to moral formation beyond obeying rulers who can maintain the peace and restrain the wicked. At best, politics can be morally rejuvenated only by subpolitical institutions in civil society like the family, or by churches (under the sovereign state), or by an extrapolitical institution like the Catholic Church in the Middle Ages. This interpretation of Augustine has merit, as evidenced by his antipolitical rhetoric in the *City of God* (Civitate Dei [CD]) that aims at dissolving the libidinous pretensions of the ambitious, such as Roman aristocrats and modern ideologues. Unfortunately, however, rhetoric here tends to obscure a more substantive message. One must not forget that Augustine himself was actively engaged in politics, not only battling heretics (discussed below) and founding the church in North Africa but also using his office, as did other African bishops, to adjudicate civil disputes among the people according to imperial laws.[11] His practical activities were not as distant from Roman politics as we have come to think.

Augustine's affirmation of political life can be seen in a few places where he appears to distinguish the usual *practice* of politics from the *essence* of politics. The essence of political life can be seen in his discussion of the social, and thus political (for Augustine appears not to distinguish the two), nature of Adam: "The underlying purpose was that a single human being should not comprise many relationships in his one self but that these connections should be severally distributed among individuals and in this way serve to weld social life more securely by covering in their multiplicity a multiplicity of people."[12] Politics is that area where a multiplicity of human beings engages in a multiplicity of relations that form their persons as images of God and help to bring about their various perfections.

The difference between theory and practice can be seen in the way he treats the founding of Rome. He compares the sanctuary founded by Romulus and Remus to that founded by Christ (although he does not equate the two):

> It is granted that Romulus and Remus, seeking a means of increasing the population of the city they were founding, established a sanctuary *[asylum]* where any man might seek refuge and be free from injury *(noxa liber),* a wondrous example *[exemplum]* of what followed in honor of Christ.[13]

The foundations of Rome and of the church are comparable insofar as both constitute sanctuaries that people seek in pursuing freedom from injury. He later states that the sanctuary created by a political founding foreshadows the remission of sins promised by the city of God:

> The remission of sins that gathers citizens for the eternal city has something in it of the famous sanctuary of Romulus, which was a sort of shadow cast ahead. For there the multitude which was to found the city was congregated for the impunity of their crimes [CD 5.17; see also CD 2.29].

Augustine treats their remission and sanctuary in the double sense of seeing Rome's original inhabitants both as thugs seeking safety from those seeking vengeance on them, and as people truly seeking safety to enable them to begin new lives. This double voice is not necessarily equivocation. Rather, it appears to be consistent with the classical view that cities, founded often by violence and for the purpose of preserving life, have their end in the good life. Augustine, of course, regards Rome's founding as paradigmatic for the practice of politics, but he also argues that Romulus and Remus need not have been dominated by the lust for domination, which caused the fratricide: "For if the goal was to glory in domination, there would of course be less domination if power was limited by having to be shared. Accordingly, in order that all power might accrue to one single person, his fellow was removed; and what innocence *[quod innocentia]* would have kept smaller and better grew through crime into something larger and inferior" (CD 15.5). His construction of this sentence in the conditional suggests that founders not motivated by the lust for domination but by an ordinate love of glory may found more just regimes. Augustine does not provide any examples of a moderate founder, but he seems to consider it possible for political life to be guided by a moderation that enables rule to be shared, in a regime that is neither too rich nor too poor.[14]

Augustine is likewise thought to have regarded the pagan civic virtues as no more than "splendid vices." However, he makes a startling claim by observing that the virtues of the noble Romans constitute the seeds of the virtues of the city of God. He calls on the offspring of Regulus, Scaevola, the Scipios, and Fabricius to awaken their "praiseworthy inborn Roman character *[indoles Romana laudabilis]*" (CD 2.29). Peter Burnell comments on this passage that "it would be difficult to find a word more redolent of nature than *indoles,*"[15] because *indoles* means inborn or native quality and genius. Addressing these political men as candidates for the city of God, Augustine calls on them to "awake more fully *[evigila plenius]*: the majesty of God cannot be propitiated by that which defiles the dignity of man" (CD 2.29). Augustine saw in pagan statesmen the potential, the "inborn" quality, that would make them sufficiently receptive to become pious members of the city of God.[16]

What was this inborn quality if not a splendid vice? Augustine warns his Christian fellow travelers not to draw this conclusion too quickly. He seems to have seen a kind of nobility in Roman heroes, one that resembles the love of God and neighbor. He writes:

Examples *[exempla]* are set before us, containing necessary admonition, in order that we may be stung with shame if we shall see that we have not held fast those virtues for the sake of the most glorious city of God, which are, in whatever way, resembled by those virtues *[virtutes quarum istae utcumque sunt similes]* which they held fast for the sake of glory of a terrestrial city [CD 5.18].

Just as Christians cannot be too sure of their own salvation, so too must they avoid the temptation of dismissing the virtue of the best non-Christians. The Romans were dominated by the love of glory, which led most of them to create a horrible empire but inspired a few heroes like Regulus, who underwent torture at the hands of the Carthaginians to preserve his oath to the gods (CD 1.15). Augustine observes that Regulus's death testifies that the Roman gods do not ensure temporal happiness. Regulus's virtue resembles that which is required for the city of God and not for the Roman civil religion. Augustine's treatment of Regulus and a few other Romans indicates that he viewed their political love of glory as pointing beyond any temporal object to the glory of the city of God: "Your purpose, therefore, is not to be seen of men, that is, a desire that they should turn and notice you *[vos converti velitis]*, for of yourselves you are nothing. Rather, 'it is that they may glorify your father who is in heaven,' and that they may turn to him and become what you are *[conversi fiant quod estis]*" (CD 5.14). Love of God and neighbor does not rule out turning others to "become what you are" when what you are doing is testifying to a higher truth, which a few Romans like Regulus were able to do. Augustine's own example and argument show that part of churchcraft involves attempting to divine the virtue within the tumult of political ambition, just as part of political soulcraft involves attempting to divine and to form the talents of one's citizens.

Augustine's understanding of Rome's founding and the ordinate love of glory is consistent with his view that the love of God and neighbor is lived out first and foremost with those in closest proximity. Augustine emphatically rejects the idea that the Christian love of all humankind leads one to forget one's family and immediate neighbor—what Charles Dickens once called "telescopic philanthropy." Love of God and neighbor necessitates loving in particular relations. He writes: "In the first place, then *[Primitus ergo]*, he has the care *[cura]* of his own household, inasmuch as the order of nature or of human society provides him with a readier and easier access to them for caring *[consulendi]* for them. Wherefore the Apostle says: 'Whoever does not provide for his own, and especially for those of his household, he denies the faith, and is worse than an infidel'" (CD 19.14, quoting 1 Timothy 5:8). Augustine indicates that the love of neighbor is practiced most fully with those neighbors who are in the immediate vicinity, such as family, friends, and fellow citizens. His invocation of Paul shows how the love of neighbor is actualized in these close ties and how these ties most rigorously test our love. It is in our relationships with family, friends, and fellow citizens that we face the constant, day-to-day difficulties of securing justice and civil peace. Such tests include fellow citizens, whose political views and programs we dispute; the poor who plead for help at inconvenient times; friends who fail us but who deserve our forgiveness; and family members whose needs divert our attention from other pursuits. These relationships test our patience with the demands of various members of our community, but they also form our personalities and help to determine who we are, as Augustine observes of Adam's social and political nature. Thus, the universal love of neighbor is most rigorously practiced (or tested) with our particular relations.

One does not choose such relationships, and one's obligations derive from their having been chosen, as it were, for one. Augustine observes that the identity of one's neighbor depends in large part on chance:

> So you should take particular thought for those who by the chance of place or time or anything else are, as if by lot *[quasi quadam sorte]*, in particularly close contact with you. Suppose that you had plenty of something which had to be given to someone in need of it but could not be given to two people, and you met two people, neither of whom had a greater need or a closer relationship to you than the other: you could do nothing more just than to choose by lot the person whom you should give what could not be given to both. Analogously, since you cannot take thought for all men, you must settle by lot in favor of the one who happens to be more closely associated *[adhaerere]* with you in temporal matters.[17]

One loves one's neighbor by loving those in proximity, which defines them as neighbors *(proximi)* (De Doctrina Christiana [DDC] 1.31.68). Their proximity is determined "as if by lot." It is tempting to interpret the above passage as Hannah Arendt does, by arguing that Augustine reduces neighbors to mere occasions of one's love.[18] It is tempting to conclude that Augustine merely aggravates the modern and postmodern tendency to treat human beings and their relations as mere accidents thrown into a meaningless world in which we treat our neighbors simply as means to our ends. Contrary to Arendt, however, Augustine does not mean that we treat people as mere occasions once they enter our lives. For Augustine, that our relations are determined "as if by lot" constitutes the link between our particular relations, which form our personalities as Americans, Texans, Canadians, or southern Alberta cowboys, and the universal love of neighbor that underscores the contingent nature of our particular relations. The importance that Augustine places on the idea of "lot" can also be grasped from commonsense experience. For instance, I would not be a friend of a person if I had not attended a particular university in a different country at a particular point of time and if I had not chosen to go to the particular party at which I met my friend. The element of chance in our choice of friends is seen when we attempt to consider the countless factors that would have prevented us from meeting had we both made different choices at numerous points along the way. This randomness is transformed into meaningfulness when we consider that each particular event in our lives constitutes, according to Augustine, a moment that leads us to turn toward (or away from, as the case may be) our proper end, to love God and neighbor, which can be discerned by natural reason.[19] Augustine's pastoral example provides a model of how lost souls in a fractured world can find their way without losing their liberties.

Finally, Augustine's affirmation of the goodness of politics can be glimpsed in his understanding of ruling. Augustine frequently uses *consulere* to describe ruling. Rowan Williams suggests that "spiritual nurture" is the best translation for this term.[20] Augustine derives his understanding of *consulere* partly from Cicero and partly from the Roman office of consul, which derived its name "from taking counsel *[a consulendo]*, not from reigning *[a regnando]* or having dominion *[dominando]*" (CD 5.12). He follows Cicero, who argued that a *populus* must be maintained by a certain amount of consultation *(consilium)*, where the consulting body (be it monarchic, aristocratic, or popular) must "always owe its beginning to the same cause as that which produced the city itself."[21] Consultation must be based upon the common sense of justice prevailing in the society.[22] Augustine understood the activity as leading or nurturing a people toward a goal (i.e., virtue) and doing so with their consent. This understanding of *consulere* is reflected in his practice of using it to signify the love of God and neighbor (CD 4.5, 5.9, 9.6, 10.5, 11.23, 11.33, 15.7, 15.25, 19.12, 19.14) and to give orders (CD 2.18, 19.16). It was seen above in Augustine's statement that we should care first for our immediate neighbors (CD 19.14). In short, it denotes a statesmanship according to which the statesman forms a people within the boundaries of their capabilities and inclinations, seeking their consultation and consent but also informing their choices.

Augustine is usually seen to unite the love of God and neighbor with its expression in Israel and the church. Israel was first the exclusive location of the love of God in a sea of pagan reprobates; after Christ, the church is the exclusive location of the love of God, and this exclusivity is often seen to promote intolerance and to justify the coercion of heretics. It is important to note that Augustine's categories of the cities of God and of man refer primarily to types of love—one of God, the other exclusively of self—and that the institutions that represent those loves experience at best an intermingling of the two.[23] This certainly does not negate the importance of sacraments, liturgy, and the practices of the church. However, it appears that Augustine cannot deny that outsiders to these institutions may possibly be members of the city of God any more than he can affirm that insiders are members of the city of God, because the best of the "pagans" are capable of performing acts of virtue that are consistent (though not identical) with the highest virtues of the city of God. Augustine's assessment of non-Christian virtue necessitates a reconsideration of the way he understands the relationship between religion and politics.

Augustine did not think that Scripture provided a historical account of the genealogy of the city of God. Rather, he writes: "I cannot bring myself to believe that none [who duly worshiped God] existed, but if all were recorded the tale would be too long, and would exemplify diligent historical research rather than prophetic providence" (CD16.2; see also 15.8, 15, 16.1, 18.1).

Scripture does not list all members of the city of God; its purpose is to display the sharpest contrast between the virtuous and the reprobate. Those outside the city of God's "official" institutional expression include Job (CD 18.47), the inhabitants of Babylon who repented (CD 16.11, 20.5), a pagan witch who cryptically prophesied Christ (CD 18.23), and Melchizedek, the Canaanite priest-king who blessed Abraham with bread and wine (Gen. 14) and to whose priesthood Jesus Christ belongs (CD 16.22, 17.5, 7). Melchizedek is distinguished not by his family and blood, like the Aaronic line of priests; rather, "each human being is chosen in accordance with the merit that the divine grace has bestowed on him" (CD 20.21). It is startling that with a Canaanite priest-king, "then first appeared the sacrifice which is now offered to God by Christians in the whole wide world" (CD 16.22). The Augustine who, in his writings against the Manichaeans and elsewhere, described pre-Christian history in terms of symbols and events that prefigured Christ, is the same Augustine who could attribute a Christian experience of grace to an individual outside what normally passes for prophetic or sacred history. Elsewhere, he distinguishes the prophetic from the institutional dimensions of the church. He distinguishes between "bishops and presbyters *[episcopis et presbyteris]*, who are now literally *[proprie]* called in the church by the mystical name priests; but just as we call all Christians 'christs *[christos]*,' because of the ritual anointing *[mysticum chrisma]*, so we call all Christians 'priests *[sacerdotes]*' because they are members of one 'holy priest *[sacerdotis]*.' Of them the apostle Peter says: 'A holy people, a royal priesthood'" (1 Peter 2:9) (CD 20.10). The church needs to recognize the difference between institutional offices and the members of the body of Christ who lend their name to church offices. Augustine's ecclesiology enables prophetic authority to check institutional authority.

What, then, is the special function of the church, and how does its mission relate to political life? Whereas political life is the place where a particular people gather to live a particular way, the church's mission is to gather all together in sacrament, regardless of nation:

> While this heavenly city, therefore, goes its way as a stranger on earth, it summons citizens from all peoples, and gathers an alien society of all languages, caring naught what difference may be in mores, laws and institutions *[moribus legibus institutibusque]* by which earthly peace is gained or maintained, abolishing and destroying nothing of the sort, nay rather preserving and following them (for however different they may be among different nations, they aim at one and the same end, earthly peace), provided that there is no hindrance to the religion that teaches the obligation to worship one most high and true God [CD 19.17].

The church or churches most explicitly represent the city of God on earth because they administer the sacraments that most explicitly express the love of

God and of neighbor. While political life is natural and can cultivate virtues that prepare one for the city of God, its partial nature makes political life profoundly unable to fulfill human beings' longings for eternal happiness. Augustine regarded the longing for eternal happiness as natural and found that only the life expressed by the church can fulfill that longing. Cities are tempted to fill this function but degenerate into tyrannical empires such as Rome when they succumb. The church places a crucial check on the city and reminds it to keep within its particular sphere of competence.

Recognizing that rogues and fools, as readily as decent and intelligent people, can occupy the offices of each side, Augustine thought that church and polity must remain within each one's respective sphere of competence and that the gray zone in between would require prudential management. Prudential management allows for more possibilities to arrange the relationship between politics and religion than that in which Augustine found himself and that was prominent for the next thousand years. Such prudence would be guided by some constants, however. The main constant, discussed above, is that political life and life in the church serve as *exempla* for each other. Most of the time, both sides lack someone with the prophetic perspective of a David, and so each must make do with referring to the other as an example to follow and as a check on itself. A concrete manifestation of this scheme would involve allowing the laity to check the church's political activities, because virtue is not restricted to offices. The liberal democratic arrangement of separating church and state is one way of institutionalizing this principle, as is state support for religious institutions such as religious education.[24] On the other hand, it perhaps also allows the church to serve as a locus for political resistance against a tyrannical government, like the Roman Catholic church served in Poland in the 1980s. Whichever form it takes, Augustine at least appears to make room for a relationship between religion and politics that moves beyond either a complete removal of religion from politics or one in which religious institutions dominate politics.

This basis for tolerance and religious pluralism within the political sphere appears to contrast with Augustine's justification of the persecution of heretics. He argued that the Donatist heretics should be "compelled" to enter the church, just as Jesus Christ told his disciples to compel outsiders to enter the house of His feast (Ep. 93.2.5, citing Luke 14:23). However, Augustine's justification addressed an emergency situation and was not intended as a general rule for politics, and nothing more than a suggestive explanation is offered here. Violence by heretics, aggravated in part by the ruthless policing by Roman imperial authorities, had made North Africa nearly ungovernable.[25] Roman authorities were often afraid to enforce any laws and were usually too brutal when they did enforce them.[26] Augustine, in response, adopted a grand, yet moderating, rhetoric by which he exhorted reluctant authorities to enforce the laws (but, perhaps impossibly, with clemency) and heretics to be in awe of the law.[27] That Augustine understood his justification as addressing an emergency situation can be seen in the fact that he prescribed violent punishments for violent heretics only; and nonviolent heretics, mostly leaders, were to receive small to moderate fines (see Ep. 104.1–2). He was interested in restricting violence instead of forcing people to convert (which is impossible to do). For instance, he opposed capital punishment and whipping with leaden rods (as Roman law required); instead, he prescribed beatings with wooden rods for violent heretics (Ep. 133.1–2), which was the same punishment meted out to unruly schoolboys such as himself in his youth.[28] The purpose of coercion, then, was to make heretics *act* virtuously, not to make them *become* virtuous or to enforce conversions:

> The thing to be considered when any one is coerced *[cogitur]* is not the mere fact of the coercion, but the nature of that to which he is coerced, whether it be good or bad: not that any one can be good in spite of his own will, but that, through fear of suffering what he does not desire *[sed timendo quod non vult pati]*, he either renounces his hostile prejudices *[impedientem animositatem]*, or is compelled to examine truth of which he had been contentedly ignorant; so that through fearing, [he] repudiate[s] falsehood that he had contended, or seek[s] truth of which he had been ignorant, and desiring to hold now what he had rejected *[ut timens vel respuat falsam de quo contendebat, vel quaerat verum quod nesciebat, et volens teneat jam quod nolebat]* [Ep. 93.5.16].

The purpose of coercion is to enable citizens to choose the right and the good, which resembles Aristotle's understanding of the coercive power of law.[29] The law cannot force a heretic to choose to *be* good. This recognition is reflected in Augustine's statement that coercion puts the heretic into the position of either renouncing his "hostile prejudices" or actively turning to the search for truth. The purpose of coercion is to clarify church doctrine to the heretic and to discipline him. After having done so, the individual heretic, freed from his initial ignorance, would have to choose whether or not to love the truth (and enter the church). Force, in this circumstance, is a necessary but not sufficient cause of conversion. The purpose of coercion, according to this passage, is to show the heretic the insufficiency of his object of worship and to teach him about the church in order to prevent his hostility toward it. To use a popular metaphor, the heretic is brought to water but is not forced to drink. Augustine addressed an emergency, violent situation by restricting the worst punishments to violent heretics. His justification of coercion was not meant to apply to the normal course of politics.

CONCLUSION

Many today worry that the gulf between the city of God and the city of man is wider than it should be. Many respond to this crisis by arguing that carriers of the city of God should build subcultures that preserve piety from the degeneracy of secular society. Others, like the Reverend Joe Wright, wish to channel God's grace directly through political institutions. Both of these responses draw from two versions of political Augustinianism. The preceding argument attempts to show that Augustine himself had a more nuanced way of rejuvenating society's moral order. In a time when technicism and heavy-handed dogma (both religious and secular) dominate political discourse, Augustine's more indirect mode of cultivating souls can elevate political life while moderating present destructive tendencies. Remembering that the cities of God and of man refer to their corresponding loves and less so to any particular institution, he thought that both loves were present in both politics and the church. He could acknowledge the virtue of Regulus and he regarded political life as intimating—distantly intimating, to be sure—the city of God. Both the city and the church have their respective functions in cultivating souls. Each function is unique, but they overlap to an extent. Augustine emphasizes their separation but also guides us as to how to negotiate between their respective functions. Thus, in building a robust bridge between the two cities, Augustine also keeps them firmly separated, thereby helping to prevent destructive attempts to combine them.

NOTES

1. John A. Dvorak and John Petterson, "Chaplain's Prayer Irks Some Lawmakers," *Kansas City Star*, 24 January 1996, C1. As of February 2002, the full text of the prayer remains posted on the website of Reverend Wright's church (www.centralcc.org/joe. html#prayer).

2. Alexis de Tocqueville, *Democracy in America*, trans. Harvey C. Mansfield and Delba Winthrop (Chicago: University of Chicago Press, 2000), 418.

3. H.-X. Arquillière, *L'Augustinisme politique: Essai sur la formation des theories politiques du moyen âge*, 2nd ed. (Paris: Vrin, 1955).

4. William Connolly, *The Augustinian Imperative* (Newbury Park, CA: Sage, 1991).

5. For a more detailed analysis of Augustine's understanding of the function of political life, see my *Augustine and Politics as Longing in the World* (Columbia: University of Missouri Press, 2001).

6. Jean Bethke Elshtain, *Augustine and the Limits of Politics* (Notre Dame, IN: University of Notre Dame Press, 1996).

7. Peter J. Burnell, "The Problem of Service to Unjust Regimes in Augustine's *City of God,*" *Journal of the History of Ideas* 54(2), 1993: 177–88; "The Status of Politics in St. Augustine's *City of God,*" *History of Political Thought* 12(1), Spring 1992: 13–29. Similarly, E. L. Fortin notes that Augustine's dialogue, *On the Free Choice of the Will*, suggests that governmental structure would have characterized Edenic life ("Political Idealism and Christianity in the Thought of St. Augustine," in *Classical Christianity and the Political Order: Reflections on the Theological-Political Problem*, ed. J. Brian Benestad [Lanham, MD: Rowman and Littlefield, 1996], 52, n.18).

8. Jacob L. Talmon, *The Origins of Totalitarian Democracy* (New York: Norton, 1970); Eric Voegelin, *From Enlightenment to Revolution*, ed. John Hallowell, (Durham, NC: Duke University Press, 1974). Notice should also be made of important attempts to recover transcendent openness within the liberal framework. See David Walsh, *The Growth of the Liberal Soul* (Columbia: University of Missouri Press, 1997).

9. Yves R. Simon, *A General Theory of Authority* (Notre Dame, IN: University of Notre Dame, 1980), 28–29.

10. Eric Voegelin, *New Science of Politics* (Chicago: University of Chicago Press, 1952), 27.

11. See Epistle 33.5. See also, Jill Harries, *Law and Empire in Late Antiquity* (Cambridge: Cambridge University Press, 1999), 204–5.

12. *City of God* 15.16. Translations are my own, but I have relied on the translation by R. W. Dyson (Cambridge: Cambridge University Press, 1998) [hereafter CD]. Political and social seem to be synonymous: "For the life of a city *[civitatis]* is certainly *[utique]* a social *[socialis]* life" (CD 19.17).

13. CD 1.34. The notion that political life distantly intimates the city of God is based on Augustine's view that the triune God becomes incarnate in creation: "therefore, let us gather up *[colligamus]*, as it were, the footprints that He left, deeply impressed in one place, more lightly in another, since they could not so much as exist, or be contained in any shape, or follow and observe any law, had they not been made by Him who supremely is, and is supremely good and supremely wise" (CD 11.28).

14. CD 4.3. See also his discussion of the Roman consuls (CD 5.12) and my extended discussion in *Augustine and Politics as Longing in the World*, chaps. 3 and 4.

15. Peter Burnell, "The Status of Politics in St. Augustine's *City of God*," *History of Political Thought* 12(1), Spring 1992, 17–18.

16. While Augustine delighted in heaping scorn on Roman pretensions for virtue and glory, he was in basic agreement with their philosophers about virtue and talent (CD 11.25). In general, see Penelope D. Johnson, "*Virtus*: Transition from Classical Latin to the *De Civitate Dei*," in *The City of God: A Collection of Critical Essays*, ed. Dorothy F. Donnelly (New York: Peter Lang, 1995), 233.

17. *De Doctrina Christiana*, trans. R. P. H. Green (Oxford: Clarendon Press, 1995), 1.29.61–2 [hereinafter DDC].

18. Hannah Arendt, *Love and Saint Augustine*, ed. Joanna Vecchiarelli Scott and Judith Chelius Stark (Chicago: University of Chicago Press, 1996), 97.

19. Frederick Crosson describes how each unique event narrated in Augustine's *Confessions* contributes to his eventual conversion and states that each event can be explained in terms of natural causation (and not reduced to natural causation) ("Structure and Meaning in St. Augustine's *Confessions*," *The Augustinian Tradition*, ed. Gareth B. Matthews [Berkeley: University of California Press, 1999], 31–32).

20. Rowan Williams, "Politics and the Soul: A Reading of the *City of God*," *Milltown Studies* 19/20, 1987, 64.

21. *De Re Publica* 1.27.43.

22. See Malcolm Schofield, "Cicero's Definition of *Res Publica*," in *Cicero the Philosopher*, ed. J. G. F. Powell (Oxford: Clarendon Press, 1995), 77.

23. See CD 1.35, 11.1, 11.34, 12.1, 14.28, 15.1, 15.22, 16.11, 18.1, 18.54.

24. See Thomas L. Pangle, "The Accommodation of Religion: A Tocquevillian Perspective," in Marian C. McKenna, ed., *The Canadian and American Constitutions in Comparative Perspective* (Calgary: University of Calgary Press, 1993), 6, 24.

25. Tony Honoré, *Law and the Crisis of Empire: 379–455 A.D.* (Oxford: Clarendon Press, 1998), 26, 133.

26. See Epistle 100, where Augustine pleads clemency for heretics who faced the death penalty.

27. On Augustine's rhetoric, see Harries, 96, and Peter Brown, "The Limits of Intolerance," in *Authority and the Sacred: Aspects of Christianisation of the Roman World* (Cambridge: Cambridge University Press, 1995), 44–46.

28. *Confessions*, 1.9–10.

29. See *Nicomachean Ethics* X:9, 1180a14–28.

3

From Moral Virtue to Material Benefit: *Dominium* and Citizenship in Late Medieval Europe

Cary J. Nederman

It is a commonplace of the literature on the history of citizenship, as well as on its theoretical principles and presuppositions, to construct a dichotomy between two widely divergent models of civic life and political identity. These two types of citizenship have been variously characterized. For Peter Riesenberg, the salient distinction is between the self-governing "citizen" of the ancient and medieval city and the inert "subject" of the modern territorial nation-state.[1] On John Pocock's account, the paradigmatic Aristotelian account of citizenship as reciprocal ruling may be juxtaposed with the Roman Law precept formulated by Gaius that the citizen is *legalis homo*.[2] Speaking more philosophically, Richard Flathman has posited a division between "high" and "low" conceptions of citizenship,[3] while Benjamin Barber distinguishes "thick" (democratic) from "thin" (liberal) ideas of the citizen.[4]

All such dichotomous taxonomies of citizenship—regardless of which notion their creators prefer—ultimately seem to share a common belief, however, that two and only two rival versions of citizenship have been available to the Western tradition of civic thought and practice. One involves an active, self-transforming conception of the *vita activa civile;* the other describes the passive individual subject to the authority of the state and its laws. We appear to be caught on a lemma whose horns are named "Aristotle" and "Hobbes." Depending upon the horn upon which we land, the cultivation of citizenship, then, has quite different implications. It entails either engagement in the vital moral/intellectual transformation of personhood or simply reminding citizens of their legal rights and obligations.

It is my contention that just such a dichotomous understanding of citizenship and civic life did in fact inform European political thought during the Latin Middle Ages. But I argue that toward the end of the medieval period, it

43

is possible to observe a theoretical challenge to the strict division between "high" and "low," or "active" and "passive," citizenship. The terms of the challenge derive directly from an attempt (couched in constructions that seem sometimes recognizably "modern") to combine, refine, and synthesize elements of the two supposedly irreconcilable poles of the tension. Admittedly, my claim here flies in the face of one of the most noticeable changes in the recent historiography of Western political thought, namely, the ongoing erosion of the once unbridgeable divide between the medieval and modern periods. Such supposedly quintessential modern political concepts as the state, liberty, natural rights, toleration, and constitutionalism have come to be interpreted by many scholars as originating in the intellectual world of medieval schoolmen, lawyers, and polemicists.[5] As J. H. Burns has observed in his introductory remarks to the *Cambridge History of Political Thought, 1450–1700*, "The differentiation . . . between 'early modern' and 'medieval' has softened. . . . The period from the late fifteenth century to the end of the seventeenth saw neither innovation nor even the unfolding of what had been implicit or latent, but rather the fuller and faster development of tendencies already explicitly present and manifest in late medieval society."[6] This judgment is supported by Brian Tierney's case that "elements of continuity existed in political and religious life (during a period of such incessant change) which might explain the survival of medieval ways of thought into the modern era."[7] The pendulum seems to have swung decisively in favor of a "continualist" construction of the terrain of European political theory between c. 1200 and c. 1700.

In many ways, this development is to be applauded; indeed, I have myself made some modest contributions to its hastening. But I fear that in the headlong rush to "medievalize" the modern—or is it to modernize the medieval?—there has been a tendency to gloss over a number of the critical changes that also characterized the unfolding of European political ideas during the centuries in question. In illustration of this point, I propose to consider a transformation in the concept of citizenship that may be noted in scholastically influenced political writing between the late thirteenth and the late fifteenth centuries—a development that carries surprising and interesting repercussions for how we conceive the citizen today. In my view, medieval political writers made a distinctive contribution to the theory of citizenship, reordering and transposing key features of classical civic discourse in unique ways. But I shall also maintain that this typical medieval approach to the conceptualization of the citizen ran its course at the dawn of modernity and was itself transmuted in order to fit new political realities and demands. Substantively, I argue that the dichotomy between forms of public identity described by current historians and philosophers can effectively be observed by reference to the widely invoked categories of *dominium politicum* and *dominium regale,* to what Burns has termed "the political theory of *dominium*" that was so common in late medieval and early modern writings.[8] I hold that as the nature of, and relationship between, these two ideas altered from their origins in Aristotle to their medieval disseminators to their eventual restatement in the work of Sir John Fortescue, the very understanding of what it meant to possess a political identity and function ("citizenship" in its most neutral sense) was profoundly transfigured. Perhaps through the lens of this conceptual structure we may begin to frame some of the dilemmas that render the cultivation of citizenship a far different enterprise than in the past: the flowering of the citizen-subject as a distinct species of political animal.

ARISTOTLE'S TAXONOMY OF ASSOCIATIONS IN MEDIEVAL EUROPE

The origins of the conceptual structure and nomenclature to be examined in this essay may be found in the first book of Aristotle's *Politics*. In the opening chapter, Aristotle famously distinguishes between four organizational principles for human association *(koinonia, communitas):* the political *(politicum),* the royal *(regale),* the familial, and the despotic. He cautions that strict distinctions are to be made between these categories: no one should imagine that mere size and scale are the bases for distinguishing between these forms of rule. It is simply untrue, says Aristotle, that the quantity of those governed or the extent of the territory determines the quality of the communal order. Rather, different forms of knowledge, different "sciences," pertain to the governance of political, royal, familial, and despotic regimes. There is a difference of kind between a large household and a small polis, just as there is between the personal rule of a king and the reciprocal rule of citizens.[9]

Aristotle then proceeds to explain in detail the divergent scientific principles at stake in the rule of each form of human association. As it turns out, the nature of the particular organization depends significantly upon the purpose of the regime itself, as conditioned by the individuals over whom authority is asserted: despotic rule, over slaves, is for the sake of the governor (master); familial rule, over wife and children, is for the benefit of the governed (family members); and political rule, for the common advantage of both governed and governor (all the citizens, who are alike and share equally in governance).[10] (Aristotle does not discuss the royal organization specifically in this context, and elsewhere in the *Politics* he seems to assimilate it to either the despotic or political forms, depending upon the goal of the king and the legal status of the subjects, viz., free or unfree.)[11] Aristotle concludes that governments "which regard only the interest of the rulers are defective, for they are despotic, while a polis is a community of the free."[12]

In Aristotle's view, then, there is a correlation between the type of government and the character of the governed. Political rule, which obviously represents for him the pinnacle of human association, is the only form compatible with citizenship per se. Other forms of governance, over various sorts of unfree persons, may be counted as "subjection" and thus incongruent with the "political" rule that corresponds to citizenship.

Once Aristotle's *Politics* returned to circulation in the Latin West after 1260, the taxonomy of communities he proposed was widely adopted by his medieval devotees. But the political terrain of thirteenth-century Europe could not have been more at variance with the polis system of ancient Greece, a divergence greatly in evidence when we examine the later interpolation of Aristotle's classifications. Medieval readers concentrated on the distinction between despotic rule (which they elided with royal governance, or *dominium regale*) and political rule *(dominium politicum)*. The distinction enjoys a long and illustrious career in the writings of St. Thomas Aquinas, as well as in Giles of Rome's *De regimine principum,* John of Paris's *De potestate regia et papali,* and a host of other important scholastic sources.[13] But surely the most famous and influential account of the ideas of royal lordship and political lordship may be found in Ptolemy of Lucca's *De regimine principum,* the continuation of the treatise *De regno* supposedly begun by Aquinas (although the involvement of the latter hand in any portion of the treatise is now much in dispute).[14] Composed around 1300, Ptolemy's extensive and systematic discussion of the topic framed much later scholastic constitutional thinking.

It is notable that while Ptolemy purports to follow Aristotle faithfully, he introduces decided and important departures from his source. Ptolemy maintains that there is no essential difference of ends between *dominium regale* and *dominium politicum.* Both must provide certain basic services (military protection, infrastructure, coinage, weights and measures, poor relief, religious guidance) to subjects;[15] moreover, both sorts of lordship aim at moral virtue (most immediately) and beatitude (more distantly).[16] Far more than Aristotle, Ptolemy concentrates upon the specifically institutional dimensions of governance. For example, in a political regime, rulers are elected, observant of law, nonhereditary, and directly accountable to their constituencies for their conduct; in a royal system, by contrast, the ruler inherits and bequeaths his office, constitutes the fount of law, and has no legal obligation to submit himself to popular judgment.[17] Ptolemy also violates Aristotle's dictum that scale is irrelevant to distinguishing forms of rule, instead advising that cities are usually best governed by political regimes, large provinces and territories by royal rulers.[18] Finally, Ptolemy leaves aside the language of citizenship that pervades Aristotle's *Politics;* whether living under political or royal regimes, in cities, or in territorial kingdoms, inhabitants are consistently "subjects."

Nevertheless, Ptolemy retains a very clear distinction between the effects of *dominium politicum* and of *dominium regale* upon their respective populaces. Even before he has fully explicated the differences between the two sorts of regimes, he explains that *dominium politicum* is conducive to "civility in governing,"[19] that is, a relationship of due respect between the governors and the governed in which they work in common concert for their mutual ends (in particular, virtue and beatitude). Ptolemy explains that "there are two reasons why the subjects of *dominium politicum* cannot be rigidly corrected, as they could be under *dominium regale*."[20] The first lies with the nature of the government itself, inasmuch as it is less secure and more directly responsive to the populace: as members of a rotating and salaried group, "political" magistrates do not have a strong motivation to discipline their subjects harshly. (Such a magistrate seems clearly modeled on the *podestà,* or annually selected professional administrator, that typified the medieval Italian civil government.) The second reason for the moderate character of political rule, Ptolemy asserts, "comes from its subjects, since, by nature, their disposition is suited to such a government."[21] This natural inclination is ascribed by him to two sources: the alignment of the constellations (which made great Rome's republican version of *dominium politicum*) and the habituation to freedom that arises from regular practice of sharing in governance. About the latter, Ptolemy remarks, "The subjects of a political government develop confidence from being released from the *dominium* of kings and from exercising *dominium* themselves at suitable times, and this makes them bold in pursuing liberty, so as not to be forced to submit and bow down to kings."[22] The experience of liberty seems to beget desire for greater liberty in at least some peoples, rendering a political regime more appropriate to their collective condition than a monarchy.

Ultimately, Ptolemy arrives at an interestingly ambiguous conclusion regarding the merits of political as contrasted with royal rule. While acknowledging that "I" (actually the author of the first book of *De regno*) had insisted upon the superiority of kingship, Ptolemy nonetheless concludes that scriptural teachings suggest that "political government . . . was more fruitful to the people."[23] He explains this contribution by once again referring to the relative circumstances of subjects. "Political government," he observes, "was better for wise and virtuous persons, such as the ancient Romans, since it imitates the state of nature" without servitude that existed in pre-lapsarian times. *Dominium politicum* accords with the purest and most divine aspects of human nature. On the other hand, once the corruption of humanity had occurred, rendering most people slaves of sin and incapable of governing themselves peacefully, royal government—with its "rod of discipline, which everyone fears"—became necessary, since it excels in controlling a servile populace.[24] Political rule is best for a free, virtuous, and wise community (of which there are but few), since it permits the greatest expression of the laudable qualities of the inhabitants. A royal/despotic regime—Ptolemy explicitly admits that the terms are interchangeable, although he later reneges on this conflation to some extent[25]—must suffice everywhere else, where those over whom authority is exercised lack the moral and intellectual qualities to escape from a state of servitude and subordination.[26] As Ptolemy succinctly concludes in Book Four, "Certain provinces are servile by nature, and despotic rule should guide these, counting regal rule as despotic. Certain others have a virile spirit, a bold heart, and confidence in their intelligence, and these cannot be ruled other than by political rule." He points to the Italian cities as examples of the latter, since "the inhabitants were always less able to be subjected than others, so that if you wanted to bring them under despotic rule, this could not be done unless the lords tyrannized."[27] Some peoples, Ptolemy apparently believes, are characteristically resistant to *dominium regale* and will rightfully refuse its imposition.[28]

In consequence, Ptolemy erects a division between political and royal regimes that is every bit as rigid as Aristotle's distinction between political and despotic forms of association, albeit the former is constructed on largely extra-Aristotelian grounds. For Ptolemy, the subject (really, citizen) under political rule is an active and responsible individual, capable of selecting the laws under which he lives and of judging the qualifications and competence of those who govern him. Indeed, he may well be prepared to take a hand in populating the magistracies of his government. In this sense, the "subject" in nations suited for a political regime—endowed with essentially the same agency as the Aristotelian citizen—can adequately express his character only under *dominium politicum*.

Nothing of the sort is true for the subject fitted for *dominium regale*: the best for which he can hope is a king who will protect him from his fellows and encourage salvation. The more fully active public expression of virtue and intellect is not available to the typical royal subject, because he would not be able to avail himself of such opportunity. This does not, however, render the royal regime illegitimate or inherently tyrannical for Ptolemy. Kingship has its appropriate role, because so many nations are filled with precisely such servile inhabitants, who require not a despot (in the Aristotelian sense) but rather a firm disciplinarian who will maintain peace and direct the subjugated masses away from sin. This is not simply to say that Aristotle has been baptized by Ptolemy and other schoolmen; instead, the categories employed by the *Politics* have been reordered in a manner befitting the religious as well as public life in late medieval Europe.

FORTESCUE ON *DOMINIUM REGALE ET POLITICUM*

Ptolemy's *De regimine principum* enjoyed a broad readership throughout the fourteenth and fifteenth centuries (albeit in the guise of Aquinas, under whose authorship the entire treatise circulated). One of the most enthusiastic members of Ptolemy's later audience was the fifteenth-century English jurist and legal theorist Sir John Fortescue. In a series of writings about the political system of England and its relation to Europe (especially, France), Fortescue appropriated and reconfigured many of Ptolemy's concepts and terms, perhaps most notably the vocabulary of *dominium regale* and *dominium politicum.* Fortescue is something of an enigma in the history of Western political thought: he has been taken both as a culmination of medieval trends and as a forerunner of modern developments. He has been crowned the last great theorist of classical natural law and also the progenitor of modern political economy.[29]

As a consequence of Fortescue's ambiguous status, there has been considerable controversy among scholars about the relationship between his writings and antecedent, especially scholastic, sources.[30] It is not my intention to address the nature and extent of Fortescue's reliance upon medieval forbears, except tangentially in connection with his reconstruction of those materials in order to delineate a very nonmedieval conception of government and political identity. Specifically, he proposes to synthesize the two categories of rule foregrounded by Ptolemy into a single, superior, and all-embracing form of government, namely, *dominium regale et politicum.* This type of hybrid regime, in Fortescue's view, is no mere theoretical construct; rather, it is embodied by the rule of the English monarchy. Corresponding to the particular characteristics of this system is an idea of the citizen quite distant from that conceived by Ptolemy and his contemporaries.

Fortescue's earliest attempt to articulate the notion of a third category that transcends the distinction between political and royal governments comes in his treatise *De natura legis naturae* (c. 1461). Having described both *dominium regale* and *dominium politicum,* he continues, "But that there is a third kind of *dominium,* not inferior to these in dignity and honor, which is called the political and royal, we are not only taught by experience and ancient history, but we know has been taught in the doctrine of St. Thomas."[31] While the later reference has induced a raging debate about whether Fortescue actually had any particular source (whether from Aquinas or Ptolemy) in mind, this should not deflect our attention from the significance of his theoretical point. For he proposes that the strict medieval classification of regimes as either "political" or "royal" need not be respected. Instead, pointing to England, where "kings make not laws, nor impose subsidies on their subjects, without the consent of the Three Estates of the realm," Fortescue asks: "May not, then, this *dominium* be called political, that is to say, regulated by the administration of many, and may it not also be named *dominium regale,* seeing that the subjects themselves cannot make laws without the authority of the king, and the kingdom, being subject to the king's dignity, is possessed by kings and their heirs successively by hereditary right, in such manner as no lordships are possessed which are only politically regulated?"[32]

Fortescue then invokes the examples of Rome during the early principate and scriptually depicted Israel under the judges as additional illustrations of mixed regimes.

Although Fortescue initially concentrates on the governmental aspects of *dominium regale et politicum,* the system equally involves for him a "mixed" character on the part of the governed: they play an active role in authorizing law, but once legislation has been approved, they are rendered passive in the face of its enforcement by the king and his officials. As he observes later in *De natura legis naturae,* "It is good for a people to be ruled by laws to which it consents."[33] This principle, for Fortescue, defines the essence of the mixed royal and political regime, conferring upon those who are governed under it the quality of citizen-subjects. Under the rule of *dominium regale et politicum,* one is both a citizen and a subject—or perhaps more properly, one alternates between these two identities according to circumstance. Thus, depending upon whether one judges from the perspective of a royal or a political system of government, the effect of Fortescue's mixed regime is either to diminish or to enhance the status of citizenship.

But why should *dominium regale et politicum* be judged superior to either *dominium regale* or *dominium politicum?* This is a question that Fortescue takes up in two of his later works, *De laudibus legum Anglie* (1468–1471) and *The Governance of England* (1471). His view is twofold: first, he insists that there are distinct advantages to the king arising from the political character of his regime; second, and perhaps more significantly, he identifies clear and tangible benefits for those who are governed by a political and royal system.

Already in *De natura legis naturae,* Fortescue had proposed that the conjunction of political with royal rule should not be construed as an infringement on the king's authority or prerogative. The fact that the monarch ruling politically as well as royally is limited by the laws that his subjects approve means only that he lacks license to decree and enforce unjust statutes. Such license is in no way appropriate to a king's true liberty; it does not fall within the legitimate power of the king to commit evil acts.[34] This theme is carried forward into *De laudibus legum Anglie,* which purports to be a dialogue between the chancellor of England (a stand-in for Fortescue himself) and the young prince of Wales regarding the study of law. The chancellor explains to Edward why English government, organized politically and royally, generates a legal structure superior to those systems found in continental Europe. For while kings elsewhere possess a wide latitude to do evil, if they are so inclined, the English ruler is prevented, as a result of the constraint imposed by the political quality of his regime, from acting contrary to just law. The political component of the king of England's governance is a check on tyranny, the will to act improperly, not on his capacity to behave rightly. "With the king ruling his people politically, . . . he himself is not able to change the laws without the assent of his subjects nor to burden an unwilling people with strange impositions."[35] Not only does this not interfere with the king's valid authority, but it yields a positive benefit: it ensures the stability of the realm and of the crown. "Rejoice, therefore, good Prince," Fortescue proclaims, "that such is the law of the kingdom to which you are to succeed, because it will provide no small security and comfort for you and for the people."[36] Fortescue points out the error that previous English kings made in scheming to rule the realm according to *dominium regale* alone: they undermined their own authority, the chancellor tells the prince, in order to satisfy "ambition, lust, [and] license, which your said ancestors preferred to the good of the realm."[37] Yet the condemnation of such rulers is notably consequentialist and temporal, rather than moral or religious, in bearing: "Hence, Prince, it is evident to you, from the practical effects, that your ancestors, who sought to cast aside political government, not only could not have obtained, as they wished, a greater power than they had, but would have exposed their own welfare, and the welfare of their realm, to greater risk and danger. . . . The power of the king ruling royally is more difficult to exercise, and less secure for himself and his people, so that it would be undesirable for a prudent king to exchange a political government for a solely royal one."[38] Fortescue's criteria for judging between different kinds of regimes and for preferring *dominium regale et politicum* are highly pragmatic: such a system of government evinces greater strength and longevity than royal rulership and thus benefits the king directly and materially. Less germane are considerations of the personal wisdom and virtue of the monarch, not to mention responsibility for promoting the moral goodness or salvation of the populace.[39]

This reflects, in turn, Fortescue's understanding of the proper aim of government. According to the chancellor, "All the power of a king ought to be applied to the good of his realm, which in effect consists in the defense of it against invasions by foreigners, and of the protection of the inhabitants of the realm and their goods from injuries and rapine by the native population. Therefore, a king who cannot achieve these things is necessarily to be judged powerless."[40] Like John Locke two centuries later, Fortescue upholds as the central (perhaps sole) responsibility of government the protection of the life, liberty, and estate of the inhabitants.[41] (It is hardly surprising, in fact, that Locke in the *Second Treatise* explicitly cites Fortescue as an antecedent authority on the nature of government.)[42]

The foregrounding of the material over the moral and religious functions and duties of government resonates in Fortescue's explanation of why subjects should prefer a king ruling royally and politically, hence shaping his conception of the character of the citizen-subject. This is evident both in his account of the origination of regimes and in his calculation of the benefits that *dominium regale et politicum* confers upon those who live under it.

Fortescue observes in *De laudibus legum Anglie* that the reason why "their authority over their subjects" differs between a king ruling royally and one ruling royally and politically stems from the manner in which each regime is instituted.[43] The former is imposed initially upon inhabitants against their will (as by conquest); only once they are assured of their own basic protection do they agree to submit themselves to the king.[44] Consequently, the subjects of a royal regime are wholly passive: "With a kingdom which is incorporated solely by the authority and power of the king, . . . such a people is subjected by him by no sort of an agreement other than to obey and be ruled by his laws."[45] By contrast, Fortescue describes the formation of a kingdom ruled by a "mixed" government as a wholly voluntary process. Although employing the traditional medieval metaphor of the body politic—according to which the head and members of the political organism cohere in a mutually beneficial reciprocal relationship[46]—he imputes to it a clearly nonhierarchical significance according to which the authority flows from the organs and limbs upward to the head. The royal head is thus firmly "bound" by the legal sinews of the body: "For a king of this sort is set up for the protection of the laws, the subjects, and their bodies and goods, and he has power to this end from the people."[47]

Fortescue's Prince Edward summarizes the relation between the royal and political king and his realm thus: "I now very clearly perceive that no people ever incorporated themselves into a kingdom by their own agreement and will, unless in order to possess safer than before both themselves and their own, which they feared to lose—a design which would be thwarted if a king were able to deprive them of their means, which was not permitted before to anyone among men."[48] If not quite a complete theory of a social compact, then the explanation of the origin of *dominium regale et politicum* offered in *De laudibus legum Anglie*—and reiterated in all essentials in *The Governance of England*[49]—clearly articulates that the people are the founding force and continuing source of public authority in such a regime. In particular, the king ruling royally and politically is responsible for guaranteeing the physical safety and well-being of the population of the realm. Fortescue's subjects are, therefore, weakly or minimally civic actors, in the sense that it is their collective will that approves the system of government and the laws by which they are governed; this is precisely the "political" aspect of the regime. But the practical impact of citizenship remains generally indirect and fleeting; for the most part, the inhabitants of a territory governed royally and politically are every bit as much passive subjects as those living under a simple royal regime.

Still, Fortescue believes that the citizen-subject who submits to *dominium regale et politicum* enjoys far greater benefit than does the subject of merely royal government. His reasons, however, are strictly instrumental. Unlike the antecedent Thomistic-Aristotelian texts that he commonly cites, Fortescue noticeably lacks any conception of civic virtue or public spiritedness as a positive or worthy goal in itself. Rather, the civic dimension of communal life is useful inasmuch as it contributes to the ability of individuals to administer, consume, and augment their personal possessions as they choose without interference from neighbors, foreigners, or magistrates. Since, as we have seen, Fortescue resists assigning spiritual and moral goals to government, he is left with material satisfaction (whether fear of its loss or desire of its increase) as the primary factor motivating a populace to acknowledge political authority. The greater the likelihood that subjects will be free to take full advantage of their bodies and properties, the better by definition that government will be.

The theme of reciprocity between regime type and the physical welfare of the people runs throughout both *De laudibus legum Anglie* and *The Governance of England*. In the latter work, Fortescue explicitly assesses the relative "fruits" of royal, as contrasted with royal and political, government by comparing the circumstances of France with those of England. The French king's royal regime, which taxes subjects arbitrarily and heavily, is held directly to blame for the immiseration of the populace. The French "commons are so impoverished and destroyed that they can barely live," since the harshness of the king's exactions ensures that "they live in the most extreme poverty and misery, and yet they dwell in one of the most fertile realms of the world."[50] Fortescue provides a very detailed depiction of this poverty—describing the diet, clothing and working conditions of the French nation[51]—and lays the blame squarely on the royal system of rule through which France is governed.[52] Just as the purely royal king causes such poverty, so he must constantly be on his guard, lest his subjects muster the courage to rise up and oppose him, contributing to the general instability of the realm.[53]

The contrast with England, and its "mixed" royal and political system, is striking. According to Fortescue, "This land is ruled under a better law; and therefore the people are not in such penury, nor thereby hurt in their persons, but they are wealthy and have all things necessary to the sustenance of nature. Wherefore, they are mighty and able to resist the adversaries of this realm. . . Lo, this is the fruit of 'political and royal law,' under which we live."[54] The major reason for this, says Fortescue, is that the English king is restrained in his ability to lay claim to the goods of subjects, should he ever desire to do so. *The Governance of England* recounts in great detail the structure of fiscal administration that bridles the king.[55] On the one hand, the English king is assured a sufficient income to perform the tasks appropriate to his office, so that he will not be tempted to pursue illegal sources of income. But on the other hand, the prerequisite of parliamentary approval, conjoined with the independent authority of royal counselors and magistrates, form a check upon and barrier to the whims to which a king who reigns royally might easily succumb.

Consequently, the royal and political ruler takes it as integral to his office not to drain income away from his subjects into his own coffers but to enact policies that enhance the wealth of the entire nation. "It is the king's honor," Fortescue remarks, "and also his duty, to make his realm rich; and it is a dishonor when he has but a poor realm. Yet it would be a much greater dishonor, if he found his realm rich, and then made it poor."[56] In turn, the wealth of subjects that arises from royal and political rule acts as an assurance of public order. Inhabitants who enjoy material well-being are, in Fortescue's estimation, more willing and able to fight for their realm; they are less likely to engage in rebellious and seditious activities; and they possess the resources, not to mention the goodwill, to subsidize the government in times of particular need. Fortescue's view, in short, seems to be that the public bearing of citizen-subjects is strictly determined by the measurable impact of government upon their private benefit. If they are contented with their physical lot, they will gladly subject themselves to the king and will perform their roles, but if their ruler adopts policies that impoverish them, they will express their displeasure directly and violently. "The greatest safety, truly, and also the most honor that may come to the king is that his realm should be rich in every estate," Fortescue observes.[57] Only a relatively short distance separates this teaching about the material roots of civic order and identity from the assumptions implicit in modern economic theories of voting and political participation.

The physical benefits accruing to those who submit to *dominium regale et politicum* are also underscored by Fortescue in *De laudibus legum Anglie*. The chancellor recommends that Prince Edward "begin with the results of only royal government, such as that with which the king of France rules his subjects; then examine the practical effect of the royal and political government, such as that with which the king of England rules over his subject people."[58] In French territories, despite the fact that they are naturally rich, the privileges of the king despoil the people of their goods. On royal authority, knights are billeted and fed without charge (or at least below market value) wherever they go in the realm; monopolies over essential commodities, such as salt and wine, compel the populace to pay extortionate prices; and the crown demands arbitrary and constant payments in the form of monetary taxes and assessments in kind and in person. "Exasperated by these and other calamities," Fortescue concludes, "the people live in no little misery." He then describes the very stark poverty that the subjects of the French king (or at any rate, the vast mass of the populace) endure, echoing the depiction presented in *The Governance of England*.[59] The royal character of French government, by permitting the king to impoverish the inhabitants of his lands with impunity, directly causes the material suffering of subjects.

By contrast, the English king, who rules royally and politically, enjoys neither the privilege of purveyance nor the right of monopoly. Moreover, his government can in no way impose "tallages, subsides, or any other burdens whatsoever on his subjects, nor change their laws, nor make new ones, without the concession and assent of his whole realm expressed in his parliament."[60] Thus, the English harvest the fruits of the earth in all their abundance, without fear of confiscation. Because it is by their own consent that subjects of a royal and political king are ruled, they cannot be involuntarily denied their goods and abused in their persons. On Fortescue's account, the immediate result of such government renders England a sort of earthly Garden of Paradise.[61] Who could fail to prefer a form of government that defends and protects the populace and its property to a system whose ruler "is so overcome by his own passions or by such poverty that he cannot keep his hands from despoiling his subjects, so that he impoverishes them, and does not allow them to live and be supported by his own goods"?[62] As in *The Governance of England,* the presumed criteria employed here by Fortescue to judge the impact of regime type on citizens are not civil, moral, or religious, but purely economic and physical. A bare notion of citizenship persists in this account, since inhabitants governed by *dominium regale et politicum* do consent to the terms of their own rule. But they are satisfied to leave the conduct of the daily affairs of government to the king and his ministers, so long as their material well-being is not imperiled. Little of the ancient, let alone the medieval, conception of citizenship remains in evidence.

CONCLUSION

Among those political theorists who are usually credited with responsibility for the undoing of the classical and medieval traditions of civic life—Machiavelli, Hobbes, and Locke, for instance—the name of John Fortescue seldom appears. Part of the reason for this may be that so much of Fortescue's writing was couched in the political and legal vocabulary of his antecedents. How can an author who quotes Aquinas and other scholastics with such enthusiastic approval be counted among the founding fathers of modern political ideas? Yet just as scholars have lately discovered the extent to which supposedly thoroughly modern writers were in fact deeply indebted to their medieval predecessors,[63] so likewise we must realize how even the most conventional forms of medieval discourse were susceptible to transformation in accordance with the requirements imposed by the emergence of distinctively modern forms of Western politics.[64]

May any theoretical lessons be plausibly drawn from this historical exercise? Does the legacy of Fortescue bequeath any inheritance that may aid us in the project of cultivating citizenship at the dawn of the new millennium? I believe that we may learn from Fortescue (and his relation to his predecessors) on several fronts. First, modern proponents of "high" or "thick" citizenship—such as civic republicans, deliberative democrats, and the like—have persistently charged that economically based theories of politics (such as one finds among rational choice and public choice proponents, as well as earlier theorists such as Joseph Schumpeter) are intrinsically incapable of justifying any activist or participatory conception of civic identity.[65] Indeed, economic approaches are often regarded as colluding with the enemies of a vital public life for citizens. But Fortescue's position reveals the possibility of a somewhat different logic. In comparison with Ptolemy, who insists upon an unavoidable choice between full-blooded Aristotelian citizenship or utterly constrained subjugation, Fortescue maintains that the material interests of both rulers and members of the community will stimulate in them a commitment to the rule of laws approved by and congruent with the interests of the citizens as a whole. Hence, behavior that may be regarded as entirely self-seeking—the maintenance and enhancement of one's possessions—translates for him by means of a very visible hand—parliamentary government—into the concrete expression of the common good. Because Fortescue gives priority to economic well-being, without, however, affording sovereign priority to the marketplace, he ultimately suggests that popular institutions and the concomitant exercise of citizenship are transparently necessary for citizens to achieve their own benefit.[66] When the people obey laws of their own authorization, the advantage of all, construed in terms of physical welfare, is sure to be served.

Fortescue's conception of citizenship is certainly "chastened" (to adopt the terminology of Flathman), then, at least when contrasted with the medieval sources on which he relied. Extramaterial considerations—the care of the soul—do not fall into the ends that Fortescue proposes for government. Priests and prelates play no significant role in public life; indeed, Fortescue characterizes lawyers as the secular "priests" of law, whose authority in statecraft equals that of the clergy in matters of soulcraft.[67]

Is Fortescue's constitutional regime ruled in accordance with laws approved by citizens, who presumably judge such statues with reference to their economic consequences, the best foundation of citizenship for which we may hope? In an increasingly fragmented public space, in which traditional ties of a civic sort are undermined as much by market-induced individualism of the crassest sort as by manifestations of religious and cultural difference, many of the claims of "high" citizenship ring hollow (except perhaps to professional political theorists). The nation-state, the primary bearer of civic allegiance for the last four centuries or so, withers daily under the pressure of globalization, on the one side, and regionalism, on the other. Meanwhile, the politics of the common good, of civic virtue, has often been distorted into a mere rhetoric of values by politicians who simultaneously promote themselves and precisely the special interests that stand at the root of social disintegration. So perhaps the real question is not "Must we settle for a position similar to Fortescue's?" but "Is even the chastened conception of Fortescue sustainable at the dawn of the new millennium?"

One substantive principle that Fortescue does assume we must adopt is a sustainable and equitable equilibrium between the demands of public and private goods. He takes as a salient quality of English *dominium regale et politicum* the fairness with which public burdens are shared among the subjects of the crown, which he believes to encourage not only social stability but also economic welfare. By contrast, he objects directly to the arbitrariness of the French policy of exempting the wealthiest members of the community (the landowning nobility) from financial sacrifices necessary for defending the realm and upholding the laws.[68] In other words, Fortescue acknowledges that a well-ordered community entails equity in the distribution of costs and benefits to its members; a primary responsibility of government, in turn, is to ensure such a distribution for citizens. While this stops short of describing a prototype of the welfare state, it suggests an ethos of public concern for private well-being that has been increasingly degraded in our own time. Far from defending the independent (and largely anticivic) mechanisms of the marketplace, Fortescue proposes to judge economic life according to a more communal criteria of material benefit. The amelioration of suffering through charity after the fact is insufficient for him; government must assess the physical consequences of its own policies in advance and must chose to act in a manner that does not impoverish (that, indeed, enhances) the circumstances of the populace. Citizens, likewise, must be cultivated to evaluate government and legislation from the standpoint of such interdependence.

If ensuring that all men, women, and children have decent food, clothing and housing—and the protection of due process under the law—does not seem a sufficiently vigorous reason for cultivating citizenship, then Fortescue's synthetic account of *dominium regale and politicum* must be declined. But if, in a world of largely conflicting and perhaps intractable moral and spiritual values, it remains possible to identify a common ground for creating what Avashai Margalit has termed "the decent society,"[69] then perhaps the path set out by Fortescue merits consideration. Without the deceitfulness of Machiavelli, the fear of Hobbes, or the essentially apolitical civil society of Locke, Fortescue affords us a general framework within which to build a leaner, yet not utterly desiccated, conception of citizenship that suits the conditions of contemporary social and political life.

NOTES

The author wishes to thank Professors Dwight Allman and Gerson Moreno-Riaño, and Ms. Bettina Koch, for their very careful readings of and useful comments on versions of this essay. In addition to the audience at a plenary session of the 1999 Baylor University Pruitt Symposium, the ideas contained in this paper were presented to a panel on "The Medieval Foundations of Constitutional Theory" at the 2001 annual meeting of the American Political Science Association, San Francisco.

1. Peter Riesenberg, *Citizenship in the Western Tradition: Plato to Rousseau* (Chapel Hill: University of North Carolina Press, 1992), 203–6.

2. J. G. A. Pocock, "The Idea of Citizenship since Classical Times," in Ronald Beiner, ed., *Theorizing Citizenship* (Albany: SUNY Press, 1995), 29–52.

3. Richard E. Flathman, "Citizenship and Authority: A Chastened View of Citizenship," in Beiner, ed., *Theorizing Citizenship*, 105–51.

4. Benjamin Barber, *Strong Democracy: Participatory Politics for a New Age* (Berkeley: University of California Press, 1984).

5. See Brian Tierney, *The Idea of Natural Rights* (Atlanta: Scholars Press, 1996); Quentin Skinner, *The Foundations of Modern Political Thought*, 2 vols. (Cambridge: Cambridge University Press, 1978); Francis Oakley, *Natural Law, Conciliarism and Consent in the Later Middle Ages* (London: Ashgate/Variorum, 1984); Cary J. Nederman and John Christian Laursen, eds., *Difference and Dissent: Theories of Toleration in Medieval and Early Modern Europe* (Lanham, Md.: Rowman & Littlefield, 1996); and Nederman, *Worlds of Difference: European Discourses of Toleration, c. 1100–c. 1550* (University Park: Penn State University Press, 2000).

6. J. H. Burns, "Introduction," *The Cambridge History of Political Thought, 1450–1700* (Cambridge: Cambridge University Press, 1991), 2, 3.

7. Brian Tierney, *Religion, Law, and the Growth of Constitutional Thought, 1150–1650* (Cambridge: Cambridge University Press, 1982), 105; cf. 106–8.

8. J. H. Burns, *Lordship, Kingship and Empire: The Idea of Monarchy 1400–1525* (Oxford: Clarendon Press, 1992), 16.

9. Aristotle, *Politics*, 1252a1–24; I am following the Greek text (ed. H. Rackham [Cambridge, Mass.: Harvard University Press, 1944]) as well as the Latin translation by William of Moerbeke (ed. Pierre Michaud-Quantin [Bruges: Desclée de Brouwer, 1961]).

10. Aristotle, *Politics*, 1278b31–1279a14.

11. Aristotle, *Politics*, 1284b35–1288b2.

12. Aristotle, *Politics*, 1279a20–22.

13. J. H. Burns, "Fortescue and the Political Theory of *Dominium*," *Historical Journal* 20 (1985): 778–80; and Burns, *Lordship, Kingship and Empire*, 24–25, 27.

14. See Ptolemy of Lucca, *On the Government of Rulers*, trans. James M. Blythe (Philadelphia: University of Pennsylvania Press, 1997), 1–5.

15. Ptolemy of Lucca, *Government*, 2.10–2.16.

16. Ptolemy of Lucca, *Government*, 3.3.7.

17. Ptolemy of Lucca, *Government*, 3.20.

18. Ptolemy of Lucca, *Government*, 4.1.2, 4.2.1.

19. Ptolemy of Lucca, *Government*, 2.8.1.

20. Ptolemy of Lucca, *Government*, 2.8.2.

21. Ptolemy of Lucca, *Government*, 2.8.4.

22. Ptolemy of Lucca, *Government*, 2.8.5.

23. Ptolemy of Lucca, *Government*, 2.9.2.

24. Ptolemy of Lucca, *Government*, 2.9.5.

25. Ptolemy of Lucca, *Government*, 2.9.1–2; cf. 3.11.9.

26. This evidence challenges the recent generalization made by Janet Coleman that all legitimate regimes, monarchic as well as civic, were regarded by medieval thinkers as promoting liberty: "Structural Realities of Power: The Theory and Practice of Monarchies and Republics in Relation to Person and Collective Liberty," in Martin

Gosman, Arjo Vanderjagt and Jan Veenstra, eds., *The Propagation of Power in the Medieval West* (Groningen: Egbert Forsten, 1996), 207–30.

27. Ptolemy of Lucca, *Government*, 4.8.4.

28. One should note that Ptolemy does not regard his position as a form of purely genetic determinism. In 24.8.3, he remarks that human beings, like other organic creatures, are capable of changing their dispositions in accordance with their environment. National "dispositions" on his treatment resemble a sort of second nature, fixed by objective conditions yet not ingrained at birth.

29. Among the scholars weighing in on this topic are: Max Adams Shepard, "The Political and Constitutional Theory of Sir John Fortescue," in Carl Witke, ed., *Essays in History and Political Theory in Honor of Charles H. McIlwain* (1936; reprint New York: Russell and Russell, 1967), 289–319; Franklin Le Van Baumer, *The Early Tudor Theory of Kingship* (New Haven, CT: Yale University Press, 1940), 4–12; Donald W. Hanson, *From Kingdom to Commonwealth: The Development of Civic Consciousness in English Political Thought* (Cambridge, Mass.: Harvard University Press, 1970), 217–52; J. G. A. Pocock, *The Machiavellian Moment* (Princeton, NJ: Princeton University Press, 1975), 9–30; Robert Eccleshall, *Order and Reason in Politics: Theories of Absolute and Limited Monarchy in Early Modern England* (Oxford: Oxford University Press, 1978), 102–9; and Neal Wood, *Foundations of Political Economy: Some Early Tudor Views on State and Society* (Berkeley: University of California Press, 1994), 44–69.

30. Especially noteworthy are: Felix Gilbert, "Sir John Fortescue's 'Dominium Regale et Politicum,'" *Medievalia et Humanistica* 2 (1944): 88–97; and J. H. Burns, "Fortescue and the Political Theory of *Dominium*," *Historical Journal* 28 (1985): 777–97.

31. Sir John Fortescue, *On the Laws and Governance of England*, ed. Shelley Lockwood (Cambridge: Cambridge University Press, 1997), 128. I have occasionally adjusted Lockwood's translations from Latin when it seemed appropriate.

32. Fortescue, *Laws and Governance*, 128–29.

33. Fortescue, *Laws and Governance*, 135.

34. Fortescue, *Laws and Governance*, 133–36.

35. Fortescue, *Laws and Governance*, 17.

36. Fortescue, *Laws and Governance*, 18.

37. Fortescue, *Laws and Governance*, 53.

38. Fortescue, *Laws and Governance*, 54; also 49.

39. Also noteworthy is the fact that Fortescue never anywhere mentions *dominium politicum* as a viable form of government, bowing perhaps to the historical realities of northern Europe, which by the late fifteenth century had taken a decisive turn toward territorial monarchies organized along national lines.

40. Fortescue, *On the Laws and Governance of England*, 53.

41. A fact not missed by some of Fortescue's commentators; see Shepard, "The Political and Constitutional Theory of Sir John Fortescue," 302–4.

42. John Locke, *Two Treatises of Government*, ed. Peter Laslett (Cambridge: Cambridge University Press, 1988), 426.

43. Fortescue, *Laws and Governance*, 18–19.

44. Fortescue, *Laws and Governance*, 19; cf. 85–86.

45. Fortescue, *Laws and Governance*, 23.

46. The basic survey of the medieval use of the organic metaphor is Tilman Struve, *Die Entwicklung der organologischen Staatsauffasung im Mittelalter* (Stuttgart: Hiersemann, 1978).

47. Fortescue, *Laws and Governance*, 21–22.

48. Fortescue, *Laws and Governance*, 23.

49. Fortescue, *Laws and Governance*, 86.

50. Fortescue, *Laws and Governance*, 88, 89.

51. Fortescue, *Laws and Governance*, 89.

52. Fortescue, *Laws and Governance*, 90–92.

53. Fortescue, *Laws and Governance*, 88, 110–11.

54. Fortescue, *Laws and Governance*, 90.

55. Fortescue, *Laws and Governance*, 92–108, 112–20.

56. Fortescue, *Laws and Governance*, 109.

57. Fortescue, *Laws and Governance*, 110.

58. Fortescue, *Laws and Governance*, 49.

59. Fortescue, *Laws and Governance*, 49–51.

60. Fortescue, *Laws and Governance*, 52.

61. Fortescue, *Laws and Governance*, 52–53.

62. Fortescue, *Laws and Governance*, 53.

63. See Scott G. Swanson, "The Medieval Foundations of John Locke's Theory of Natural Rights," *History of Political Thought* 18 (1977): 399–459; Janet Coleman, "*Dominium* in Thirteenth- and Fourteenth-Century Political Thought and Its Seventeenth-Century Heirs: John of Paris and Locke," *Political Studies* 33 (1985): 73–100; Cary J. Nederman, "Amazing Grace: Fortune, Free Will and God in Machiavelli," *Journal of the History of Ideas* 60 (October–December 1999): 617–38.

64. For instance, see Cary J. Nederman, "Bracton on Kingship First Visited: The Idea of Sovereignty and Bractonian Political Thought in Seventeenth-Century England," *Political Science* 40 (July 1988): 49–66. I do not mean to suggest that Fortescue's emphasis upon economic criteria for judging political institutions and systems had no predecessors in the Middle Ages. In fact, in a book manuscript (entitled *The Virtues of Necessity*) that I am currently completing, I argue that he may properly be regarded as the culmination of a growing late medieval trend toward positing material well-being as a standard of good government. But this relationship with medieval forbears differs markedly from the one that scholars have standardly ascribed to Fortescue, as we have seen already.

65. See Adrian Oldfield, *Citizenship and Community: Civic Republicanism and the Modern World* (London: Routledge, 1990), 1–28, 145–74.

66. I have detected a similar position in another famous late medieval figure, Marsiglio of Padua, who is even more explicit about the congruence of self-interest with the public will; see Cary J. Nederman, "Society and Self-Interest: Political Theory and the Profit Economy in Marsiglio of Padua's *Defensor Pacis*," presented to a conference on "Material Culture and Cultural Materialisms in the Middle Ages and Renaissance," sponsored by the Arizona Center for Medieval and Renaissance Studies, Tempe, February 1999.

67. Fortescue, *Laws and Governance*, 6–7.

68. Fortescue, *Laws and Governance*, 51.

69. Avashai Margalit, *The Decent Society* (Cambridge, Mass.: Harvard University Press, 1996).

4

Lockean Liberalism and the Cultivation of Citizens

Nathan Tarcov

John Locke was one of the great philosophic originators of modern liberalism. By modern liberalism I mean not the particular ideology that distinguishes most adherents of the Democratic party from most adherents of the Republican party in the United States today, but rather the broader and more fundamental doctrine that the end of government is, as Locke argued, the preservation of the liberty of each of the members of society as far as possible. This doctrine is more fundamental than the principles that distinguish what are called liberals in contemporary American political debate from what are called conservatives. It is indeed a doctrine common to contemporary American liberals and conservatives, both of whom understand their respective principles as the best interpretation of it.

Identifying the purpose of government with the preservation of liberty is such a hackneyed cliché of our political rhetoric that Americans may hardly be aware of the range of alternatives to it. Americans may imagine that political debate can be only about the elaboration, interpretation, or application of that doctrine, rather than about the choice between it and the alternatives. Americans so take it for granted and are so unaware of the alternatives that they may not notice when we do depart from it toward an alternative. In contrast, Locke and the other originators of the liberal conception of the purposes of government had to argue against the previously taken for granted views of the purposes of government, the preliberal views.

Before considering the cultivation of citizens specifically in a Lockean liberal society and polity, it is useful to make some general distinctions relevant to the relation between soulcraft and statecraft or the cultivation of citizens in various kinds of societies and polities. We can distinguish, first of all, among qualities and beliefs that are understood as necessary 1) for the salvation of one's soul; 2) for the perfection of one's soul; 3) for the success and preservation of any society (e.g., law-abidingness and willingness to fight for the preservation of the society); and 4) for the success and preservation of liberal society in particular. These might be called: 1) salvific virtue and doctrine; 2) moral virtue and doctrine; 3) generic civic virtue and doctrine; and 4) specific liberal virtue and doctrine. We can also distinguish among at least the following agencies and their characteristic modes of cultivating such virtues and beliefs: 1) government, which uses coercion; 2) the family, which uses habituation; and 3) churches, teachers, writers, and others who use persuasion.

On the basis of these distinctions, I will suggest the following. First, Lockean liberalism claims that the end of government is the protection of rights, not the cultivation of salvific or moral virtue and doctrine, and therefore that it may not use coercive force for their cultivation. Second, liberal society nonetheless requires citizens who possess civic and liberal virtues that need to be cultivated and who adhere to civic and liberal doctrines that need to be propagated, and liberal government may use force for the cultivation and inculcation of civic and liberal virtue and doctrine or at least for the suppression of antisocial and illiberal vice, crime, or doctrine. Third, the primary responsibility for cultivating liberal virtues and propagating liberal doctrines belongs, however, not to government but to other agencies in a liberal society: to families, churches, teachers, and writers like Locke. Fourth, ultimately the arguments for liberalism by such nonstate agents rest not merely on claims about civic and liberal virtue and doctrine but also on claims about salvific and moral virtue and doctrine. Fifth, Locke finally makes his argument for liberalism on the basis of his reader's desires to be a particular kind of human being, to possess particular virtues, and to pursue the truth.

THE ENDS AND REQUIREMENTS OF LIBERAL GOVERNMENT

Lockean liberalism argues that the end of government is not the cultivation of particular kinds of human beings, the inculcation of particular virtues or dispositions, the development of particular capacities, or the propagation of particular truths or doctrines but the protection of rights. In other words, in terms of the distinctions we started with, Lockean liberalism denies that the state can use coercive force for the cultivation of salvific or moral virtue.

The fundamental hypothesis of Locke's political theory in the *Second Treatise*[1] was what he called the state of nature—that is, his claim that the condition all human beings are naturally in is one of freedom and equality. By nature human beings are free to act, constrained only by their own reason (the dictates of which Locke called the law of nature), not by the will of another human being (2T: 4, 6, 15, 22). No human being has by nature a right to rule other human beings otherwise than as they reciprocally have the same power over him or her. The natural inequalities among human beings do not entitle one to rule another (2T: 54, 70), given our "common nature, faculties, & powers" (1T: 67; 2T: 4). This hypothesis contrasts sharply with that of Aristotle and his scholastic successors, that natural inequalities subordinate some human beings to others.

This fundamental hypothesis of natural freedom and equality implied that the individual is prior to society, in that society must be understood as serving individual purposes that could in principle (though not effectively in practice) be pursued without society. It also implied that the common good must be understood as derived from the good of every particular member of society (1T: 92). It further implied that liberty is prior to authority—that is, that the purpose of authority and law is "not to abolish or restrain but to preserve and enlarge freedom" (2T: 57). Finally, it implied that rights are prior to duties in that our duties are to respect the rights of others (2T: 6).

Just as Locke conceived of individuals as possessing rights to life, liberty, and property in a state of nature, so he regarded the end of government as the protection of the lives, liberties, and properties of all the members of society as far as possible. Locke often called this end of government the preservation of "property" (2T: 88, 124, 134, 138), thereby including all three of these rights, since each of them is conceived of as property, as something belonging to individuals that they cannot be rightfully deprived of without their own consent (2T: 87, 138, 140). This limited end of government is the heart of modern liberalism and contrasts sharply with preliberal conceptions of the end of government as the improvement or salvation of souls, the punishment of vice or sin, the propagation of the truth, or the glorification of God.

This limitation and contrast are especially clear in Locke's *Letter Concerning Toleration,* where he argued explicitly that the civil power is confined solely to the care and advancement of civil goods (such as life, liberty, bodily health and freedom from pain, and possession of external things such as land, money, and furniture) and that it neither can nor ought to be extended to the salvation of souls. On the contrary, the care of every man's soul "belongs unto himself, and is to be left unto himself."[2] Not only is the purpose of government limited to civil goods rather than the care of the soul, but it is also limited to protecting those civil goods from harm by others, not from self-inflicted harm (LCT 35).

This liberal restriction on the purpose of government precludes government from having not only a religious concern with the salvation of our souls but even a moral concern with the improvement or perfection of our souls. Locke argued in the *Letter* that "Covetousness, Uncharitableness, Idleness, and many other things are sins, by the consent of all men, which yet no man ever said were to be punished by the Magistrate. The reason is, because they are not prejudicial to other men's Rights, nor do they break the publick Peace of Societies" (LCT 44). In Locke's earlier "Essay on Toleration," he made this denial more sharply: "However strange it may seem, that the law-maker hath nothing to do with moral virtues and vices . . . otherwise than barely as they are subservient to the good and preservation of mankind under government"; indeed "he is not bound to punish all, i.e., he may tolerate some vices."[3]

These limitations on the ends of government rest on Locke's claims that whereas individual pursuit of the material goods required for bodily preservation can affect their pursuit by others and be interfered with by the violence of others, individual pursuit of salvation and perfection neither interferes with their pursuit by others nor can be interfered with by the violence of others (LCT 47). Similarly, the physical force wielded by government can prevent interference with the pursuit of the property required for bodily preservation but cannot facilitate the pursuit of salvation or perfection. These limitations rest therefore not on indifference to the goods of the soul or the means of achieving them, but on claims about the differing nature of the pursuit of the goods of the soul and the pursuit of the goods of the body.

Just as Locke denied that government ought to be concerned with the religious salvation or moral perfection of our souls, so he made clear in the *Letter* that "laws are not concerned with the truth of opinions, but with the security and safety of the commonwealth and of each man's goods" (LCT 46). The aim of government, according to Locke, therefore is not the cultivation of a particular kind of human being, the inculcation of a set of moral virtues, or the establishment of a body of official truths but the protection of rights.

LOCKE ON THE CULTIVATION OF VIRTUE

It would be a grave misunderstanding of Lockean liberalism to think that because it denies the legitimacy of the state's using coercive force to promote salvation or perfection, it also denies the state's right to promote civic or liberal virtue by force or other means, let alone the rights of other agencies to promote salvific, human, civic, or liberal virtues. On the contrary, liberal society requires the cultivation of particular kinds of human beings, the inculcation of particular virtues or dispositions, the development of particular capacities, and the propagation of particular truths or doctrines—in short, the cultivation of both generic civic virtues and specific liberal virtues. It requires the cultivation of liberal human beings who seek mastery not over others but over themselves, who defend their own rights and those of others—tolerant human beings who examine their own opinions, refuse to accept the opinions of others on authority, and do not seek to impose their own opinions by authority on others. It requires the inculcation of the virtues taught in

Locke's *Some Thoughts Concerning Education: self-denial* (the ability to deny one's own desires for the sake of what one's reason tells one is best); *civility* (respect for the opinions, feelings, and reasoning abilities of others); *liberality* (a willingness to share what one does not need with others who need it); *justice* (respect for the rights and property of others); *courage* (willingness to risk bodily harm and even death for the sake of what one's reason tells one is best); *endurance* (willingness to accept bodily pain for the sake of what one's reason tells one is best); *humanity* (avoidance of infliction of pain on others); *curiosity* (desire for knowledge useful to human life); *industry* (willingness to take pains and labor to produce things useful to human life); and *truthfulness*. A liberal polity also requires among its citizens the virtues taught in Locke's *Two Treatises*: *vigilance* against the abuse of power and the violation of rights, but also *prudence* in weighing the violated rights against the trouble and cost of vindicating them (2T: 176, 208–10, 220, 230). A liberal society and polity require the cultivation of *rationality* and the *pride in rationality*, which were for Locke the ultimate basis of the *love of liberty*, rather than ambition for mastery over others, and the promotion of *concern for winning the freely given esteem of others* rather than the glory of conquest over others.

Although a Lockean liberal society exists for the sake of protecting rights rather than for the cultivation of particular kinds of human beings, the inculcation of particular virtues or dispositions, the development of particular capacities, or the propagation of particular truths or doctrines, it has the authority to use force when necessary against those kinds of human beings, vices, dispositions, and doctrines that violate the rights of others or the public good. In terms of the distinctions I started with, Lockean liberalism allows the state to use coercive force for the cultivation of generic civic or liberal virtue, or at least the suppression of antisocial and illiberal vice or crime. Locke did not rule out this kind of moral concern by government. The statement quoted above from the "Essay on Toleration,"[4] that the lawmaker has nothing to do with moral virtues and vices, did not end there; it continued, "otherwise than barely as they are subservient to the good and preservation of mankind under government." The lawmaker therefore is concerned with moral virtues and vices insofar as their promotion or curtailment is conducive to the good and preservation of mankind under government. Similarly, although civil society is not concerned with the truth of opinions as such, it must establish the opinion of toleration itself. Liberal politics requires a liberal public opinion in favor of liberty.

Locke's *Letter Concerning Toleration* argued that diversity of opinions cannot be avoided (LCT: 55) and is even politically useful, since under conditions of liberal toleration "all the separate Congregations, like so many Guardians of the Public Peace, will watch one another" (LCT: 53). Nevertheless, while Locke insisted on unlimited toleration for what he called "speculative" opinions, those that have no effect on conduct, he limited the toleration of practical opinions that do influence conduct on the basis of their effect on the safety of the commonwealth and of every particular man's goods and person (LCT: 46). He therefore granted no right to toleration for opinions contrary to civil society or to the moral rules necessary for its preservation. Such opinions in his time were most likely to take the form of such claims as that promises do not have to be kept with heretics, that excommunicated rulers forfeit their power, that dominion is founded on grace, or that obedience is owed to a foreign ruler (LCT: 33, 49–50).

Positively put, Locke insisted on a common opinion transcending the diversity of opinions. He suggested that the law of toleration should oblige churches "to lay down Toleration as the Foundation of their own Liberty; and teach that Liberty of Conscience is every mans natural Right" (LCT: 51).[5] Liberal toleration itself becomes a kind of established civil religion undergirding the diversity of nonestablished religions. The *Two Treatises of Government* themselves may be understood as an effort to *dis*establish Filmer's doctrines of absolute monarchy, which led rulers to violate their subjects' rights and inclined subjects to let them get away with it, and to *establish* instead Locke's liberal doctrines.

Nevertheless, the primary responsibility for cultivating liberal human beings, civic and liberal virtues, liberal dispositions, and liberal doctrines belongs not to coercive government but to other agencies in a liberal society: to families, churches, teachers, and writers like Locke. In the *Second Treatise* Locke distinguished the family from government by granting to the former the power of education and to the latter the power of life and death (2T: 55–58, 69–71, 170–71). In the *Letter* he called the magistrate's power that of the sword and the church's the right of instruction; he required the clergy to teach both private persons and magistrates the duties of goodwill, charity, and toleration, whereas he did not expect the civil magistrate to play any special role as teacher of virtue (LCT 27, 31, 33–35).

While the end of government according to the *Second Treatise* is limited to the protection of rights rather than the cultivation of virtue, Locke was directly concerned in other works with the education of human beings who would possess the virtues required for liberty.[6] In *Some Thoughts Concerning Education* he showed how children could be educated in the virtues needed in a free society not through coercion but through appeals to their love of liberty and pride in rationality. In *An Essay concerning Human Understanding* he argued against the doctrine of innate ideas, which he regarded as a justification for subservience to prejudice, superstition, and intellectual tyranny, and he encouraged his readers to question the opinions others would impose on them by authority and likewise to refrain from imposing their own opinions on others by authority.

Although liberal government can promote or oppose certain types, qualities, and opinions not for their own sake but only inasmuch as they serve or obstruct its purpose of the protection of rights, ultimately the arguments of those writers like Locke who argue for liberalism must rest on claims not merely that these types, qualities, and opinions are necessary for the success of liberal society but that these are the types of people we should want to be, that these are the virtues we should want to have, and that these doctrines are true. They must argue on the basis of some conception of perfection or salvation. Ultimately, it cannot be enough to persuade reasonable people to become a certain kind of person because that is the kind of citizen required by a liberal polity, or to strive for certain kinds of virtues because they are the qualities needed by a liberal society, let alone to believe in certain opinions because they are supportive of a liberal polity and society. It would be necessary to persuade people first that they want to become whatever kind of person is needed by their society, that virtue is whatever qualities are required by their society, and that truth is whatever supports their society; such subordinations of the individual, of morality, and of truth to the requirements of society can hardly be the doctrines of liberalism, at least of a reasonable or Lockean liberalism. In other words, in Aristotle's terms,[7] it is never sufficient to consider the cultivation of good citizens without also considering the cultivation of good human beings. In terms of my initial distinctions, liberal society requires that nonstate agencies concern themselves with human and even salvific virtue as well as civic and liberal virtue. Locke appealed for toleration in the *Letter* on the basis not only of the distinctions he made there between the ends of civil society and of churches but of the claim that Christians are required to be tolerant to be saved (LCT 23–25). He made his argument for liberalism, above all in the *Essay*, on the basis of his readers' desire for their own minds to be free to pursue the truth.

Locke's *Two Treatises* are not only the elaboration of a doctrine about the rights and duties of governors and subjects but a complex effort to check certain human propensities and encourage others, to cultivate the kinds of human beings needed as governors and subjects in a free society. He distinguishes tyranny from lawful government by the tyrant's directing his actions to "the satisfaction of his own Ambition, Revenge, Covetousness, or any other irregular Passion" (2T: 199). Doctrines like Filmer's that dress up power "with all the Splendor and Temptation Absoluteness can add to it" flatter and give a greater edge to "the natural ambition of man, too apt of itself to grow and encrease with the Possession of any Power" (1T: 10 and 106). Ambition corrupts men's minds into mistaking true power and honor, and it teaches princes to have interests distinct from those of their peoples (2T: 111). Ambition fills the world with disorders, war, and conquest (2T: 175). The pride and ambition of private men as well as rulers have caused great disorders (2T: 230).

Yet it would be a great mistake to think that Locke attempted to crush every form of pride in favor of narrow, fearful self-interest or mere pursuit of comfortable self-preservation. Human pride of a certain kind plays a positive role in Lockean liberalism. The *First Treatise* opens with the following sentence: "Slavery is so vile and miserable an Estate of Man, and so directly opposite to the generous Temper and Courage of our Nation; that 'tis hardly to be conceived, that an *Englishman* much less a *Gentleman* should plead for it." This contempt for slavery that Locke ultimately appeals to, however, is less a national and class pride than a species pride, a pride in human rationality and superiority to the irrational animals. This pride affirms natural human equality and rejects any subordination instituted "as if we were made for one anothers uses, as the inferior ranks of Creatures are for ours" (2T: 6). This pride expresses indignation at rulers who treat their peoples like herds of cattle (IT: 156; 2T: 93, 163) and indeed would treat those who do that as themselves wild beasts to be destroyed (2T: 10, 11, 16, 172 n, 181, 182). Our pride, or sense of what is due to us as rational creatures, makes us potential partisans of liberalism.

Locke's arguments for liberalism appeal to human pride in human rationality, our sense of "what may be suitable to the dignity and excellency of a rational creature."[8] The granting of liberty is the most prudent as well as the most rightful way of governing human beings—above all because of human beings' desire to "be thought rational creatures," "to show that they are free, that their own good actions come from themselves, that they are absolute and independent" (STCE: 41, 73). The sense of my own rationality, my own ability to direct my conduct, brings with it a desire for liberty and resistance to those who would deprive me of it and treat me as if I were not a rational creature.

CONCLUSION

The sense of one's own rationality is compatible with ambition to master others only when one does not regard them as equally rational; it is rendered compatible with respect for the liberty of others when it recognizes their presumptive rationality too. Locke showed we can plausibly want to be free from the will of others without having to impose our will on them, at least so long as we are willing to resist those who would impose their will on us or others. But to do so he had to restore the sense of human dignity debunked in various ways by Machiavelli and Hobbes, a new modern egalitarian sense of what is presumptively owed to every one of us as rational creatures, equal not merely in our propensity to kill and be killed, as in Hobbes, but in our claims to be treated as free and rational.

The *Essay* argued on behalf of liberalism not as a set of political institutions or doctrines, as do the *Treatises* and the *Letter*, but as a set of moral dispositions supportive of such institutions or doctrines. Following the opinions of others has the same consequence as being obligated to follow the legally established religion: it would give people "reason to be Heathens in Japan,

Mahumetans in Turkey, Papists in Spain, Protestants in England, and Lutherans in Sueden."[9] The *Essay* urged its readers not to be "content to live lazily on scraps of begg'd Opinion," and neither to assume an authority of dictating their opinions to others nor to accept the opinions of those church or party leaders who would impose them by authority (ECHU: Epistle, IV xv 6, xix 2, xx 17–18).

Locke was concerned not only with trying to get the possessors of authority not to use that authority to impose their opinions on others. In itself that would perhaps ultimately not matter very much for him, unless he could accomplish a more fundamental objective. That deeper objective was to get his readers to question authority, to examine their opinions, and to think for themselves. Without that intellectual freedom, that mental liberation (which is hardly captured by the term "toleration"), toleration would amount only to what one group that accepts its opinions out of subjection to one authority affords to another group that accepts different opinions on another authority. All the individual members of those groups would remain "enslaved in that which should be the freest part of Man, their Understandings," just as they are in places where people are "*cooped in* close, *by the Laws* of their Countries" (ECHU: IV xx 4).

Locke's argument for toleration or liberalism in the *Essay* attempted to unite the duty to examine one's own opinions with the duty to let others do so too. He tried to unite these two by claiming that "those, who have not thoroughly examined to the bottom all their own Tenets, must confess, they are unfit to prescribe to others" and that "those who have fairly and truly examined . . . are so few in number, and find so little reason to be magisterial in their opinions, that nothing insolent and imperious is to be expected from them" (ECHU: I iv 22, IV xvi 4). Conversely, Locke argued, "assuming an Authority of Dictating to others, and a forwardness to prescribe their opinions" is a constant concomitant of being one who "tyrannizes over his own mind" (ECHU: IV xix 2). Locke appealed above all to our desire to believe that our own minds are free, so as to restrain us from trying to enslave the minds of others.

Locke's liberalism ruled out as the *direct* aim of government the cultivation of a particular human type, the salvation or perfection of our souls, the inculcation of a particular set of moral virtues, or the establishment of a particular body of orthodox opinions for the sake of truth and replaced those goals with the preservation of the life, liberty, and property of the members of society as far as possible. Lockean liberal government promotes particular types, virtues, and opinions not for their own sake, as they are necessarily pursued by thoughtful human beings, but only insofar as they are conducive to its direct goals. It must try to cultivate neither tyrants nor slaves but free human beings, who love liberty, possess liberal moral virtues, and profess liberal opinions. As long as men are creatures guided by imagination, passion, and custom as well as by reason, there is no guarantee that liberal institutions alone can preserve themselves or produce those human beings, virtues, passions, and opinions. That will always remain a challenge for the public policies of liberal governments and the private efforts of liberal educators.

NOTES

1. References to Locke's *Two Treatises of Government* will be contained in parentheses. They refer to *Two Treatises of Government*, ed. Peter Laslett (Cambridge: Cambridge University Press, 1988). For the *First Treatise*, I use the designation (1T) and for the *Second Treatise* (2T), followed by the relevant section number(s) into which Locke divided each of these texts.

2. See Locke's *Letter Concerning Toleration*, ed. James H. Tully (Indianapolis: Hackett, 1983), 26, 35. I will use the designation LCT, followed by the page number, to identify further references to the *Letter*.

3. "An Essay on Toleration," in *Political Essays*, ed. Mark Goldie (Cambridge: Cambridge University Press, 1997), 144, 146.

4. See p. 64 above.

5. "Liberty of Conscience is every mans natural Right" is William Popple's free translation or insertion. Cf. the more literal translation of Locke's Latin in Locke, *Epistola de Tolerantia/A Letter on Toleration,* ed. Raymond Klibansky, trans. J. W. Gough (Oxford: Oxford University Press, 1968), 134–35: "to teach, and to lay down as the foundation of their own liberty, the principle of toleration for others."

6. Locke thus defies the distinction between liberals, concerned simply with "how government should treat its citizens," and republicans, whose first question is "how citizens can be cultivated capable of self-government." See Michael Sandel, *Democracy's Discontent: America in Search of a Public Philosophy* (Cambridge, MA: Harvard University Press, 1996), 27; also below, p. 139–40.

7. See Aristotle, *The Politics,* 12766.16–12776.6.

8. *Some Thoughts Concerning Education* 31, in *Some Thoughts Concerning Education and of the Conduct of the Understanding,* ed. Ruth Grant and Nathan Tarcov (Indianapolis: Hackett, 1996); henceforth cited in the text as STCE with Locke's section numbers as given in that edition.

9. *An Essay Concerning Human Understanding,* ed. Peter H. Nidditch (Oxford: Oxford University Press, 1975), IV xv 6; henceforth cited as ECHU with Locke's book, chapter, and section numbers as given in that edition. See also LCT, 27–28.

Part II

CULTIVATING CITIZENS AS A CONTEMPORARY PROBLEM

5

Who Are We?
Taking Stock of the Culture

Jean Bethke Elshtain

I will approach this theme by donning theological garments, loosely draped, in order to explore the ground and structure of hope for all citizens—most particularly, for those citizens called *Christian*. In so doing, I will not abandon the ground of political and civic theory—the work with which I am associated—but, rather, I will critically explore certain convictions, which I and millions of others share. These convictions help to give form and texture to a way of being and knowing that imbeds strong norms for action. Another way of making this point is to say that we are called to be good stewards and wise and faithful servants. We are called to live within and to act upon projects on the ground of hope. My aim in moving this direction is not to exclude citizens who do not embrace Christian hope but instead to display the ways in which that hope can help to sustain the critical and constructive civic projects and identities that promote our collective well being as a people, whether one is claimed by the name *Christian* or not.

The advent of a new millennium, rather like what Samuel Johnson is said to have observed about the prospect of hanging, concentrates the mind wonderfully. We take stock. We look back in order to peer ahead. Having looked back, and having surveyed the shipwreck that is too much of the twentieth century, we ask ourselves: Do we dare to hope? Taking stock honestly and forthrightly, refusing to avert our eyes, it is clear that optimism isn't warranted. But, then, optimism about human prospects never is. Hope, however, is something else. While optimism proffers guarantees that everything will turn out all right and that all problems are solvable, hope, that great Christian virtue, urges us into a different stance, one aware of human sin and shortcoming but aware also of our capacities for stewardship and decency and our openness to grace. I shall argue that citizens of this great democratic

73

society can find reasons to hope and that citizens who call themselves *Christian* are, above all, claimed by hope.

HOPE AND LANGUAGE

The question of cultivating citizens gestures toward an active process of the formation of selves capable of sustaining certain virtues and ways of being. Martin Luther, in an Augustinian mode, insisted that our speech should stay close to the ground, or ordinary usage, and that language should not be misused, made purposefully misleading, euphemistic, or obfuscatory. Sound speech, for Luther, drew one close to the reality one was describing.[1] The first concrete project for citizens who live in hope is, therefore, to insist that we name things accurately and appropriately, in the conviction that there is a structure and order to being that can be named and described. Why is this vital? One extraordinary sign of our times is a process of radical alteration in language, understanding, and meaning. We are, or ought to be, painfully aware of what happened when totalitarian regimes had the power to control language and to cover mass murder with the rhetoric of the improvement of the race or even of mercy and compassion. But we are much less attuned to the ways in which our own language and, hence, our understanding of the world may be distorted by drawing us away from, rather than closer to, that which we are depicting.

Consider, for example, the appropriation of the word "community" by enthusiasts of cyberspace.[2] Community is derived from the Latin *communis,* from which communion, communicate, even the reigning image of the person in Christian anthropology as one born *in communio,* all usher. Community is grounded. It must begin with the concrete, the tactile, the relational, the fleshly. It implicates us in a world of others, who bind us to them as well as to a time and a place. In 1938, as the world was collapsing and turning vicious all around him, Dietrich Bonhoeffer penned an urgent work, *Life Together.* In this text, Bonhoeffer meditated on the nature of a Christian community, having in mind his own community, in which he and his seminarians shared a life together as pastors and pastors-in-becoming of the Confessing Church before the Gestapo forced the closing of their community. Community cannot exist without the physical presence of others. Why? Because: "A human being is created as a body; the Son of God appeared on earth in the body for our sake and was raised in the body."[3] Scripture uses the metaphor of a body—the body of Christ—to describe the church.[4]

Bonhoeffer attacks all spurious forms of idealism that would have us live in psychic "reality," or in "a dream world . . . abandon[ing] ourselves to those blissful experiences and exalted moods that sweep over us like a wave of rapture. For God is not a God of emotionalism, but the God of truth."[5] Wishful dreaming makes us "proud and pretentious." But no "visionary ideal" ever binds people together. The Christian community is "not an ideal we have to realize, but rather a reality . . . in which we may participate."[6] Real community is mediated as we are stirred to love of neighbor through shared love in and through Christ. This actual community never excludes "the weak and insignificant, the seemingly useless people, from everyday Christian life in community"—no, for "in the poor sister or brother, Christ is knocking at the door."[7] Bonhoeffer credits these lessons in concrete embodied community to the people of Israel and their experience as handed down to us in Scripture. He also picked up something of the rhythms and flow of communal monastic life during his visits to Rome and his stay in a monastery.

By contrast to the concrete, nitty-gritty, tactile nature of real community, think of so-called "cyber-community" and that "reality" called virtual. This is a form of gnosticism that is parasitic upon the concrete realities that thoroughgoing cyberites disdain, with their labeling of people who are not totally hived or caught in the web as PONAs, people of no account. Writes Mark Slouka: "Already, we are told, technological prostheses had begun to 'liberate' us from the limitations of the human body. The possibilities were endless. Within the span of our children's lifetimes, we are assured, it would be possible to link the human nervous system directly to a computer, to download the human consciousness into RAM (random access memory), effectively preserving it in some artificial state. Within the foreseeable future, the dividing line between nature and technology—a false dichotomy, we were told, since at least the invention of agriculture—would be erased; genetic engineering in general, and the Human Genome Project in particular, had already blurred the line forever."[8] Divorced from our bodies, so the scenario runs, all boundaries between self, other, male female, anything and everything would disappear. We could be anyone we want. We could go anywhere we want. We could do anything we want. Reality would lose all meaning. And so, I submit, would, and does, community, when it involves no concrete, living relations of human bodies one to another, whether in a given moment or in situ. Once one acquiesces in euphemisms, from "community" for cyberspace to such horrible and familiar substitutes as "pacification" for harrying and hounding peasants, destroying and looting their homes, and forcing them to become desperate refugees; or "compassion" for killing helpless, imperfect human beings; or "choice" for a nigh-unlimited "right" to withdraw the boundary of moral concern from unborn children at any stage of fetal development; or "liberation" for our freedom from any socially or ethically sanctioned relations or commitments—one deepens a radical loss of meaning.

What does it mean to *name* things correctly? It does not mean embracing a simplistic, designativist account of language, nor does it commit one to a correspondence theory of truth. Rather, the task I urge upon those who live in hope is to pay more attention to the ways in which the abuse of language creeps up stealthily on cat's paws and thus may insinuate itself unawares. Living in hope means being attuned to the ways in which language simultaneously frees us and binds us. Those who aim to unloose language entirely from coherent tethering diminish the potent role of language in constituting and structuring human relations in ways befitting the complexity of persons as creators and creatures. There is a structure of human hope, even as there are structures of all other complex human possibilities. Hopelessness is one by-product when meanings spiral out of control. When words implode, so do worlds. In his great work, *The Peloponnesian War*, Thucydides ties the loss of clear meanings of words to Athens's subsequent degradation and decline. He clearly intends this as a kind of civic object lesson: beware when words lose their meaning.[9]

Words and their meanings are connected to debates about truth. The deformation of language characteristic of totalitarian regimes was an integral feature of their playing fast and loose with facts, and thereby undermining any possibility of shared truth-claims as a feature of political and personal life. People were vanished from photographs, written out of history. Events were obliterated or invented. Those of us who never experienced such horrors underestimate how important truth is to people who lived for years within a tissue of state-sponsored lies. This came home to me at a conference in Prague on "Truth and Politics" in 1994 at which philosophers from Central and Eastern Europe who had fought the good fight against totalitarianism expressed their perplexity at the blithe attitude evinced by many Western philosophers concerning the question of truth.

My paper on that occasion consisted of an analysis of Hannah Arendt's complex reflections on this topic. Arendt, one of the premier political thinkers of this century, had insisted that the political world is utterly dependent upon facts, for life in the plural must tend to "factual truth."[10] Arendt argued that there is such a thing as a historical record and that we are not permitted to "rearrange the facts" in order that they might better comport with our own perspective. She cites the French premier Georges Clemenceau, who, when asked what future generations would say about responsibility for the outbreak of the First World War, replied that he wasn't sure how the war-guilt question would finally be ironed out. "But I know for certain that they will not say Belgium invaded Germany." This stubborn fact—what Arendt calls the "brutally elementary data"—will remain, and if it is destroyed, much more will have been lost than this one forlorn fact. For at the sad moment when a power monopoly can eliminate from the record "the fact that on the night of August 4, 1914, German troops crossed the frontier of Belgium," "power interests" will have utterly shut down a public world of freedom depending upon the stubborn reality of certain humble truths.

HOPE AND REASON

Now let us turn to a second claim on those who live in hope, namely, to be prepared to offer a reasoned defense of one's positions and to engage one's interlocutors and fellow citizens from a stance of openness and respect. Now more than ever, Christians must cultivate and defend human reason. One of the most ardent defenders of human reason in the world today is Pope John Paul II, who shares Augustine's insistence that God's righteousness and human righteousness are linked and that this linkage extends to our capacity, in freedom, to seek the truth. In his work, John Paul taps the love of wisdom and the desire for the truth that he takes as part of our very constitutions. There is, he claims in the encyclical *Fides et Ratio*, a kind of epistemic urgency characteristic of human beings. Our sense of wonder is awakened by contemplation of creation. Now the danger is that this quest for knowledge may become what John Paul calls "philosophical pride" should we, for example, take but one stream of thought for the whole. At its best, however, our searches strengthen our capacities as "free and intelligent" subjects who have the "capacity to know God, truth and goodness."[11] This is an extraordinary gift that should not be squandered. Thus, the church has no quarrel with the natural sciences or the other great disciplines as a matter of principle.

John Paul insists that too simple a fideism fails to recognize the importance of rational knowledge and philosophic discourse for an understanding of the faith. Those who live in hope keep the window to transcendence open as part of thinking faith—for to believe is to "think with assent."[12] John Paul then gestures toward one of the "most significant aspects of our current situation," the crisis of meaning to which I have already referred.[13] This crisis consists of radical doubt that throws us into nihilism, the triumph of instrumental thinking, a rejection of the "sapiential dimension as a search for the meaning of life,"[14] and the sheer "fragmentation of knowledge" itself.[15] John Paul frets throughout *Fides et Ratio* about contemporary anti-intellectualism, whether in the church or not—and if anti-intellectualism and simplistic fideism are not the problem, the pridefulness of philosophical totalizers and systematizers is likely to be. In the eloquence of John Paul's argument on behalf of reason, one finds a display of robust Christian hope—that human beings might think, believe, and act in ways that are generous and large-hearted.

When John Paul notes that St. Anselm "underscores the fact that the intellect must seek that which it loves [, that the] more it loves the more it desires to know," he locks horns with a modern reason that believes reason unaided can lead us to wisdom. If Christians need philosophy, philosophy needs love and illumination by faith. Otherwise the person is drawn to forms of modern reason that "lured people into believing that they are their own absolute master, able to decide their own destiny and future in complete autonomy, trusting only in themselves and their own powers."[16]

Live in hope: reason, argue, explore joyfully. This is the only way we can come to know one another. As Francis Cardinal George proclaimed in his installation homily as Chicago's archbishop:

> What the church brings to any society or neighborhood is the experience of making differences public so that they can be shared to create a richer unity. In the church every racial and cultural difference must be made public so that everyone can come to know how Christ can be black or white or brown or yellow or red. If I do not know any Mexicans or Russians or Africans or Chicagoans, I cannot experience how Christ can be Mexican or Russian or African or Chicagoan. The differences must be made public, but always in a way that they can be shared, so that they can enrich everyone.[17]

This process is the work of reason in faith and love.

The third difference that those who call themselves Christian can and should make in order to roll back the scrim of modern meaninglessness is to display what incarnational being-in-the-world is all about. We are called to cultivate citizens who make visible before the world the fullness, dignity, and wonder of creation—the horror, then, at its wanton destruction. This sounds mysterious, but it isn't. Modern deadness is all around us—the conviction that the world is so much matter to manipulate; that abstract signs and symbols entirely of our own creation capable of whirring around the globe in milliseconds are the reality that counts; and that individuation as a kind of radical aloneness simply is the human condition.

Christianity, by contrast, is a remarkably enfleshed way of being. The body is no mere container for the soul but our very essence. We are not individuals whose sociality is the result of voluntaristic motion but persons whose sociality is given. Kenneth L. Schmitz calls the notion of the person "extravagant," even lush, here remarking on the Trinitarian vision.[18] As humans moved into modernity, the transcendent dimension of this complex concept that fused together dignity, intimacy, relationality, interiority, and other features of persons began to fade. Unsurprisingly, the dominant metaphor for political organization by the seventeenth century had shifted from anything suggestive of the corporate to everything generated by contract. Colin Gunton argues that the presupposition underlying social contract theorizing is that: "Social existence is not essential to our being as humans, but a more or less unfortunate necessity. . . . Both Hobbes and Locke found their concepts of the social contract on a deficient sociality, a failure to consider the essentially social nature of human being."[19] This contract metaphor implicates us in a contraction of personhood, and the only "value" or "dignity" we have is what the contract permits and what, nowadays, the market will bear.

Let us look at some concrete instances of the loss or bleeding away of incarnate reasoning and being and at, by contrast, examples of words made flesh.[20] Consider, for example, that we are now urged to think about death in the language of rights—specifically, a right to die. Despite its pervasive use, this notion should retain the capacity to startle us. People die. One scarcely needs a right to do that. But the "right"-to-die enthusiasts claim a legal right to an "easeful" death. The architect of much of the current hoopla surrounding the issue is self-promoting pathologist Jack Kevorkian, who rails against any and all who refuse to take on board his insistence that people should have the "right" to kill themselves and to have medical assistance in doing so whenever they see fit. This is but one among a cluster of views Kevorkian holds. Others include the right to experiment on convicted murderers before their executions—they are going to be killed anyway, so why preserve any integrity to their bodies before execution?—and, as well, he has, in print, "excused Nazi doctors for having experimented in death camps, because at least some physiological knowledge emerged thereby from the general slaughter."[21] Kevorkian's "philosophy," if such a crackpot melange of bone-chilling opinions can possibly be said to constitute such, is the crudest utilitarianism imaginable. As Anthony Daniels notes:

> Assisted suicide and euthanasia are but stalking horses for Kevorkian's wider social vision of routine experimentation upon dying people and walk-in municipal suicide centers where the ill and merely disgruntled will be helped (at public expense) to shuffle off this mortal coil. They will be manned by salaried specialists in death called obitriatists, who practice patholysis, the dissolution of all suffering.[22]

Kevorkian would not have gotten as far as he did, or gotten away with what he did so long as he did, were there not widespread support for what he seemed to be for and what he seemed to be against, no matter how strange Kevorkian himself. He presented himself as a Child of the Light, deploying the dominant terms of our discourse—compassion (let's end suffering now!) and wants-as-rights. Those opposed to him were Children of Darkness. He singled out for special abuse the Catholic Church, medicine, even the press, which, of course, helped to "make" him in the first instance. They would hold things back and stop people from doing what they "want" and had a "right" to do. If we have embraced the view that we are all alone without "rights" (having denied relational personhood), why should we be queasy about exercising that right alone at the end, in a van in a parking lot somewhere, dumping the bodies that are the end product on the doorsteps of hospital emergency rooms or leaving them for police to find? There are many ways to ill-dignify the bodies of the ill and dying, and this is surely one.

When people think twice, they blanch before the horrors of a Kevorkian. Perhaps this is why the incarnational dimension has not been altogether quashed. Ezekiel Emanuel points out that support for "euthanasia and assisted suicide has declined rapidly among those who must administer it," and, as well, that the more people find out about how this actually works, the more they are disinclined to favor changing the laws to sanction the practice. Instead, what people want—and what they wanted all along—was not an absolute right to state-sanctioned death but more effective ways to minister to the bodies of the dying. The public was reflecting a rightful abhorrence at the excessive medicalization of death and the often cruel prolongation of life in ways that constitute an assault on embodied dignity and sociality as the dying person is entubed, encased, ensheathed in multiple forms of medical paraphernalia, and removed from the tactile world of loved ones.

The incarnational moment reasserts itself as part of what the Pontifical Academy for Life calls "an authentic culture of life, which should . . . accept the reality of the finiteness and natural limits of earthly life. Only in this way can death not be reduced to a merely clinical event or be deprived of its personal and social dimension."[23] I submit that in the depths of our being we know this. It is awareness that can be clouded over. It goes into the shadows and reappears as phantoms and hauntings, but it cannot be altogether quashed. That is why one lingering horror of Nazi genocide is the image of all those bodies—piles of them—being bulldozed into pits once the camps were liberated, being given the closest thing to a decent burial affordable in such desperate circumstances. But we know people deserve better. We know that every single one of these anonymous bodies was somebody's mother, father, son, daughter, wife, husband, child, grandparent, friend. These are the folks by whom we should be accompanied as we move through life toward death, a surround that speaks to our dignity as persons and that, therefore, puts pressure on excessively clinical, utilitarian, or simply, à la Kevorkian, ghoulish and macabre, approaches to life's end.

HOPE AND CONTEMPORARY CULTURE

Finally, citizens who are Christian and are called, therefore, to live in hope must ensure that their churches play a critical role as interpreters of the culture to the culture. There are few such public sites available, especially in this era of media saturation. Recall the complex position of the Christian as pilgrim, poised between the twin poles of *amor mundi* and *contra mundum*. This means one is gifted with the power to transform a wounded culture, not as a messianic project but as a work of grace and love. In recognizing and holding ever before our eyes the dignity of the human person created in God's image, one is called to talk about and work to achieve a common good, not as enforced homogeneity but as a type of community that turns on and recognizes the particular gifts each brings to the banquet table of life.

You cannot engage the culture if, in common with too many contemporary cultural critics, you loathe and despise it or have given up hope for it entirely. One cannot hate that which one would transform. There is something good in every culture. It would be astonishing were this not so. Indeed, I would say it would be impossible, because that would mean that that culture had been utterly denuded of any access to the good and that it was living in a barren wilderness of the spirit. At one point in our culture, this denunciatory tack was the purview of the political left, with its violent negations of all things 'Amerikan.' Now such voices are heard more from the right of center. America is construed as one seething fleshpot, ready to implode. The voice that prevails in such critiques is that of condemnation. But if the culture were really beyond redemption, it would cast doubts on creation itself and its goodness. Surely that cannot be bleached out entirely! Let us look at a few signs of the times that cultural critics (rightly) point to as evidence of disorder or moral catatonia. But let us 'read' these signs in a more hopeful way, following an Augustinian commitment to charitable interpretation.

An issue evoking something akin to despair—deeply and ardently felt— and, at times, the most severe language of condemnation is the current abortion regime. But a charitable interpretation of our current situation would point to such hopeful signs as the fact that the latest reliable surveys indicate that over 70 percent of Americans think access to abortion should be limited in some circumstances. Only 16 percent of the public think abortion should be illegal under all circumstances; some 27 percent that abortions should be permitted in all circumstances. Interestingly enough, however, the number of people who call themselves "pro-choice" has declined since the triumph of what many have called an "abortion culture" in the wake of *Roe v. Wade,* even as the number identifying themselves as "pro-life" has risen.[24] Working with such figures, one can patiently and charitably engage strong pro-choicers and ask them to explore their own moral queasiness about an unlimited abortion right—which we have evidence is widespread. Doesn't this perhaps speak to a deep uneasiness about narrowing the boundary of moral concern where human life in situ at any stage of development is concerned? Shouldn't Christians live out an alternative by showing a generous concern for the lives of all children, born and unborn? Shouldn't this voice and concrete, hands-on programs of help and nurture prevail?

My next example of the church and Christians as cultural hermeneuts is drawn from the arena of popular cinema. Movies have been taking lots of hits from critics recently, and for good reason. Much of what is out there is either pap or authentically degrading, representing human beings at their most debased, hideous, selfish, and cruel as entertainment for profit. I am not here thinking of serious films, like Steven Spielberg's *Schlinder's List*—which, necessarily, depicts Nazi cruelty and debasement—but instead of so many of the horrifically stupid and graphically violent "entertainments" put out for consumption by teenagers. But there is much else going on. Blanket targeting of films that display any violence simply falls wide of the mark and suggests to many young people (and not they alone) that Christians are hermetically sealed-off grumps.

Consider the 1995 film *Seven,* which many "Christian" voices enjoined people not to see because of its graphic representations of the aftermath of grotesque crimes of murder. (We don't actually see the murders committed, but we see pictorial representations of these murders in most instances, though thankfully not in the case of the final murder.) What hits Detective Somerset (Morgan Freeman) right from the start is that the first murder is an "act that has meaning." He knows the murders are just beginning. Why? Because of the methodical, deliberate nature of what was done and how it was done, with the word GLUTTONY scrawled in grease on the wall of the kitchen of an obese man who had been forced to eat himself to death. Detective Somerset, in his quest to understand, cites Milton. He predicts that six more murders will come. His brash young partner, Detective Mill, who has just recently been assigned to this detective division, is impatient and finds Somerset unintelligible—a little loony himself. The guy [the killer] is "just a psycho," a crazy who pees all over himself and blabs nonsense. Somerset knows it is far more serious and haunts the public library after closing hours. (He is friends with the night custodial crew and watchmen.) He begins to reread and to consult Dante's *Purgatorio,* Chaucer's *Canterbury Tales.* He consults the *Dictionary of Catholicism.* He recommends these to Mill. Mill, almost crazy with impatience, throws a volume of Dante, having tried without success to read it. The dominant Western tradition, with its reflections on questions of good, evil, Satan, God, and theodicy, elude Mill entirely. He is a child of the media era. He bounces around erratically and says "whatever" a lot—and he resorts to *Cliff Notes* versions.

Cliff Notes—the film suggests that that is the way our culture at present knows its great tradition, if at all, through a summary outline in which others have done all of the work. One has not the patience any longer to do the hard work of learning. One has lost access to a yet-vibrant and enriching wellspring of human knowledge, identity, complexity, and purpose. If Monday's murder was GLUTTONY, Tuesday's is GREED. A wealthy lawyer has bled to death, forced to cut off one pound of his own flesh. *The Merchant of Venice* is the relevant textual reference point. Somerset notes that this leaves SLOTH, WRATH, PRIDE, LUST, and ENVY to go. It will continue.

The film plays out in a kind of inferno. It is always raining, gray, bleak. Sidewalks are dirty. Paint peels on walls. There is no color save a kind of brownish, greenish, grayish hue—colors of decay. Somerset muses that the murders are like "forced contrition." The victim is contrite not because he or she has come to "love God" but becomes he or she is forced to undergo a violent expiation, and then killed. Detective Mill is agog with disbelief at Somerset's hermeneutical strategy and approach. The murderer has left a message at the GREED murder scene: "Help Me." Mill interprets this as just another sicko whimpering. He bleaches the meaning out of all the signs. Somerset mordantly describes the task he and Detective Mill are undertaking in general as homicide detectives: We are picking up the pieces. Putting things in neat piles. So many corpses unavenged.

By Thursday, they think they've got a fingerprint match to the killer, or so the signs tell them. But no, they've been faked out. The seven-deadly-sins killer has cut off the hand of a victim whom he has kept methodically and cruelly tied up for over a year, even to the point of using antibiotics for bladder infections, in order that he can, through forced inactivity, display the contrition attendant upon SLOTH. The severed hand provides the fingerprints that lead the police to a room where, bound to a bed, is a rotting, barely alive corpselike entity, starved and effectively brain-dead. Somerset keeps thinking. He is deeply frightened. The killer has purpose. He focuses on the details. He is playing a complex game. At this point, Detective Mill's beautiful young wife, Tracy, meets with Somerset, a sympathetic, older African-American gentleman of the "old school," just to have someone to talk to. She hates the drab, decaying world they find themselves in. She can't bear the elementary schools she has visited (she was a fifth-grade teacher "upstate")—they are such terrible environments for children. She is lonely and sad, and she is pregnant but hasn't told her husband. Somerset, trying not to advise, nevertheless tells her that if he had it to do over again, he would have the child he succeeded in urging the woman he never quite married to abort. There isn't a day that passes, he tells Tracy, that he doesn't regret that decision. "Spoil the kid every chance you get," he urges Tracy, steering her in the direction of life.

In the meantime, the meticulous killer goes about his work. Somerset says, "These murders are his sermons to us." Mill is incredulous. "The guy's a whack job." Saturday turns up the death labeled LUST. A woman has died horribly in a sexual act into which her partner, the precipitate cause of her horrible death by evisceration, was coerced at pain of his own death. Somerset warns Mill. "This isn't going to have a happy ending;" he notes that "Satan himself couldn't live up to the expectations that are building," for the killer will be "just a man," here revisiting the theme of evil as diminished, not grand.[25] Wearily, Somerset notes that he is tired of living in a place that "nurtures apathy as a virtue." Sunday is the murder designated as PRIDE, a beautiful woman whose nose has been "cut off to spite her face." Astonishingly, at this point, the killer, bloodied, shows up at police headquarters to turn himself in to Detectives Somerset and Mill. He has already had one shoot-out with them, for they tracked him down to his apartment through the signs he had left everywhere and the books he has checked out—you are what you read.

Some read the works the killer has absorbed as a way to think about the theodicy question and as object lessons in what happens to a human being itself, absent a transcendent reference point. The killer has made himself his own point of reference. He claims that he was "chosen." Somerset challenges him, noting that "if your hand was forced, you shouldn't enjoy it." A real messiah doesn't exult and gloat. The killer is proud of his death-dealing tasks and proclaims their necessity—he was wiping out people who embodied deadly sins. They were not "innocent." Of course, in Christian theology, none of us is. The killer confidently predicts that what he is doing will be "followed forever." He is the arbiter of life and death.

Having taken the two detectives to a deserted, barren, desert wasteland, where the sun is glaring brutally and all is empty, he awaits the end result of his grotesque, cruel handiwork. It comes in the form of a box that contains the severed head of Tracy, Mill's wife. (We do not see this. We see only the look of horror—a soul-shuddering moment—as Somerset opens the box, Mill having been given task of guarding the murderer.) The killer starts to describe his handiwork to Mill. Somerset is screaming for Mill to drop his gun. He doesn't want the chain of violence to continue. The killer taunts Mill—he, the killer, was overtaken by ENVY of Mill and his life and his wife, so he "took her pretty head," and now he must die at the hands of Mill made WRATH. Somerset cries out to Mill, "He wants you to shoot him." "Please," Somerset begs, "If you kill him, he will win." Mill, twisted and screaming in pain and disbelief, crying "No! No!," shoots the eagerly anticipating killer once, then empties his gun into him.

Evil, it seems, has won. The film ends with a voice-over by Somerset. "Ernest Hemingway once wrote, 'The world is a fine place and worth fighting for.' I agree with the first part." We are left drained. The cycle of vengeance goes on. Perhaps the most wounded victim in this gallery of grotesque deaths is Detective Mill. He will go on living, knowing he has enacted the killer's last "sermon." But the film is an allegory on what happens when signs have lost their meaning. The signs left by the killer lost their meaning to all but Somerset, who cannot get things on an interpretive track intelligible to others, who have lost access to the tradition of thinking about good and evil. A critical hermeneutic would see here on display a twisted theodicy and the defamed fruits of a cruel self-absorption of a particularly megalomaniacal sort. That our culture seems to throw up more and more such representations—and living exemplars—should be a matter of deep concern. The response should be loving regard and a recognition that hope yet shines its steady light. But we must push back the scrim of darkness to see that light.

Think here of the horror of the Columbine High School massacres and the shocked lamentations that succeeded it—proof positive, to some, that young people were going to hell. Two young men were, quite assuredly, in hell. Captured by the darkness and representations of evil, they struck out, targeting explicitly students who voiced their belief in the God of creation. Some of the wounded were shot, they tell us, because they said they believed and were carrying Bibles. Rachel Scott was shot first in the leg and then through the head when she said she believed in God. Cassie Bernall, having answered yes to the question, "Do you believe in God?" was shot through the temple. Who can imagine such courage under such terrible circumstances? But look what students did during the course of the massacre and after: at risk of their own lives, they ushered frantic and paralyzed classmates to safety. (This is how one young man died.) They struggled to keep their coach and teacher, Dave Sanders, alive, staunching his wounds with their torn tee-shirts and fashioning a stretcher from table legs. When it was clear that he was bleeding to death, they held him, prayed with and for him, and showed him pictures of his family. They created prayer circles as the siege continued. They loved and cared for one another. In the aftermath, they put up signs and crosses and offered prayers and devout promises to help rebuild a community that would constitute a living memorial to their classmates who had perished. This is, to put it bluntly, a hell of a thing for kids to go through. But the way in which these young people went through it should help us to savor living hope rather than to dwell exclusively on the violence and lament and condemn all things adolescent.

Let us return, one last time, to the culture of films. It is the top-grossing film of all time, *Titanic,* that I want to explore in closing. *Titanic* was a cultural event of titanic proportions, with huge throngs going week after week—men and women of all ages in every country in which it played. What were they coming by the millions for? Many cultural critics put it off entirely on "chick flick" teen enthusiasm for the (admittedly) extraordinary young actor, Leonardo di Caprio, who plays the self-sacrificing romantic lead, Jack Dawson. But this misses the boat. Viewers told of being "drawn back to" the film again and again. Experts were dumbfounded. Forty percent of those who had seen it wanted to see it again, compared with 2 percent for the average film. More than one-third of the audience was over the age of twenty-five. Graves of *Titanic* victims were thronged. There was a popular pilgrimage never imagined possible to cemeteries in Halifax, Nova Scotia, where a number of the *Titanic* dead are buried, including one "Jack Dawson." What was—is—going on here?

I have tried this interpretation out a few times and it wasn't regarded as crazy, so let me unpack it as another example of how Christian symbols and concepts afford an interpretive site for dominant cultural phenomena. What *Titanic* offers is a penetrating view of the cost of human arrogance and pride. The villain, one Caledon Hockley (Billy Zane), gloats that "God Himself could not sink this ship." Even the name *Titanic* can be construed as a kind of thumbing one's nose at divinity. The titans, after all, were underworld destroyers who, if unleashed, could only destroy. Bruce Ismay, the ship's builder (not her decent architect) extols the mechanical brilliance of the ship's supremacy—it was "willed into solid reality." Sheer size is proclaimed a good in itself. Due to prideful arrogance, an insufficient number of lifeboats have been installed, it having been considered a waste of good deck space to put in enough to accommodate all passengers. Why bother, as no one would ever be in need of saving? All were already, so to speak, rescued. They were on an unsinkable ship.

The film veers back and forth between life in steerage and the world of the upper class (and the American rich were very rich indeed, this being in the days before a graduated income tax), as the ship that cannot sink moves over the glassy sea. On the upper decks all is diamonds, furs, shimmer, and glamour, as privilege closes ranks and every whim is catered to by a huge, properly obsequious staff. Beneath her decks is a blazing inferno where giant boilers roar and engines—the biggest ever on a ship—grind, exuding power. A transgressive love affair builds between Rose DeWitt Bukater (upper class) and Jack Dawson (steerage), a good-hearted itinerant artist living on "God's good humor." Jack understands that "life's a gift. You never know what you're going to be dealt." One must, therefore, "make each day count." Everyone knows the story as a sustained allegory on human chance and the hideous fruits of pride that strike most deeply into the company of the least privileged. So Hockley proclaims in response to Rose's cry that there are sufficient lifeboats for only half, that half must die—and "not the better half."

Jack and Rose cling together. If you jump, I jump. The film shows acts of cowardice, chicanery, stupidity, grace, and courage. Some comport themselves with dignity and sacrifice themselves for others, including "lesser" sorts. The "ship of dreams" has turned into a sinking horror, with intimations of all that is best, and ample scope for all that is lowest about us. A priest prays the rosary as others cling to him. "I saw a new Heaven and a new Earth. . . . [T]he former world had passed away." The band plays "Nearer my God to Thee" and perishes, comforting people until the end—an act that can be taken as folly or grace, depending upon one's interpretive site. Jack saves Rose. "I've got you. I won't let go." He pleads with her, "Do me this honor. Promise you'll survive. Promise you won't give up." He gives up his own life for her, as a door fragment afloat on the icy water that serves as a precarious life raft would capsize were more than one person to attempt to occupy it. Fifteen hundred human beings go into the sea; only six are pulled to safety. Boats float half-empty.

Now, I've heard complaints from a Christian perspective that the film contains a pernicious message in that Rose describes Jack as having "saved her" in "all the ways a human being can be saved." She says this as an old woman remembering her experience, recalling the way she was slated for an endless "parade of balls and cotillions" and witless chatter as the rich reveled in their richness. The "ship of dreams" was, for her, a slave ship meant to take her into a forced marriage to an arrogant man of means who believed that money could buy anything—including life and death, as we see when he bribes a ship's steward in an attempt to get into a lifeboat ahead of women and children of the "lower sort."

Life merges into death at the film's beginnings, with its underwater images of the ship's forlorn, majestic ruin. At the film's end, the dead are powerfully reborn into a new life on a very different *Titanic*. Rose dreams a paradisiacal dream. The ship is recreated. Alive once more, there is beauty and music and camaraderie. In Rose's transformed vision, those separated by status and office are all together, forming a great circle above and at the base of the grand staircase in order to bless a young love. It is a dream of reunion. People are gathered without distinction and resentment in a way that is reminiscent of the communion scene in *Places in the Heart*, where the sheriff and his young killer, who have been parted by violence and fear, take communion side by side, and are thus reunited under the sign of Christ's sacrifice and God's grace.

We do well not to minimize or mock or belittle these moments. They speak to hunger and a search for meaning and grace. Although Rose utters what can be taken as heretical (Jack cannot save her in all the ways a human being can be saved), she also embodies, with her words and her dream, a transcendent reference point that she cannot fully articulate, or chooses not to. In discussing those who, like Ismay, saved, and hence ill-dignified, themselves as they let so many children from steerage go to desperate, watery deaths, Rose comments that they were "waiting for an absolution that would never come"—not if they hoped to absolve themselves from themselves, and by their own powers. But it is Rose's dream of reunion and in-gathering that is so powerful. We are struck because—or so I submit—the most plausible and powerful way to read her dream is as an instantiation of the of the Kingdom of Heaven, where all are gathered together, where resentment is known no more. The poor have not replaced the rich or the captain or others of power in her dream. Instead, all have been mixed up, mingled, and joined together. They are united because they are focused on something other than themselves. They are united in and through Jack and Rose's love. This is not enough for our hungry hearts. But it affords us glimpses of what a community of love and a God who so loved the world is all about. We still see through a glass darkly, but the film, charitably interpreted, helps us to see more and deeper. So many kept returning because they wanted to understand why they were returning. The film was nurture of some sort. What need, what good, was here hinted at?[26] Read the signs of the times. Love the world enough to want to know it. Know the world enough to love it.

Despite it all—the troubles, the pain, the frustrations, the dangers of either self-pride or excessive self-abnegation—through it all remain trust, hope, and for Christians, the greatest of all these: love. Let us add thankfulness—gratitude—to the list. One of our grandsons, dear Bobby, now three, said to me when he was just barely two and I was swinging him in the backyard on a sunny, crisp day with a slight breeze stirring the leaves in the trees: "Everything is everywhere." This he said as he looked at me after having gazed for a time at the sun, the rustling leaves, the expanse of yard, a cat frolicking nearby: Everything is everywhere. It is that childlike awe and wonder, in words as beautiful to me as any I have ever heard, that is the warp and woof of hope and love. Delight and wonder are part and parcel of hope and trust; for, as Augustine would say, without hope and trust our hearts are locked away. He was right.

NOTES

1. Martin Luther, "The Bondage of the Will," in *Martin Luther's Basic Theological Writings*, ed. Timothy Lull (Minneapolis: Fortress Press, 1989), 173–226.

2. I am not here referring to those who regard the internet as a complex tool for research or as a way of quickly sending out functional messages; rather, I have in mind those who have become publicists of cyber-reality and who debunk the puny stuff of that which most of us know as the "real world."

3. Dietrich Bonhoeffer, *Life Together: Prayerbook of the Bible*, Dietrich Bonhoeffer Works, vol. 5, trans. Daniel W. Bloesch and James H. Burtness (Minneapolis: Fortress Press, 1996), 29.

4. Bonhoeffer, *Life Together*, 29.

5. Bonhoeffer, *Life Together*, 35.

6. Bonhoeffer, *Life Together*, 38. An interesting discussion of "The Ecclesiology of John Paul II," by Fr. Avery Dulles, SJ, appears in *Origins* 28(44) (April 22, 1999): 759–63. Fr. Dulles points out that John Paul's preferred category for ecclesiology is communion and that this communion is the "integrating aspect, indeed the central content of the 'mystery' or rather, the divine plan for the salvation of humanity" (759).

7. Bonhoeffer, *Life Together*, 46.

8. Mark Slouka, *War of the Worlds* (New York: Basic Books, 1995), 18–19.

9. Thucydides, *The Peloponnesian War* (London: Penguin, 1982), 3.82.4.

10. Arendt's views appear at various places in her work. I here concentrate on her essay, "Truth and Politics," which appears in the collection *Between Past and Future: Eight Exercises in Political Thought* (New York: Viking Press, 1968).

11. John Paul II, *Fides et Ratio* (Boston: Pauline Books and Media, 1998), sec. 4, 12.

12. *Fides et Ratio*, sec. 79, 99.

13. *Fides et Ratio*, sec. 81, 101.

14. *Fides et Ratio*, sec. 81, 102.

15. *Fides et Ratio*, sec. 81, 101.

16. *Fides et Ratio*, sec. 107, 129.

17. Francis Cardinal George, "What the Church Brings to the Neighborhood," *Origins* 27(1) (May 27, 1997): 3.

18. Kenneth L. Schmitz, "Reconstructing the Person: A Meditation on the Meaning of Personality" *Crisis* (April 1999): 28.

19. Colin E. Gunton, *The One, The Tree and the Many: God, Creation and the Culture of Modernity* (Cambridge: Cambridge University Press, 1993), 220.

20. A tremendously complex discussion is Josef Seifert, *Back to "Things in Themselves": A Phenomenological Foundation for Classical Realism* (New York/London: Routledge and Kegan Paul, 1987). See especially Part II: "Objective knowledge of 'things in themselves'; constituted, unconstituted, and unconstitutable being."

21. Anthony Daniels, "A Bit of His Own Medicine," *The Independent* on Sunday (November 29, 1998): 30. This is an extensive and sober piece in a London newspaper, and it contrasts—in its favor—with much of the media coverage in U.S. newspapers, which tended to take on Kevorian's own self-congratulatory view of himself as a martyr to a righteous cause. One exception is *The New Republic,* which ran a series of critical pieces on Kevorkian, including his disproportionate selection of women as ideal death-subjects.

22. Daniels, "His Own Medicine." Once again one sees how the stuff of dystopian science fiction yesterday turns into today's proposals and, God forbid, tomorrow's realities.

23. Pontifical Academy for Life, "The Dignity of Dying People," *Origins* 28 (41) (April 1, 1999): 707.

24. Richard Benedetto, "Abortion Poll Reflects Public's Deep Divisions," *USA Today* (May 5, 1999): 15A.

25. See my discussion of Augustine and Hannah Arendt on this issue in *Augustine and the Limits of Politics* (Notre Dame, IN: Notre Dame University Press, 1996).

26. Even a film like *The Matrix,* much condemned in the wake of Columbine High School, points to that which it cannot itself make manifest. The film is riddled with violence, yes, but there is talk of the "one" and of "Zion" and of getting out of a world in which one is forced to live falsely. The theology, however, is very weak. A chosen one doesn't become such at the moment he begins to "believe in himself." This is a very New-Agey pop-psych substitute for serious theology, but it is a cut above a standard slasher, bomber, gasher film.

6

Higher Education and the Cultivation of Citizenship

Alexander W. Astin

That higher education plays a central role in shaping civic life in modern American society seems beyond dispute. Our colleges and universities not only educate each new generation of leaders in government, business, science, law, medicine, the clergy, and other advanced professions but are also responsible for setting the standards and training the personnel who will educate the entire citizenry at the precollegiate level. Higher-education institutions can also exert important societal influences through the scientific, technological, and cultural knowledge produced by their faculties.

While the United States is generally regarded as having the finest postsecondary education system in the world, there is mounting evidence that the quality of civic life and engagement in this country has been eroding in recent years.[1] The list of problems is a long one: shaky race relations, growing economic disparities and inequities, excessive materialism, decaying inner cities, a deteriorating infrastructure, a weakening public school system, an irresponsible mass media, declining civic engagement, and the increasing ineffectiveness of government, to name just a few. In a democracy, of course, citizen disengagement from politics and governmental ineffectiveness not only go hand in hand but also cripple our capacity to deal constructively with most of the other problems.

If higher education is indeed such a central player in the shaping of civic life in America, then one might reasonably ask, where have we gone wrong? That our system has the capacity, not to mention the responsibility, to begin focusing more of its energy and resources on such problems is reflected in a number of recent developments, including the rapid growth of the Campus Compact (which now numbers nearly seven hundred member institutions that have pledged themselves to promote engagement in public and community service), the involvement of the American Association for Higher Education in a major effort to encourage service learning across the disciplines, and the commitment by the American Council on Education to undertake a "national initiative on higher education and civic responsibility."

Despite these promising developments both inside and outside academe, the American system of higher education still has a very long way to go before it can claim to be genuinely committed to the task of renewing and revitalizing civic engagement and democracy in the United States. In the classroom, faculty continue to emphasize the acquisition of knowledge in the traditional disciplinary fields and the development of writing, quantitative, and critical thinking skills, giving relatively little attention to the development of those personal qualities that are crucial to civic life and effective democratic self-government: self-understanding, listening skills, leadership, empathy, honesty, generosity, and the ability to work collaboratively.

Most of these qualities exemplify what Daniel Goleman would call aspects of "emotional intelligence."[2] One seldom hears mention of these qualities, or of "civic responsibility," or of "citizenship" in faculty discussions of curricular reform, even though such concepts are frequently found in our catalogues and mission statements. While there have been some very promising developments in the curricular area—an increased emphasis on issues such as multiculturalism and the environment, for example—most of our undergraduates have little exposure to coursework that focuses directly on issues of contemporary American civic life and democracy: the central role of information and the mass media, the possible causes of declining civic engagement and declining trust in government, the escalating role of money in politics, the growing corporate influence, and so on. Finally, in our hiring, tenuring, and other personnel practices, collegiality and service to the institution and to the community continue to receive little, if any, weight.

THE CENTRAL ROLE OF BELIEFS

The cultural essence of any organization, such as a university, is the shared beliefs of its members. The more I reflect on the problems confronting higher education and the larger society, the more I become convinced that at the heart of our problems in trying to revitalize American democracy and civic life are issues of beliefs. By this I mean our beliefs about the meaning and purpose of an undergraduate education, as well as our notions about educational excellence and, especially, our view of the role that higher education should play in the larger society. The problem is not so much that we might differ in our beliefs about these matters but rather that these beliefs remain unexposed and unexamined while we discuss and debate the educational policies and practices that emanate from them.

As a starting point, let's take the issue of the relationship between higher education and society. Different people can hold very different beliefs about this relationship. An extreme view, which would probably be endorsed by only a small number of hard-core purists like Robert Maynard Hutchins, is that the university should remain walled off from the external world of practical affairs so that the students can study and learn, and faculty can pursue truth unencumbered by worldly distractions. While this "ivory tower" concept of higher education has a certain appeal for some scholars I know, it never could, nor will, represent a viable conception of higher education in modern American society. Like it or not, American higher education is a creature of society, is sanctioned and supported by that society, and has in turn pledged itself to serve that society in its mission statements, catalogs, and other public pronouncements.

An alternate belief system, which seems to dominate in discussions of educational "policy" these days, is what I like to call the "pegboard" view. Under this view, the outside world is like a giant board containing an array of differently shaped job slots, and the role of higher education is to produce the right-shaped people—the "pegs"—who will fill these slots. This is the dominant belief system not only of our captains of industry but also of most politicians and policy makers, not to mention many students, teachers, and parents. The pegboard view is also what drives the "competitiveness" argument, namely, that higher education must deliver more people with expertise in science, technology, and modern management techniques so that America's economy can remain "competitive" with the economies of Western Europe and, especially, the burgeoning economies of countries on the Pacific Rim.

My main concern with the pegboard view is that it represents an extremely limited conception not only of the role of higher education but also of the larger society. When we consider the major problems plaguing contemporary American society, it is ludicrous to argue that they can all be summed up in the issue of economic competitiveness. Competitiveness in the international marketplace bears only a marginal connection to the domestic issues of racial polarization, poverty, joblessness, crime, a deteriorating infrastructure, environmental degradation, political apathy, and distrust of social institutions. There is nothing inherently wrong with higher education's attempting to produce graduates who possess more of the job skills required by modern business and industry, but it is naive to think that this will make much of a dent in our myriad social problems. Indeed, becoming more "competitive" economically may well be antithetical to any effort to deal constructively with problems like the infrastructure, crime, the maldistribution of wealth, and especially the environment.

Still another conception of the role of higher education in society is what I call the "private economic benefit" viewpoint, which, simply stated, maintains that the role of higher education is to provide opportunities for individuals to obtain higher-level and higher-paying jobs and in general to live a more comfortable and affluent lifestyle. This is obviously a close cousin of the pegboard view, in that it focuses on employment, upward economic mobility, and the development of "human capital." One might also call this the "consumer" viewpoint, in the sense that it sees individual students as consumers, who invest time and money in higher education in order to receive greater economic benefits later on. This idea of a trade-off, an investment for a later return, is what economists have in mind when they calculate the "rate of return" to higher education. Proponents of higher education who tout the "increased earnings" associated with higher education are also operating from this same belief system. Even if one accepts the argument that private economic benefits provide the main justification for higher education, this particular belief system is extremely limited, because it has little to say about how the society as a whole is served by such an approach. In other words, while it may be a laudable goal to contribute to the economic comfort and well-being of those citizens who are fortunate enough to enter and complete higher education, this viewpoint has little to say about what is going to happen to people who are not able to complete higher education, nor does it say anything about how, if at all, the many other social and economic problems of our society will be addressed by such an approach.

An entirely different kind of belief system is implied in the various public pronouncements that American colleges and universities make in their catalogs and mission statements. In certain respects these statements reflect our highest sense of mission and purpose. Thus, if we were to study the mission statements of a randomly selected group of American higher-education institutions, we would seldom, if ever, find any mention of private economic benefits, international competitiveness, or slots in the labor market. On the contrary, when it comes to describing its educational mission the typical college or university will use language such as "preparing students for responsible citizenship," "developing character," "developing future leaders," "preparing students to serve society," and so forth. In other words, if we are to believe our own rhetoric, those of us who work in the academy see ourselves as serving the society and of promoting and strengthening our particular form of democratic self-government. We might call this the "citizenship" view of higher education's role. While such a belief system does not preclude individual economic benefits or the preparation of people to serve the needs of employers, its central focus is on responsible citizenship and service.

Clearly, our capacity to contribute to the solution of our many social problems and to the rehabilitation of democracy and civic life in American society will depend heavily on which belief system we embrace. The problem, of course, is that if you look at the typical American college or university—

its curriculum and co-curriculum, its teaching and personnel practices, and the values that govern its administrative policies—it's very difficult to find evidence of a core commitment to preparing students for responsible citizenship. Most institutions, in short, have simply not put their "citizenship" and "service" commitments into practice.

Perhaps the most pressing reason to begin taking our public pronouncements about our societal mission more seriously is the sorry shape of contemporary American democracy. Most citizens don't vote, negative campaigning reigns, and public distrust, contempt, and hostility toward "government" has reached unprecedented heights. The most recent freshman surveys conducted by the Higher Education Research Institute indicate that student interest and engagement in politics is at an all-time low.[3] While academics frequently comment on this sorry state of affairs, they seldom suggest either that higher education may have played a part in creating these problems or that it can or should attempt to do anything about them.

BELIEFS ABOUT "EXCELLENCE"

Closely connected to our beliefs about our societal mission are our beliefs about academic "excellence." For a number of years now, I've been very critical of our traditional approaches to making ourselves academically excellent, which often seem to be reduced to acquiring as many resources as possible and building up our institution's reputation so we can move up as far as possible in the institutional pecking order. My concern about these approaches is that they fail to address directly our basic societal purposes of teaching and public service. Not that we don't need reputations or resources in order to teach and serve, but rather that a unidimensional focus on resource acquisition and reputation building as ends in themselves can ultimately cause us to neglect our basic educational and service missions.[4] Paradoxically, it can also cause us to neglect our research mission, because we become focused more on acquiring top scholars and researchers than on developing the scholarly talents of the incumbent faculty.

The roots of many of our seemingly most intractable problems can be found in this preoccupation with resource acquisition and reputational enhancement: the valuing of research over teaching, the struggle between equity and excellence, and the lack of community that we find on many campuses. We value research more than teaching, because we believe that outstanding scientists and scholars will add more to our reputation and resources than will outstanding teachers or mentors. When we define our excellence in terms of the test scores of our entering freshmen—the high-scoring student being viewed here as a "resource" that enhances our reputation—we set our sense of excellence in direct conflict with our desire to promote educational opportunities for those groups in our society whose test scores put them at a competitive disadvantage. Finally, when we place the highest value on the individual scholarly accomplishments of our students and faculty, we reinforce their competitive and individualistic tendencies, making it very difficult for them to develop those qualities that help to promote a sense of community on the campus: good colleagueship, collaboration, community service, citizenship, and social responsibility. These latter qualities, of course, are the same ones that are needed to make any democracy work.

CITIZENSHIP AND LEADERSHIP

The problems that plague American democracy and civic life are in many respects problems of leadership. By "leadership" I mean not only what elected and appointed public officials do but also the large and small civic acts performed by countless individual citizens who are actively engaged in making a positive difference in the society. A leader, in other words, is anyone—regardless of formal position—who serves as an effective social-change agent; in this sense every student—and every faculty and staff member—is a potential leader.

Discussions about the frail state of American democracy typically make reference to such problems as lack of citizen engagement, distrust of government, racial divisions, unethical politicians, the excessive influence of money, and an irresponsible mass media. While each of these problems needs more of our attention, the biggest problem with contemporary civic life in America may be that too few of our citizens are actively engaged in efforts to effect positive social-change. Viewed in this context, the "leadership development" challenge for higher education is to empower students, to help them develop those special talents and attitudes that will enable them to become effective social-change agents. While the list of relevant "leadership talents" is a long one, it would almost certainly have to include such qualities as communication skills (especially listening skills), empathy, generosity, commitment, caring, self-understanding, honesty (i.e., the ability to develop trust), and the ability to work collaboratively with others. Once again, these are some of the same qualities that are needed for effective citizenship.

Most of us probably think of democracy primarily as an external process, where people do things like discussing issues and politics, campaigning for candidates, or voting. While these activities are indeed important elements of a healthy democracy, none of these "external" behaviors is likely to occur in the absence of appropriate "internal" conditions: an understanding of how democratic government is supposed to function, an appreciation of the individual's responsibilities under such a form of government, and a willingness, if not a determination, to be an active participant. In other words, democratic behavior is most likely to occur when the person has acquired certain knowledge, understanding, beliefs, and values. These "internal" qualities are precisely the kinds of qualities that educational institutions are in an ideal position to foster.

The problem here for us in the higher education community, in a nutshell, is that we have not done a very good job of developing these qualities in our students, because we have been preoccupied with other things. While many of my faculty colleagues may argue that the failure or success of our system of representative democracy is not higher education's responsibility or concern, they forget that promoting "good citizenship" and "developing future leaders" are two of the most commonly stated values in the mission statements of colleges and universities. Like it or not, we are publicly on record as committing ourselves and our institutions to promoting leadership and citizenship.

CREATING A TRUE "CITIZENSHIP CURRICULUM"

If we really want to make good on our professed commitment to democracy and citizenship, we need to examine all aspects of our undergraduate programs, with the following questions in mind: Does this course, or this requirement, or this teaching technique, or this educational policy contribute to the student's ability to become an informed, engaged, and responsible member of society? Are there alternative approaches that might be more effective in helping us realize these goals?

A real "citizenship curriculum" would no doubt include much of what we currently call "the liberal arts," but the "packaging" and "delivery system" might be very different. The new curriculum would also include a number of new elements. Most importantly, it would be designed around a thoroughgoing conception of 1) what students need to know about contemporary American democracy and how it actually works, and 2) what skills and attitudes students need to develop in order to become engaged and effective citizen-participants.

My own sense about such a curriculum is that it would enrich, rather than diminish or dilute, the traditional "liberal education" now being offered in most of our colleges and universities. In particular, the humanities and social science requirements that so many students now find "boring" or "irrelevant" could be given new life and meaning if the content and pedagogical approach were more directly connected to issues of citizenship and government. Contemporary American democracy and society and its problems afford countless opportunities to explore concepts such as truth, honesty, self-knowledge, power, and the law, and to deliberate on fundamental value issues like competition versus collaboration, the individual versus the community, material versus spiritual values, freedom and responsibility, equity versus excellence, and the distribution of wealth.

Pedagogy would also have to change, of course, in recognition of the fact that civic life and engagement is not just something one talks or thinks or writes about but also something one does and experiences. Although I may well be accused of oversimplification, I would submit that there is currently available to all of us who teach the liberal arts a simple but extremely powerful tool that not only promises to enhance higher education's capacity to address our myriad social problems but provides us with an opportunity to strengthen some of the most important features of a classical liberal education. I am speaking here of what has come to be known as "service learning."

The basic idea behind service learning is to use a community or public-service experience to enhance the meaning and impact of traditional course content. Service learning can not only enrich traditional course content by giving the student an opportunity to "test" or "demonstrate" abstract theory in the real world but can also improve the quality of the service being performed, by giving it an intellectual underpinning. Although increasing numbers of institutions are giving serious consideration to the idea of expanding their service-learning opportunities for students, this particular pedagogical innovation is still a relatively infrequent, if not marginal, activity on most college campuses. The obstacles to more widespread use of service learning are many, including lack of faculty experience and expertise, the absence of a campus center to facilitate the development of service learning courses, the belief that it may incur additional costs, faculty resistance, and the question of efficacy: Does service learning really work?

Recently at the Higher Education Research Institute we have completed a series of empirical studies of how students are affected by participation in community service, and the findings are nothing short of remarkable. In one national longitudinal study,[5] we compared service participants with nonparticipants using 35 different outcome measures covering three broad areas: academic development, civic values, and life skills. What was especially remarkable about the findings was that every one of the 35 student outcomes was positively influenced by service participation. Other recent research also indicates that these favorable outcomes are enhanced if the service is not merely volunteer work but rather is performed as part of a course.[6]

In another longitudinal study[7] we sought to determine if there are any lasting effects of the undergraduate service experience that extend into the first five years after college. Once again we found uniformly positive effects on a range of postcollege outcomes, including enrollment in postgraduate study, commitment to community values, participation in community service after college, and satisfaction with the extent to which the undergraduate experience prepared the student for postcollege employment. Also—of special interest to college presidents and directors of development—is the finding that undergraduate participation in community service increases the likelihood that the alumnus will contribute money to the alma mater!

Turning now to the question of costs, there is no question that service learning—properly done—involves significant additional costs. Our site visits to campuses that had received service-learning grants from the Corporation for National Service convinces us that any significant program of service learning requires a staff of experienced professionals who can develop field placement opportunities in the community and who can work directly with faculty to assist in the development of service-learning components in courses. This is no work for amateurs. In other words, if the faculty have to do this on their own, it will be very difficult to expand service-learning significantly. Even with professional help, however, service-learning tends to require more faculty time and effort than does traditional classroom instruction. It also, of course, requires much more engagement from the student. One obvious and simple way to deal with these "cost" issues is to award more credit for courses that incorporate service learning. Such an approach would certainly seem to be justified, given the additional faculty and student effort involved.

One of the most attractive features of service learning is that it affords us an opportunity to incorporate, in one learning experience, some of our most powerful but currently underutilized pedagogical techniques. One of these is cooperative, or collaborative, learning. Service learning readily lends itself to collaboration, where small groups of students work together, teaching and learning from each other. According to a large and growing body of research,[8] collaborative learning is more effective than traditional individualistic or competitive learning. This form of learning capitalizes on the power of the peer group, which recent research[9] has shown to be the most potent source of influence on the undergraduate. Students are more likely to invest time and energy in the learning experience if they know that their efforts will be scrutinized by peers, or if they know that they are part of a larger effort where fellow students must depend on each other.

Service learning also incorporates another powerful pedagogical device: reflection.[10] Service learning typically involves a good deal of this, where students reflect on the service experience, not only in terms of its significance for the theoretical course content but also in terms of what it means to them personally.

It seems to me that reflection connects directly to another one of our themes—the notion of "soulcraft." For me, the process of considered reflection on one's life and one's experience—whether it takes the form of quiet meditation or prayer, introspective writing, or group "processing"—comes closer than almost anything else we can do in our classroom teaching to promoting a real understanding of oneself and others. While the ancient injunction to "know thyself" is at the core of almost all of our great philosophical and religious traditions, it typically receives very little attention in contemporary curriculum and pedagogy. This lack of emphasis is especially ironic, in light of the fact that the notion of self-understanding is at the heart of the classics that provide the principal philosophical basis for a liberal arts education.

My many years of involvement as a practitioner and scholar in higher education convinces me that service learning—perhaps more than any other innovation I know of—has the potential to transform our institutions of higher learning in positive ways. Beyond the direct benefits to students just discussed, more widespread use of service learning would also:

- Enliven and enrich the teaching and mentoring activities of faculty by introducing a "lab" component into coursework that provides them and their students with an opportunity to test out theoretical concepts in a real-world environment.
- Break down the artificial distinction between "academic" and "student" affairs by involving student affairs staff in the development and implementation of service components in formal coursework.
- Strengthen the sense of meaning, purpose, and community on the campus by engaging many more of its faculty, staff, and students in the mission of serving others.
- Cultivate a much stronger positive connection between the campus and its surrounding community.

REVITALIZING DEMOCRACY AND CITIZENSHIP

At the risk of sounding like an alarmist, I'd like to suggest that our more arcane discussions of higher education "policy" sometimes make me wonder if we are just fiddling around while Rome burns. If higher education doesn't start giving citizenship and democracy much greater priority, then who will? Corporate business? The news media? The church? Politics? How can we ever expect the democratic dream to become more of a waking reality unless education changes its priorities? Some of my academic colleagues might respond that a "traditional liberal education" is the best thing we can do to prepare young people for the responsibilities of citizenship. While there may be some truth in that argument, the uncomfortable reality is that whatever we are currently doing— call it liberal learning if you like—simply isn't getting the job done. Most of our citizenry—and that includes most of our college-educated citizenry—seem neither to understand what democracy is all about nor to accept their individual responsibilities to make it work. Judging from the choices that those relatively few who do bother to vote make when they go to the polls, it seems clear that we have not done an effective job of showing our students how to avoid being bamboozled by politicians and the major news media. What I am really suggesting here is that the future of American democracy is to a certain extent in our hands, and if we want to do anything to improve the current state of democracy, we have to change some of our ways of doing business.

It would be a mistake, I think, to construe my argument simply as an appeal to our sense of altruism or social responsibility. On the contrary, higher education has an enormous personal stake in producing graduates who understand the key roles that information and education play in our democracy. We continually need to remind ourselves that our students are the same people who will be voting on education bond issues and choosing among candidates who are either friendly or hostile toward education. The quality of their experience in our institutions will be a prime determinant of how they will view education later on.

What other societal institution has the resources, the understanding, or the will to undertake such a major rehabilitation and renewal of our faltering democracy? The point is simply this: We in the higher education community don't have to be content with simply griping about the conduct of the media and the ignorance and indifference of the electorate; we are actually in a position to do something about it.

SOME FINAL THOUGHTS

Our students and our colleagues are going to be influenced at least as much by what we academics do as by what we say in our mission statements, classroom lectures, and faculty meetings. In other words, we are modeling certain values in the way we conduct ourselves professionally: how we treat our students in and out of class, how we deal with each other as professional colleagues, and how we run our institutions. If we want our students to acquire the democratic virtues of honesty, tolerance, empathy, generosity, teamwork, cooperation, service, and social responsibility, then we have to model these same qualities not only in our individual professional conduct but also in our curriculum, our teaching techniques, and our institutional policies.

What I am really suggesting here is that a genuine commitment on the part of our higher education system to renewing civic life and civic engagement in American society will require that we be willing to embrace significant changes in our curricula, teaching practices, reward systems, and community relations and, most importantly, in our institutional values and beliefs.

In light of the reduced funding and other external pressures that many colleges and universities are experiencing today, it seems only fair to ask whether it's realistic to think that higher education has the wherewithal to undertake the kinds of reforms I have been suggesting here. However, in our haste to man the barricades to defend ourselves against external threats, we are inclined to forget that the autonomy that we seek to protect may be the most powerful tool that we have for reshaping higher education in the interests of promoting democracy and citizenship. There is no one standing in our way except ourselves. We still retain control over practically all of the decisions that really matter: whom to admit and how to admit them; what courses and what work to require of our students; what to teach and how to teach it; how we assess and evaluate our students; how we structure our co-curriculum programs; how we hire, reward, and tenure our colleagues; what policies and procedures we utilize to govern ourselves; and what subject matter we choose for our research and scholarship.

The implications here are clear: If we genuinely believe that it would be in our own best interests—not to mention those of our students and of the society that supports us—to introduce a central focus on democracy and citizenship into our curriculum and other campus activities, we have both the autonomy and the intellectual skill to do it.

NOTES

1. See, for example, Robert Putnam's *Bowling Alone: The Collapse and Revival of American Community* (New York: Simon and Schuster, 2000).

2. Daniel Goleman, *Emotional Intelligence: Why It Can Matter More than IQ* (New York: Bantam Books, 1995).

3. Cf. L. J. Sax, A.W. Astin, W. S. Korn, and K. M. Mahoney, *The American Freshman: National Norms for Fall 1998* (Los Angeles: Higher Education Research Institute, 1999). Also, A. W. Astin, S. A. Parrott, W. S. Korn, and L. J. Sax, *The American Freshman: Thirty-Year Trends, 1966–1996* (Los Angeles: Higher Education Research Institute, UCLA, 1997).

4. A. W. Astin, *Achieving Educational Excellence: A Critical Assessment of Priorities and Practices in Higher Education* (San Francisco: Jossey-Bass, 1985).

5. A. W. Astin and L. J. Sax, "How Undergraduates Are Affected by Service Participation," *Journal of College Student Development* 39, no.3 (1998): 251–63.

6. A. W. Astin, L. J. Vogelgesang, E. K. Ikeda, and J. A. Yee, *How Service Learning Affects Students* (Los Angeles: Higher Education Research Institute, UCLA, 2000).

7. A. W. Astin, L. J. Sax, and J. Avalos, "Long-Term Effects of Volunteerism during the Undergraduate Years," *The Review of Higher Education* 22, no. 2 (1999): 187–202.

8. D. W. Johnson, R. T. Johnson, and K. A. Smith, *Active Learning: Cooperation in the College Classroom* (Edina, MN: Interaction, 1991).

9. A. W. Astin, *What Matters in College? Four Critical Years Revisited* (San Francisco: Jossey-Bass, 1993).

10. J. Eyler and D. E. Giles, Jr., *Where's the Service in Service Learning?* (San Francisco: Jossey-Bass, 1999).

7

Citizenship, Faith, and Christian Higher Education

Michael D. Beaty

In his address to the nation on November 8, 2001, President George W. Bush suggested that the events of September 11 might give birth to a reinvigorated civic life. He said,

> The enormity of this tragedy has caused many Americans to focus on the things that have not changed—the things that matter most in life: our faith, our love for family and friends, our commitment to our country and to our freedoms and to our principles. . . . Since September the 11th, many Americans, especially young Americans, are rethinking their career choices. They're being drawn to careers of service, as police or firemen, emergency health workers, teachers, counselors, or in the military. And this is good for America.

President Bush is not the only one to make this observation. In an article entitled, "Can Patriotism Be Turned into Civic Engagement?" Professor William Galston recently claimed that the terrible events of September 11 have produced a surge of patriotic feeling among young Americans.[1] Galston's hope is that this outpouring of love of country and civic feeling will make possible a renewed commitment to public life. He observes that if this surge of interest in public life could be sustained, it would represent a significant shift in outlook for a group of Americans previously characterized by a detachment from civic life. He cites the University of California at Los Angeles long-term study of matriculating college freshmen from 434 of the nation's baccalaureate colleges and universities, showing that since the mid-1960s, "every significant indicator of political engagement fell by at least half. By last year [2000], only 28 percent of freshmen felt that keeping up with politics was important, down from 60.3 percent in 1966."[2] However, Galston hopes that the events of September 11 and afterward may have changed a generation of college students' angle of vision on public life. He puts it this way:

> For many, it is their first experience of public service as meaningful; of national leaders, local leaders, police officers, firemen, and their fellow citizens as virtuous, even heroic. But no civic invisible hand guarantees that these effects will endure. At best, we have an opportunity—which may prove fleeting—to solidify this new civic sense.[3]

Galston makes an important point. If these altered perceptions on civic responsibility and public life are to take root and flourish, these nascent perceptions and initial decisions will require supporting institutions, and perhaps a renewed understanding of public life. How best are we Americans to take advantage of this opportunity? How should American educators respond? What new initiatives ought we to undertake?

Alexander Astin wrote fairly recently in the *Chronicle of Higher Education* of the lamentable state of American democracy and decried the poor job American higher education has been doing in preparing students for democratic citizenship.[4] Like most American universities, Christian universities and colleges have long embraced the cultivation of good citizens as one of their primary and most important educational aims.[5] Both Astin and Galston identify civic education as one of the primary goals of our universities. Galston insists that we must "restore the civic mission of our educational institutions,"[6] and Astin prescribes that "citizenship development . . . be viewed as an integral part of the educational program" rather than "an add on, to be pursued only if new money ever becomes available."[7] Astin asks,

> If higher education doesn't start giving citizenship and democracy much greater priority, who will? Corporate business? The news media? Politicians? How can we ever expect the democratic dream to become a reality unless education changes its priorities? The future of American democracy is, to some extent, in our hands, and if we want to improve it, we have to change some of our ways of doing business.[8]

Are Christian colleges and universities doing enough to educate our students to be good citizens of a democratic culture? Civic education, or education for citizenship, remains an expressed goal of the educational mission of many religiously identified institutions, but especially of Protestant colleges or universities. For example, the mission statement of my own institution, Baylor University, expressly states: "Established to be a servant of the church and of society . . . Baylor strives to develop responsible citizens. . . . Baylor provides expanded opportunities for civic education and for church and community service at home and abroad."[9] What should be the educational aims of such institutions if they take seriously their own mission statements?

If Christian colleges and universities are not doing enough, to whom can Christian educators turn to develop an educational strategy whose aim is the formation of better citizens of a democratic culture? Perhaps Christian educators find an answer to this question in Martha Nussbaum's recent book, *Cultivating Humanity: A Classical Defense of Reform in Liberal Education*. Professor Nussbaum argues "for a particular norm of citizenship" and makes "educational proposals in light of that ideal."[10] She insists that the primary goal of education is not equipping students for careers and professions but rather preparing them for world citizenship. In this goal, she underscores her agreement with Cicero and the Stoics. More specifically, she contends that a liberal education in our own day is education for democratic citizenship, and in this way her proposals cohere with much of the education that took place in nineteenth-century America.[11] Baylor's own motto, *Pro Ecclesia, Pro Texana*, adopted in 1845, suggests this very understanding of a university education. Though clearly provincial, this formulation fits with the American notion, especially among Protestants in the nineteenth century, that a classical college education ought to equip students to be good citizens of both the church and the state, and to enable them to perform well a variety of roles—citizen, deacon, minister, lawyer, physician, and teacher—in both the *ecclesia* and the *civitas*.

Professor Nussbaum's book is relevant to Baylor University and other religiously identified colleges and universities, because she examines fifteen institutions chosen as representative of the different types of colleges and universities in the United States. Among those institutions are several religiously identified institutions, including Belmont University, a Baptist liberal arts institution. She focuses special attention on the University of Notre Dame and Brigham Young University, with which Baylor is comparable.[12] Interestingly, she argues that "for institutions whose religious identity more centrally [than Brandeis, for example] shapes campus life, the available choices seem to lie between these two [institutions]."[13] They provide, she thinks, two very different conceptions of the task of cultivating citizens for contemporary democracy in a Christian university.

Nussbaum insists that the present and future of American higher education is healthy. She defends higher education in America against several recent jeremiads by critics who accuse it of corrupting our youth through multiculturalism, African-American studies, gender studies, and courses about human sexuality, to include gay and lesbian studies. By contrast, Nussbaum claims that these are valuable reforms, reforms needed to produce "citizens of the world," a phrase she takes over from the ancient Stoics, whom she admires greatly. Socratic self-examination and a narrative imagination that allows us to appreciate the point of view of other cultural traditions are essential features of a genuinely liberal education, she argues. Such an education produces "world citizens" with "minds of their own" who view "humanity" as the community of their first allegiance.

My own aim in this essay is to argue that her proposal for a particular conception of liberal education and its ends ought to be unpersuasive for Christian colleges and universities who are serious about their Christian identities.

I focus on her characterization of a "world-citizen," whose formation is the aim of a genuinely liberal education.[14] I contend that the ideal of world citizenship recommended by Nussbaum cannot be embraced by Christians, and by extension, that it cannot be the aim of a Christian university. My strategy is to outline briefly her initial proposal, to discuss why Christians will find many aspects of her proposal attractive, to identify and discuss why Christians will find the core of her proposal unacceptable, and to conclude with some remarks on Christian faith, citizenship, and liberal education.

NUSSBAUM ON CITIZENSHIP AND LIBERAL EDUCATION: THE INITIAL PROPOSAL

According to Martha Nussbaum, the primary or ultimate aim of a liberal education is to enable students to "learn to function as citizens of that entire world."[15] She points out that Diogenes first coined the term "citizen of the world" but that it is the Stoics who made this idea "respectable and culturally fruitful."[16] They hold that "the good citizen is the *citizen of the world*"[17] rather than a good citizen of one's local political community, whether city, county, state, or nation.[18] Further, she argues that the kind of education that forms "world citizens" is a liberal education. While this sort of education has its roots in the kind of inquiry Socrates called "the examined life" and in Aristotle's reflections on citizenship, Nussbaum suggests that it matures in Stoic notions of "liberal." On this view, "liberal" means the liberation of the mind from bondage so that the person is able to function with sensitivity and alertness to the whole world. Liberal education, then, is what Seneca meant by the "cultivation of humanity."[19]

Nussbaum contends that the cultivation of three capacities is essential for a liberal education: 1) the capacity for Socratic examination of one's self and one's traditions; 2) the capacity to see oneself as a citizen of the world rather than merely the citizen of some local community and group; 3) the capacity for a narrative imagination that allows one to understand the world from the point of view of another person, who differs with respect to race, religion, gender, or sexual preferences. Since a colleague and I have provided previously an extensive discussion and critique of Nussbaum's misleading characterization of Socratic thinking and of her portrait of Socrates as a proponent of democracy, here I shall focus on Nussbaum's account of world citizenship.[20]

WHAT CHRISTIANS MIGHT FIND ATTRACTIVE ABOUT NUSSBAUM'S PROPOSAL

While I will later argue that Christians ought to reject Nussbaum's understanding of citizenship and liberal education, first it is important to notice the numerous features of her account that are attractive to Christians. To begin, among her heroes are Socrates and Diogenes. Both of these men disdained the traditional marks of status—wealth, power, and popularity—lived rather simply, and mingled with the lower classes in their societies, treating its members no differently than they treated the wealthy, influential, and the powerful. Both were willing to call into question many of the moral conventions of their communities for the sake of norms that transcended their local customs. Socrates believed that his penetrating examinations of himself and his fellow citizens in Athens promoted virtue in the individual and the health of the city. Christians will see in Socrates and Diogenes analogies to the prophets of the Hebrew Scriptures and to Jesus of the Gospels, for spurning wealth, power, and popularity. They too lived simply among the weak in their communities. Jesus frequently challenged the conventional understanding of the Torah held by Sadduccees and the Pharisees. Moreover, Christians will admire Nussbaum's insistence that each human being ought to regard all human beings as possessing a moral status deserving of respect, just treatment, and even benevolence—not merely those of one's immediate family or community but also those separated from us by race, ethnicity, gender, and sexual orientation. Additionally, Christians will see analogies in Nussbaum's injunctions to their notion that all human beings are equally children of God and that we are obliged to love not only our neighbors but also our enemies. Her frequent admonitions that the world citizen take into account those who have been marginalized in society by poverty, hunger, tragedy, or oppression resonates well with biblical demands that God's people champion justice and offer hospitality to the alien, the widow, and the poor.

However important our local place, its associations, and its attendant loyalties and obligations are, Christians will agree with Nussbaum that there is something more fundamental about us than our particular place and its stations or roles, and that this more fundamental something is the basis for our obligations to those with whom we share neither kinship nor friendship.[21] Nussbaum's appropriation of Seneca's characterization of the human being as a member of two communities, the first one assigned to us at birth and the second the community of all human beings, will remind the Christian of Augustine's suggestion that Christians live in two cities, the earthly city of man and the city of God. Finally, Nussbaum's insistence that human beings ought to recognize that their first allegiance is neither to merely human forms of government nor to merely temporal power[22] is something Christians will accept as a fundamental mark of Christian identity.

WORLD CITIZENSHIP AND LIBERAL VALUES

World Citizenship

How, then, should Christians think about Nussbaum's claim that the aim of a liberal education is to form world citizens? Admittedly, some Christians insist that "citizenship" ought never to be the aim of Christian education.[23] My purpose in this essay, however, is to discuss whether or not Nussbaum's proposal is acceptable for those Christian colleges and universities that embrace the cultivation of citizenship as a goal of the education they have chosen to provide. So, I am going to set aside the objection that "education for citizenship" is not an appropriate end for Christian universities until the final section of the essay.

As you remember, Nussbaum's specific suggestion is that liberal education ought to form "world citizens." What are we Christians to think of this proposal? First, it is reasonable to ask if the notion of "world citizenship" is a coherent notion. For *civis*, or "citizen" is a social and political role in a *civitas*, a politically organized community. The role of citizen has attached to it legal freedoms or rights and also duties. One learns how to be a citizen by a variety of socially constructed and/or politically conceived forms of education and, thereby, learns one's freedoms, rights, and duties while acquiring the virtues necessary to excel in the role of citizen. But there is no world *civitas* or government such that it, or some representatives of it, grants or acknowledges freedoms or rights and assigns duties; there are only smaller more discrete communities within which the notion of "citizenship" is practically applicable and by virtue of which we could answer questions such as "What are the appropriate rights, duties, and virtues of citizenship in *X*?" given that *X* is some particular community, political state, or government such as the United States of America. In the absence of a world government is "world citizen" a coherent notion? It seems possible, though highly unlikely, that in the future there would be a world government that performs the tasks identified above. So, perhaps one should say that the notion is coherent but practically impossible to realize. If "world citizen" has no referent in practice, and such a practical reference is highly unlikely to be realized, then it is hard to see how it is useful in establishing a normative notion of citizenship.

Let me press the point a bit more. Our world is made of many different states or ways of organizing the governing structures of a society—when we understand "society" as referring to a group of people who are bound by common cultural and geographical identity. Among them are a multitude of democratic and nondemocratic states. Consequently, there are many different particular notions of citizenship. For example, the role of a citizen in a liberal democracy differs in significant ways from the role of a citizen as understood in classical republican political theory, and that differs even more from how citizens or subjects are understood in nondemocratic societies. Thus, when Nussbaum insists that a liberal education is to form "world citizens," is she speaking with a fairly specific meaning, or is she speaking metaphorically? For example, from Aristotle we learn that a polis shares a common conception of the good. A good community is governed by individuals of practical wisdom who establish a system of education—intellectual and moral formation—in light of the good for human beings. This telos finds expression in a fully flourishing human life, which is realizable only within a properly ordered polis. In such a polis, citizens will perform their specified duties and exercise their specified freedoms. On this Aristotelian view, it is crucial to the community or the nation that education impart to all citizens a shared concept of the good, so that citizens will develop those virtues that will sustain and express the good. On such an understanding, it is possible that the shared conception of the good be religious in nature. If so, then, on some religious conceptions, the good for human beings would include a right relation to God. In such a homogeneous society, tolerance—first a political policy or legal arrangement for avoiding conflicts between individuals who differ radically in their notion of the good—will be unnecessary. As a dispositional characteristic, tolerance will be indifference to the trivial preferences of others. If so, citizens in such a polis would have a duty, one could imagine, to vote for laws that sustain and encourage a right relation to God, and, since it would be evil to hamper anyone from being properly related to God, it would be intolerable to behave otherwise.

Liberal Values

In the United States, our understanding of democracy is largely animated and informed by political liberalism.[24] On this view, democracy is a way of governing that grants to all its citizens equal protection under the law and an equal opportunity to govern by allowing participation in elections of officials and the like. As a strategy of governing, it is arguably consistent with the Aristotelian conception of the polis discussed above. In our democratic culture, however, political liberalism often adds the non-Aristotelian notion that government must be neutral toward the comprehensive metaphysical, moral, and religious views held by its people.[25] It is commonly held that this principle of neutrality with respect to the practices of governing our democratic culture requires citizens of a liberal democratic society to exercise a particular kind of restraint when engaging in the characteristically political practices of democracy.[26] Call this the "liberal-democratic" conception of citizenship. On this view, it is commonly argued that the role of the citizen requires one to restrain oneself from appealing to religious reasons, for example, in adopting certain public policies toward abortion.[27] Moreover, according to this liberal-democratic view, to restrain oneself from appealing to one's religious views as motives or justifications for political decisions is to exercise the virtue of tolerance. It seems to follow that on this conception of citizenship, one has a duty not to vote for laws if they encourage or sustain right relation to God.[28] To refuse to do so is to act intolerantly or intolerably.

What could it mean, then, to insist as Nussbaum does, that a genuinely liberal education would educate students with respect to world citizenship when the world contains competing and incompatible notions about what it means to be a citizen and about the rights, duties, and virtues appropriate to that role? For surely she cannot mean that every university ought to educate students with respect to all these different ways of being a citizen. Indeed, some of them are contradictory. Of course, that there are contradictory norms or patterns of citizenship is no problem if by education Nussbaum merely means informing students of the wide range of possible ways of being a citizen in our world. But clearly Nussbaum means both more and less than that. She is not as intent on informing students of the wide range of particular political understandings of citizenship being realized in various political communities of the world as she is on advocating or promoting a particular ideal of citizenship. For Nussbaum, the notion of a "citizen of the world" is not being used in its strictly political sense but as a metaphor for humanity, the moral community of human beings worldwide to which, Nussbaum asserts (without argument) each human being owes his or her first or ultimate allegiance.[29]

Even when "citizen of the world" or "world citizens" is used in this metaphorical sense to pick out the moral community of human beings, it gets whatever value it has for practical reasoning from familiar, nonpolitical uses of "citizen." For example, when Augustine refers to Christians as citizens of the city of God, he has a particular and discrete community in mind. Members of this community, the church, thought Augustine, are guided by the truths revealed in Scripture and interpreted by the *magisterium*. Similarly, when the Stoics are thinking of world citizens, they have in mind a community of philosophers who take their bearings from nature or Logos. In both cases, the existence of a particular community and the wisdom accessible to its members make it possible for them to live independently of the views and conventions that prevail in the particular earthly city in which they find themselves.[30]

Let me pull together the main threads of my argument. Nussbaum's thesis is that a liberal education cultivates—that is, educates or forms students to become—world citizens. But I have suggested that there are different and competing political conceptions of "citizenship in the world." The practical implication for education in the university is this: either these different conceptions will be presented as various roles one might—or might not— try on from the smorgasbord of options available to students, who, in turn, are made ever more sophisticated by the increasing number of choices, or they will be presented as options to be evaluated from some more fundamental point of view, with this philosophical conception providing the content and normative implications of "world citizenship."

According to Nussbaum, liberal education is the cultivation of world citizens. In this context, "cultivation" is being used as a metaphor that suggests nurturing and providing sustenance to produce something of a very definite sort. The charitable interpretation of Nussbaum's project is that we must appeal to a specific philosophical tradition, or family of positions,[31] in order to make Nussbaum's notion of cultivating or educating for world citizenship a coherent proposal. It is quite clear from Nussbaum's narrative that she has positioned her proposal within the philosophical tradition called political liberalism, mentioned above, which extends from the Stoics like Cicero and Seneca through Kant and Mill to contemporary thinkers such as John Rawls, Richard Rorty, Robert Audi, William Galston, and Stephen Macedo. Central to this tradition of liberalism is the Stoic insight, one deepened by Kant in his essay on perpetual peace, that "each human being owes his first and primary allegiances to no mere government, no temporal power, but to the moral community made up of all human beings."[32] What problems, if any, then, does this particular philosophical account of citizenship present Christian educators who are serious both about achieving academic excellence as a university and preserving the institution's ecumenically orthodox Christian identity?

THE "NEW" LIBERAL EDUCATION, VIRTUES, AND CITIZENSHIP: A THEOLOGICAL CRITIQUE

In the conclusion of the book, Professor Nussbaum asserts that we live in a culture divided between two conceptions of a liberal education. Both "fit citizens for freedom," but the older is inferior, because it aims at acculturating one in the customs and traditions to which one is born, which are both local and provincial.[33] The second, says Nussbaum, liberates the mind from the bondage of habit and custom, producing citizens who are not free because of faith or birth but because they have become acquainted with some rudiments of the major non-Western cultures and minority groups and the history and variety of gender and sexuality, and have become rigorous and critical in argument.[34] Of such citizens, we can speak of them being able to "call their minds their own."[35] According to Nussbaum, "to call one's mind one's own" is to have "ownership of one's [own] thought and speech," and this ownership imparts to all who have acquired the status of being able to call their minds their own "a dignity beyond the outer dignity of class and rank."[36] How should we read Nussbaum's credo? Quite clearly, Nussbaum intends to affirm the sovereignty of the individual over all other loci of authority, and this orientation is hardly surprising, given the fact that she locates her understanding of citizenship within the tradition of political liberalism. But is it innocent, at least for those faithful to the Christian tradition? I think not.

First, notice that Nussbaum insists that what "fits citizens for freedom" is what the citizen has done for him/herself by virtue of becoming acquainted with at least one non-Western tradition or minority group, by becoming acquainted with the history and variety of gender and sexuality, and by having acquired a sufficiently rigorous and critical mind. In short, one becomes "fit for freedom" by virtue of what each individual has done for himself or herself rather than what has been done for one by others. Of course, the theological truth most at stake here for Christians is the contention that we are fit for freedom only by virtue of what God has done for us, first in his covenantal relationship with the Jews and then in Jesus Christ's redemptive life, death, and resurrection. What God had done for us is what we could not have done for ourselves, and it is this work that fits us for every real and valuable form of freedom, be it moral, political or religious; moreover, it is an enabling condition for being and doing well, both as individuals and also as members of various human communities and in the fulfillment of various roles one might occupy in different associations and societies. If Christians accept Nussbaum's admonitions uncritically, then, they fail to ground their understanding of themselves, of human communities, and of social and political arrangements on this most fundamental of all Christian claims.

Second, Nussbaum suggests that "calling one's mind one's own" is "to have ownership of one's [own] thought and speech." What distinction does Nussbaum have in mind? Perhaps a personal vignette will be illustrative here. When I first went off to college, my luggage was not my own. It was luggage bought and owned by my father. He lent it to me. I used it to carry my clothes. The clothes I carried in the luggage were mine—not because I had bought them with my own money but because they had been bought for me by my parents and given to me. The clothes weren't hand-me-downs from an older sibling. While the clothes were not bought with my own money, I considered them, nonetheless, "my clothes," and so did my parents and friends. Legally, the clothes were mine. Existentially, they were mine, for they suggested my identity by giving shape and form to my presence and to my movements wherever I went; they mediated my relation to others, and they communicated, at least to some extent, my personality to others. The clothes in Dad's luggage were mine, though the luggage was not.

Perhaps Nussbam thinks of students and the ideas they bring with them to college more like hand-me-downs from their parents, older siblings, and significant others in the community, or like the luggage in which these clothes were carried. Maybe what she has in mind is that until students "own" the ideas they bring with them to university the way my father owned the luggage, or stand in a different relation to their ideas than I stood to my clothes, "their minds are not their own."

What do the clothes I called my own and the luggage I did not own have in common? Neither cost me any money. Neither cost me any toil, labor, or effort to acquire them. All were in effect gifts to me, acquired effortlessly on my part. The investment of time, money, skill, and disciplined work habits that made the luggage and clothing objects of use for me were all contributed by my father. In short, they were not acquired by my own efforts. So, perhaps Nussbaum is making the point that a liberal education reorders the student's relationship to items that he has received by the work and sacrifice of others. A good liberal education forces students to examine even the ideas they bring with them with respect to their understanding of truth, how those ideas fit with other truths, and what implications for larger views of human beings, society, and the world their ideas have. Such critical examination is hard work. It requires attention, disciplined work habits, and a growing awareness of a large and complex world of diverse viewpoints, traditions, customs, and conceptions of the good life. Perhaps Nussbaum means to suggest that even if students' views change little in the sense of what they regard as true, unless what they now regard as true is the result of a disciplined effort to think rigorously and imaginatively about our complex world, then they stand as a borrower of ideas and not as people who have "ownership of their thought and speech."

If this construction is what Nussbaum means, then there is little or nothing with which Christian educators will disagree. Christians have no fear of the "examined life" when this phrase identifies the educational goal of developing the intellectual and moral disciplines of students so that they stand in a different relation to their own ideas as young adults from what they did as adolescents. The aim of the examined life would be to enable students to own the contents of their minds in the way in which a man who inherits a farm might own a farm, not only by virtue of his father giving him the legal title to it but also by virtue of the years of hard work he devoted to it. It is the relation to his inherited land that is attained by studying the land, by learning its strengths and weaknesses as both tilled soil and pasture, and by improving its capacities for cultivation and fruitful harvest. This relation is consistent with persons so educated, recognizing all the while their utter dependence on what had been given to them and apart from which all their efforts would have been in vain.

Third, another interpretation of "having ownership of one's own thought and speech" is available, one that raises trouble for Christians who find some features of Nussbaum's understanding of liberal education and citizenship attractive. To own something gives one authority over it. One is entitled to use it as one wills. When another owns something and you want to use it, you are subject to the owner's will, interests, and authority insofar as you wish to make use of what he owns. To put it another way, the owner is sovereign over what he owns and is free to use it, to shape it according to his own judgments, preferences, and interests. In short, ownership confers authority. That this is what Nussbaum means when she claims that a liberal education gives students ownership of their own thoughts and speech is suggested by the tradition of political liberalism within which Nussbaum is situated. How so?

According to Stephen Macedo, liberalism is importantly associated with Isaiah Berlin's negative conception of liberty: "Political liberty in this sense is simply the area within which a man can act unobstructed by others."[37] Normal persons, says Macedo, have a moral claim on our forbearance, our non-interference, with respect to their formulation, pursuit, and execution of their own plans of life.[38] Recognizing the freedom of others to choose their own ideals, or to live without ideals, is to recognize their autonomy.[39] "Autonomy," then, is the freedom to shape one's own plan of life. reflectively, creatively, and experimentally in a way that actively develops one's own individuality without interference from others.[40] Surely, Nussbaum and Macedo might say, if individuals own anything, they own their own life plans. Macedo commends liberalism because it "liberates persons from inherited roles, fixed hierarchies, and conventions that narrowly constrain individuality and the scope of choice."[41] In so doing, he suggests, liberalism secures the conditions within which autonomous individuals may flourish. Macedo's ideas may help us to understand what Nussbaum means when she connects liberal education with helping students to "call their minds their own," or helping them to "have ownership of their own thought."

What difference should attention to Christian education make to our disposition to accept, or reject, the claim that all genuine liberal or university education ought to form "world" or "liberal" citizens? First, insofar as the aim of a liberal education is to form autonomous individuals who are first and foremost maximally independent and self-directed, and for whom an individual's own choices about moral ends and practices are the ultimate authority, where ends and purpose are never given or fixed, and experimentation and novelty are prized, Christians must reject it. It is deeply at odds with Christian education understood as, in part, the formation of Christian persons—persons, who think, will, and behave Christianly. Christians see in their Trinitarian confessions the implication that human beings are fundamentally relational creatures, because reality is, at its deepest level, relational. Moreover, the Christian narrative depicts the greatest human good not as one to be achieved in maximal independence and maximal experimentation with a variety of possible ends, but rather as a life lived in communion with others, in mutual dependence and mutual self-submission. Finally, the apostle Paul calls on Christians to take on the mind of Christ, not to call their minds their own. His admonition reminds Christians that neither our minds nor our bodies belong to ourselves but rather to God and to one another, as we are bound to one another by Christ in the church.

Furthermore, according to Macedo, a liberal society is not characterized by neutrality but by agreement on liberal ideals, values, and virtues.[42] These virtues are pervasive because they "override competing commitments and claim authority in every sphere of our lives."[43] The institutions, laws, and public morality cannot be neutral to the ideals, practices, and virtues that are constitutive of our public life. These values are substantive.[44] They "require the highest allegiance of liberal citizens, values that override or preclude many, and condition all other projects." A liberal society grudgingly concedes that some persons embrace illiberal values because of their involvement in authoritarian communities like the church but insists that "citizens" adopt a public/private distinction that separates the church from liberal society. Thus, illiberal values may be cloistered in the private lives of individuals and their communities. Nonetheless, for a liberal society, insists Macedo, liberal ideals, virtues, and practices are understood to be normative for every aspect and institution of our pluralistic and democratic culture. They are to shape and structure the private lives of citizens as well.[45] The most important liberal values are autonomy, respect for diversity, tolerance, a commitment to equal rights and to the rule of law to secure those rights. According to Macedo, because liberal citizens should act from liberal ideals and values, we may speak of "liberal virtue."[46] For Macedo, "autonomy" is the desired ideal of the properly educated person, a commitment to tolerance and to liberal justice its chief virtue,[47] liberal citizenship its ultimate expression, and liberal institutions, such as the university, and liberal education the primary vehicles for its cultivation and promotion.[48]

There necessarily exists a second major disagreement between Christians and the notion of "world" or "liberal" citizenship. Both Nussbaum and Macedo insist that for citizens who truly understand democratic ideals, one's ultimate loyalty is to these liberal ideals (autonomy, tolerance, diversity, equality in the law, and equality at the polls). On their view, the moral community constituted by these shared ideals is every reasonable person's first and primary duty. This, however, cannot be the case for Christians. Our faith, as expressed in our creeds and liturgies, reminds us that our primary loyalty is to the Triune God and to Christ's church. Neither the ideals of world citizenship nor the ideals of constitutional democracy, as congenial as these ideals are to liberty-loving Christians, can be the ultimate objects of allegiance. To acknowledge liberal ends and liberal virtues as primary and pervasive is to trivialize or even emasculate faith for the sake of "world" (or "liberal") citizenship.

For these reasons, the ideal of "liberal citizenship" as understood by Stephen Macedo, or "world citizenship" as articulated by Nussbaum, cannot be the aim of a university education as understood by Christians. Being a faithful Christian includes a confession that God is the creator and sustainer of the universe, and that God has acted in Christ's death and resurrection. It is a confession that says that Christ came to save us as sinful human beings and that God continues to work among us in the form of the Holy Spirit. Being a Christian involves an identification with, and submission to, a specific community whose confession is Trinitarian and whose beliefs and practices are framed and shaped by the acceptance of the canonical Christian scriptures. To participate in Christian education, then, is to allow the Christian

Trinitarian confession, the communal identification with Christians in the church, and the Scriptures to shape one's formation—intellectually, morally, and spiritually. It means, more particularly, letting the Scriptures, the creeds, and Christian intellectual traditions help shape one's thinking about citizenship in a democratic culture. Inasmuch as Nussbaum's account advocates notions of freedom, individualism, and civic allegiance that either precludes or co-opts the above marks of Christian faithfulness, the fundamental convictions of her account cannot be accepted by Christians who want to develop educational objectives and a credible curriculum of cultivating Christians as citizens in a democratic culture.

CONCLUSION

Some 160 years ago, Tocqueville observed American democracy with astonishment. He noted that much of America's democratic energy and commitment was born and nourished in American churches. Ironically, liberalism has failed to recognize that the Christian's contribution to democratic citizenship does not come from allegiance to the ideal of autonomy but from membership within a fundamentally illiberal institution, the church. In the Scriptures Christians find that we often have desires that will ultimately harm us and that injustice is not merely procedural but is often substantive. In liturgies we are reminded that injustice mars our souls, and we desire to be rid of our dispositions toward injustice. In catechesis we begin to receive the moral formation that will help us become the people we should be. Acknowledging the church's authority, we submit ourselves to others who are wiser than we are and to a tradition that has existed longer than we have. In the practice of its disciplines, we are able to see that some pleasures are better than others and that due to our shortsightedness or concupiscent nature, we sometimes need to be told which pleasures are better. Having listened to one who sees far better than we and to others who hear better than we, we begin to become good Christians. What informs our ideal of a faithful Christian also supplies content to what we believe a good citizen of a liberal democracy should be. We accept democracy as both a gift and a responsibility, and we aim to be good democratic citizens. Nonetheless, we do not give our primary allegiance to democracy. By affirming our allegiance to something that transcends democracy, we remind democracy of its temporality. It, too, is an institution destined to pass away.[49]

NOTES

Versions of this paper has been read at the Society of Christian Philosophers meeting at Westmont College, at the 1999 Pruit Memorial Symposium at Baylor University, and at Research Day at Baylor University. I am grateful to the constructive criticisms offered by colleagues on all these occasions. Even more, I am grateful to Dwight Allman, Anne Bowery, Barry Harvey, Doug Henry, Scott Moore, Robert Roberts, and Ralph Wood for many substantive and stylistic suggestions that have made this paper much better than what it would have been without their attentive assistance. I owe special thanks to John Basie and Tom McCasland for many valuable suggestions each made while carefully editing earlier versions of the paper.

1. William A. Galston, "Can Patriotism Be Turned into Civic Engagement?" *Chronicle of Higher Education*, 16 November 2001, B16–17.

2. Galston, "Patriotism," B16. See also the UCLA study online at www.seis.edu/heri /00_exec_summary.htm.

3. Galston, "Patriotism," B17.

4. Alexander Astin, "What Higher Education Can Do in the Cause of Citizenship," *Chronicle of Higher Education,* 6 October 1995, B1.

5. Speeches by Baylor presidents during the nineteenth century, for example, included the cultivation of good citizens as one of Baylor's aims as a university. Baylor is a typical example, in this respect, of an old-time Protestant college.

6. Galston, "Patriotism," B16.

7. Astin, "Higher Education," B1.

8. Astin, "Higher Education," B1.

9. *Baylor University Catalogue, 2001–2002,* 4.

10. Martha Nussbaum, *Cultivating Humanity: A Classical Defense of Reform in Liberal Education* (Cambridge, MA: Harvard University Press, 1997), ix.

11. Cf. William Carey Crane, "Who Ought to Supply and Control the Education Needed by the People," Texas Collection, Baylor University, 3–13.

12. Larry Lyon and Michael Beaty, "Integration, Secularization, and the Two-Spheres View at Religious Colleges: Comparing Baylor University with the University of Notre Dame and Georgetown College," *Christian Scholars Review* 29, no. 1 (Fall 1999): 73–112; Larry Lyon, Michael Beaty, and Stephanie Litizette Mixon, "Making Sense of a 'Religious' University: Faculty Adaptations and Opinions at Brigham Young, Baylor, Notre Dame, and Boston College," forthcoming in the *Review of Religious Research*.

13. Nussbaum, *Cultivating Humanity,* 290–91.

14. Nussbaum, *Cultivating Humanity,* 8.

15. Nussbaum, *Cultivating Humanity,* 7.

16. Nussbaum, *Cultivating Humanity,* 56 and 58.

17. Nussbaum, *Cultivating Humanity,* 59.

18. Speaking anachronistically, of course.

19. Nussbaum, *Cultivating Humanity,* 8.

20. See Michael Beaty and Anne Bowery, "Cultivating Christian Citizenship: Martha Nussbaum's Socrates, Augustine's Confessions, and Contemporary Academia," forthcoming in *Christian Scholars Review.*

21. Nussbaum, *Cultivating Humanity,* 61.

22. Nussbaum, *Cultivating Humanity,* 59.

23. See, for example, the following essays by Stanley Hauerwas: "A Christian Critique of America," in *Christian Existence Today: Essays on Church, World, and Living in Between* (Durham, NC: Labyrinth Press, 1988), 171–91; "The Politics of Witness: How

We Educate Christians in Liberal Societies," in *After Christendom? How the Church Is to Behave If Freedom, Justice, and Christian Nation Are Bad Ideas* (Nashville: Abingdon Press, 1991), 133–52. Also see, Barry Harvey, *Another City: An Ecclesiological Primer for a Post-Christian World* (Harrisburg, VA: Trinity Press International, 1999).

24. See John Rawls, *Political Liberalism* (New York: Columbia University Press, 1993), for one elucidation and defense of how our fundamental democratic institutions, practices, and roles (democratic citizenship) are to be understood and justified.

25. See Rawls, *Political Liberalism*, 190–94. Rawls views the term "neutrality" as unfortunate but develops the notion that liberalism endorses a "neutrality of aim" when this phrase means 1) that the state is to do nothing to favor in particular a comprehensive moral, religious, or metaphysical view; 2) the state is to secure every individual's equal opportunity to advance any conception of the good that he/she freely affirms, as long as it is not inconsistent with the priority of the right. What the latter point means is that the state need not let citizens pursue conceptions of the good that are inconsistent with the political conception of justice as fairness, even if freely chosen. See also Michael Sandel's discussion of liberalism's commitment to neutrality, what he calls "procedural neutrality," in *Democracy's Discontent: America in Search of a Public Philosophy* (Cambridge, MA: Harvard University Press, 1996), 4. Some critics of liberalism deny that neutrality is possible. See how Rawls attempts to blunt such charges in passages cited in this footnote. Others contend that such a commitment to "neutrality" stands as, or is embedded in, a comprehensive moral, religious, or metaphysical point of view.

26. Robert Audi and Nicholas Wolterstorff, *Religion in the Public Square* (Lanham, MD: Roman & Littlefield, 1997), 75.

27. Robert Audi offers two conditions that must be satisfied with respect to advocacy of public laws or policies. A good citizen ought to have both a secular reason and a secular motivation. See Audi, "Liberal Democracy and Religion in Politics," in Audi and Wolterstorff, *Public Square*, 24–35.

28. Of course, according to some Christian views of the relation of moral truths to the civil law, the epistemic justification for a civil law is overdetermined. That is, there is often both a nonreligious epistemic justification and a religious epistemic justification for the civil law. Also, the Christian recognizes that when a citizen has a nonreligious epistemic justification for a civil law, for which there is a religious justification, that law has, as a byproduct, promoted right relation of the individual to God. This is so even if that person does not have as a motive the promotion of right relation to God. Take, for example, those who observe prohibitions against murder, incest, rape, etc. Because such prohibitions express moral truths known by reason and not by revelation, observance of them plausibly promotes right relation to God, even when the motive of the agent who is acting in accord with such prohibitions has nothing to do with promoting right relation with God. On this view, complying with such prohibitions is surely a necessary condition to right relation with God, even if not a sufficient condition. I thank my colleague Douglas Henry for bringing this point to my attention.

29. Nussbaum, *Cultivating Humanity*, 59. The lack of argument for this claim, ironically, is in conflict with her Socratic ideal of the examined life that stipulates that no one ought to accept any belief unless it is justified by a good argument. The phrase "being justified by a good argument" is ambiguous. Does it mean that "there

is a good argument for the conclusion" even though you don't know of it and could not produce it, or does it mean that the person believing the claim has a good argument for the conclusion and can produce it? My sense is that typically Nussbaum means the latter; thus her failure to advance such an argument for this crucial claim is at the very least curious, and more dramatically, it makes her account of world citizenship inconsistent with her own Socratic ideal. What follows from this incoherence I leave for the reader to ponder.

30. I thank Dwight Allman for pointing out this salient fact.

31. Audi and Wolterstorff, *Public Square*, 74.

32. Nussbaum, *Cultivating Humanity*, 59. Nussbaum indicates that Diogenes Laertius responded to the question about where he came from by saying, "I am a citizen of the world." She also notes that he regarded himself as an exile, for the sake of philosophy. We may suppose that he saw these two states as being intimately related. Thus, rather than regarding "world citizenship" as a metaphor for membership in some abstract moral community comprising all human beings, as Nussbaum supposes, we may just as easily surmise that Diogenes meant to insist that insofar as he was in exile from the cities of Athens, Corinth, Thebes, and the like, and the citizenship they afforded free-born men like himself, he was bound to no city, thus to no community of men and women.

33. Nussbaum, *Cultivating Humanity*, 293.

34. Nussbaum, *Cultivating Humanity*, 295.

35. Nussbaum, *Cultivating Humanity*, 293, 295.

36. Nussbaum, *Cultivating Humanity*, 293.

37. Stephen Macedo, *Liberal Virtues: Citizenship, Virtue, and Community in Liberal Constitutionalism* (Oxford: Clarendon Press, 1991), 213.

38. Macedo, *Liberal Virtues*, 215.

39. Macedo, *Liberal Virtues*, 216.

40. Nussbaum, *Cultivating Humanity*, 269.

41. Macedo, *Liberal Virtues*, 207.

42. Macedo, *Liberal Virtues*, 253, 258–65.

43. Macedo, *Liberal Virtues*, 264. See the entire section entitled "The Private Life of Liberal Virtues," 262–65, for in it Macedo claims that liberal virtues ought ultimately to pervade and order every aspect of a person's life, if they live in a constitutional democracy.

44. See also, Rawls, *Political Liberalism*, 191.

45. Macedo, *Liberal Virtues*, 265.

46. Macedo, *Liberal Virtues*, 259.

47. Nussbaum likewise identifies "autonomy" as the chief product of Socratic inquiry. Consider, as just one example, the following passage: "Distinguishing patient's rights from patient's interests, for example, as reflections about Socrates' example helps us to do, proves crucial in organizing people to oppose the excessive control of a professional medical elite and to vindicate their autonomy." Nussbaum, *Cultivating Humanity*, 25.

48. Macedo, *Liberal Virtues*, 263.

49. I do not agree that locating the discussion of citizenship within an eschatological framework changes everything for the Christian, as my theologian colleague and friend Barry Harvey does. He insists that "since the world and every human in-

stitution is destined to pass away, including democracy, the goal of Christian education is to make good and faithful use of the (inferior) goods of our shared democratic culture rather than to educate students to be good citizens of a constitutional democracy. Placing the discussion in an eschatological framework, as Christians must do, clearly explains why Christians will both recognize Nussbaum's proposal as ultimately unacceptable, while admitting that, given her commitments, perhaps, she has done as well as one can" (e-mail correspondence). Does it follow from embracing a Christian eschatological framework that Christian universities and colleges ought not educate students to be good citizens of constitutional democracies? It does not follow. Such an education includes teaching students to make good and faithful use of a limited, though important, good—citizenship in a constitutional democracy—that contributes to our earthly flourishing. I concede that this assertion should be defended, but to do so would require more work than is compatible with the limits of this essay.

8

Have Americans Lost Their Virtue?

Alan Wolfe

In 1741, Jonathan Edwards delivered the most famous sermon in American history. With all the certainty of a man sure of his position, Edwards told his Northampton, Massachusetts, parishioners that God holds them "over the pit of hell, much as one holds a spider, or some loathsome insect, over the fire" and that he "abhors you, and is dreadfully provoked; his wrath toward you burns like fire; he looks upon you as worthy of nothing else, but to be cast into the fire."[1] Notwithstanding transformations in the way we live that render Edwards's eighteenth-century village foreign to our sensibilities, the grandchildren of Jonathan Edwards still make themselves heard in late-twentieth-century America. Their language is not as harsh. It is not outward piety but outward profanity that disturbs them. Some of them turn away from his theology in favor of an analysis rendered in secular terms—even, at times, in the language of social science. (This is not as odd as it may at first seem; Edwards himself believed that the scientific revolution of Newton and Locke supported his theology.) Others find the problem to lie not in the moral depravity of individuals but in structures within which individual choices are made. Yet for all these differences, there is nonetheless a widespread feeling in the land, akin to the Great Awakenings of America's past, that something has gone profoundly wrong with the country's moral character—and that someone has to bring the matter up for urgent public attention.

Perhaps the one contemporary voice that resonates most with the tone of moral opprobrium so characteristic of Jonathan Edwards is that of Robert Bork, former professor of law at Yale University, just down the highway from where Edwards preached. Turning to the Old Testament for the title of his book, *Slouching toward Gomorrah*, Bork writes that morality cannot be based on reason but instead presupposes the unquestioned authority of religious texts and practices. While religion was at one time "rigorous" and in that way served the function of instilling respect for authority, its demands will win no hearing in a society devoted to egalitarianism and individualism. "As life became easier and diversions more plentiful," Bork continues, "men are less willing to accept the authority of their clergy and less willing to worship a demanding God, a God who dictates how one should live and puts a great many bodily and psychological pleasures off limits."[2] In theory, it might be possible for individuals to reflect on their experience and from that deduce moral rules to govern their lives. This, however, would work only for a few people, Bork believes: "To suppose that an entire society may be made moral in this fashion is merely laughable. We are not a community of over 250 million reflective men and women able to work out the conditions of contentedness and willing to sacrifice near-term pleasure for long-term benefits."[3]

Similar ideas have been expounded by other thinkers, none with as large an audience as former secretary of education William Bennett. From a wide variety of sources—the Bible, great literature, children's stories, history— Western societies, he believes, came to a broad agreement on the importance of the virtues. But if such virtues as friendship, loyalty, work, and faith are not taught well, especially to the young, they turn into vices. Bennett leaves no doubt that such vices are omnipresent in contemporary America. Surveying the moral landscape, he is disturbed by rising rates of divorce, out-of-wedlock births, crime, and other potential indicators of decline. Indeed once one starts looking for them, signs of moral degeneration seem to be everywhere: basketball players strangling their coaches; cadets at austere military institutions participating in cheating rings; the entertainment industry purveying sex and violence to ever-younger watchers and listeners; gays demanding acceptance of their sexuality; and most disturbing of all, a president engaging in sordid and illicit sex and then lying about it on television and in the courts. Moral health is like physical health: to find out whether the body is sick, you take its temperature. No matter how you measure it, Bennett believes, America's moral illness gets worse day by day. A society in which vice triumphs over virtue is morally flabby; we do what is in our best interest, shirk our responsibilities when they prove burdensome, lie to get ahead, and, as afraid of administering punishment as having it administered, persuade ourselves that everyone deserves a second—or third or fourth—chance.[4]

The analysis of Bork and Bennett is not just an academic exercise. Their views overlap significantly with those of Christian activists influential in the Republican Party. Of all those worried about the moral situation of the United States, only conservative Christians have the confidence to call themselves a "moral majority," a term coined by the political activist Paul Weyrich. Overcoming a history of suspicion toward political activity, Christian conservatives organize their followers around an analysis of what went wrong in America that can be summarized in the form of a few basic propositions. The primary source of morality, as Robert Bork emphasized, is religion. It therefore followed that for a society to have a common morality, it also must share a common religion. Once upon a time, this story continues, America did have that common religion; not only were most Americans Christian, but most Americans saw nothing amiss with prayer in school, Christ in Christmas, or God in the national motto. Those days are long past, not because America now has so many Jews—conservative Christians see themselves as friends of Israel—but because the dominant religion of America is secular humanism. Under the sway of that view of the world, the indicators of moral decline identified by William Bennett cannot be a surprise. Only by returning the country to an appreciation of its religious heritage can the moral decline of the United States be reversed. That will be done, as the term "moral majority" implies, through a kind of grassroots populism, allowing traditionally silent Christians in their local communities to make their voices heard.

My final example of those who believe that something has gone seriously wrong with morality in contemporary America comes from a wide variety of journalists and social critics who believe that we no longer live with the moral integrity of those who came before us. Among the most eloquent and honest of those voices is that of the journalist Alan Ehrenhalt, who brings to life the world of 1950s Chicago. Whether discussing the lives of those trapped in black ghettos, those tied both to their local Catholic parishes and to the political machine of Mayor Daley, or those attracted to mass-produced housing in the nearby suburbs, Ehrenhalt emphasizes the degree to which limited lives could, in their own way, be considered good lives. Chicagoans of that time no more thought of morality as a range of choices from which one chose the appropriate response than they thought of a world in which television might some day offer more than a hundred competing stations. They accepted authority for what it was and shaped their lives to conform to its commands. The preoccupations of their lives—sin, obedience, standards, respectability, and togetherness—seem worlds away from ours. Yet this world, from which so many of the baby boomers fled the minute postwar prosperity allowed them to do so, stands in retrospect as a world governed by a decided moral integrity.[5]

Because he is willing to use an unfashionable word like "authority," Ehrenhalt's social criticism is clearly of the conservative variety. But liberals and leftists also find much that distresses them about the moral state of the contemporary world. In searching for effective ways to make their points, they also look back to the 1950s, indeed to many of the same phenomena—and in the same city—brought to life by Ehrenhalt. Ray Suarez, the radio talk-show host, understands that the Chicago of the 1950s was a vibrant city, not yet cut into unlivable districts by highways and characterized by hideous public housing projects. It is nonetheless an undeniable fact that since the 1950s millions of Americans have voted with their cars against the presumed moral advantages of urban life. When they address the question of why they did so, most liberals rely on the same explanation: racism. The moment cities began to fill up with African-Americans whose roots lay in the South, middle-class whites suddenly found the attractions of suburbia irresistible. In a leftist tradition that finds causes for discontent in the priorities of social structures rather than the behavior of individuals, it is easy to find villains among the bankers and real estate brokers who profited from white flight. To them can also be added the automobile manufacturers and construction trades, which lobbied government for the subsidies to build the highways that carried people away from the cities. But structural explanations can only take us so far. "Can you assign culpability to a crime with ten million accomplices?" Suarez asks.[6] The answer must be yes. For liberals and leftists, racism is a moral vice fully as corrosive as hedonism is for conservatives. America's cities hollowed out because so many Americans, acting out of fear and ignorance, refused to honor the moral principle of treating all their fellow human beings as equally worthy of respect. In leaving the cities, their behavior was not only shortsighted; it was wrong.

I believe the critics I have been discussing, despite the rhetorical power of their analysis, have not had a significant impact in changing America in the direction they favor. To be sure, Bork's and Bennett's books became bestsellers. No one can doubt that for a significant period of time conservative Christians had strong influence within one of our two major political parties. Just because historical social criticism is nostalgic does not necessarily mean it is wrong: Ehrenhalt is correct to suggest that an earlier generation of Chicagoans respected authority more than the present generation—and Suarez is also right to suggest that they were more racist. Yet I think it fair to say most of these critics miss the mark. Despite initial enthusiasm for their insistence that America has lost its virtue, the tide has begun to turn away from them. Of course one could respond to the fact that Americans do not seem to be listening to their message by arguing that their inattention is precisely what is wrong with America. Critics of our decline are in the odd position of having their message well received—in which case America really cannot be so bad—or in having their ideas about America confirmed—in which case their message is not well received. But I think there is another reason why their analysis of the American condition eventually fails: There is something wrong with the substance of what they are saying. I want here to offer an analysis of what it is that they get wrong.

THE AGE OF MORAL FREEDOM IN AMERICA

The same question that bedeviled Jonathan Edwards also bedevils his grandchildren: If society is irredeemably bad, can the people who compose it ever be good? Putting the same question another way, what happens if the problem with America turns out to be Americans? The institutions that together constitute the social capital of America—families, religious congregations, neighborhoods, clubs—are not, as we know from Tocqueville, imposed from above. They are voluntary organizations made strong by the individual decisions of millions of individuals pursuing what Tocqueville called "self-interest rightly understood." By that very same logic, they are also made weak when individuals avoid their obligations to pursue self-interest wrongly understood. It would therefore seem to be impossible to argue that such institutions are in decline without in some way implying that, morally speaking, it is Americans themselves who are really in decline.

The source of this moral decline, from the point of view of many who speak in the contemporary tones of Jonathan Edwards, is the fact that increasingly Americans are applying the same freedom they have in economics and politics to the moral questions with which they have to deal. Morality defines our duties to self and others. It includes, but is not limited to, timeless questions like these: What is the difference between right and wrong? What does it mean to lead a good life? What is virtue, and what is vice? In what—or whom—should a person believe? What is forbidden, and what is allowed? How binding is the marriage vow? What do parents owe their children? Can a person be compelled against his will to obey a law with which he disagrees? What obligations do citizens have to their countries, and are they more or less important than their obligations to humanity in general? What is justice? Is there a duty to help the needy? If so, should it be undertaken voluntarily or compelled through law? Are all human beings deserving of equal respect? When is it justifiable to take from some in order to give to others? What rights do people have? How fundamental are they?

As if questions like these were not difficult enough to answer, people who live in the modern world find themselves facing an entirely new set of moral issues posed by changes in human social practices, politics, and technology. Is an abortion ever justified? Should sexual relations between people of the same sex be extended the same moral stature as sexual relations between people of opposite sexes? Should research into cloning be permitted? Is it right to kill animals to serve human needs for food and fashion? Is a sexually promiscuous person immoral? Should people with disabilities be treated in the same way as those without disabilities? Is the nuclear family the best form for the family to take? When should children be considered responsible adults? Are drug addicts responsible for their actions? Is there an obligation to discourage someone from smoking? Does respect for religious diversity include respect for nonbelievers? Should we try to regulate the content displayed on the internet? Ought we to permit euthanasia? Under what conditions and whose supervision? If we discover that behavior traditionally considered immoral, such as violence, has biological or neurological origins, should we change our conceptions of morality? Should we, if we could, make people who violate received ideas about morality feel a sense of shame?

Moral freedom is the principle that individuals should determine for themselves their duties to self and others. They, and they alone, should provide the answers to both those perennial questions and the more contemporary questions moral inquiry has addressed. To be sure, they can consult moral authority in the form of God's commands, tradition and customs, the advice of the wise, the laws of the state, or the practices of institutions, but when an answer has to be given, they must look as deeply as possible into themselves— at their own interests, desires, needs, sensibilities, identities, and inclinations—before they decide what they ought to do. Moral freedom is a more radical concept than political or economic freedom, because its scope is so much greater. Although political freedoms—the right to speak one's thoughts or vote for candidates of one's own choice—are enormously important, they are restricted to one sphere of human activity: obtaining and exercising political power. The same is true of economic freedom, which, by definition, is limited to such essential, but also essentially mundane, matters as the buying and selling of commodities. Moral freedom involves freedom over the things that matter most. The ultimate implication of the idea of moral freedom is that there are no questions the answers to which must be found outside the purview of freely choosing people.

Because the idea of moral freedom is so radical, it has not been an idea that has ever possessed much currency among the West's great moral theorists. Even those who made passionate arguments in defense of freedom in general did not extend their argument to moral freedom. Indeed, the common position among most Western thinkers has been to argue the necessity for moral constraint as a precondition for freedom in all other aspects of life. Typical of them is Immanuel Kant. Kant was one of the great theorists of freedom in the Western tradition. In no other thinker can one find such eloquent efforts to secure a grounding for the proposition that the greatest value to human beings lies in their capacity for autonomy. But we can only be autonomous, according to Kant, to the degree that we act in accord with timeless moral precepts not chosen by us. Moral action, in Kant's view, was the exact opposite of a do-as-you-please affair. Instead, we must imagine what would happen if all other people act as we are tempted to do, a thought experiment that makes immediately clear why acting selfishly or short-sightedly would be wrong. Should I nonetheless decide to act in ways contrary to the categorical imperative—should I, for example, conclude that under the circumstances in which I find myself at the moment I would be best off lying, or taking my own life, or taking advantage of another—I would not have been morally free but the opposite. For if everyone else had made the same decision as I did, the result would be a form of anarchy in which nothing, including autonomy, would be possible.

Religious freedom is yet another realm of liberty that is not the same as moral freedom, one indeed that, to come into existence, generally requires the definite absence of moral freedom. The freedom to hold and to act upon one's religious beliefs is not the same thing as the freedom to decide for oneself what and how to believe. John Locke's *Letter Concerning Toleration,* a classic text in the history of religious freedom, does not extend tolerance to all, for, in grounding the concept of toleration in Christian teachings, it leaves Jews to the mercy of their own conceptions of justice and excludes entirely those "who deny the Being of a God." By the time the idea of religious toleration came to the United States, its basis was broader than Locke's. But for America's eighteenth-century theorists, religious freedom was still freedom for religions and only incidentally freedom for believers—or, even more improbably, nonbelievers. The free-exercise clause of the U.S. Constitution countered the idea of an established church. It imagined a world in which Baptists and Catholics would have the same right to practice their religion as Congregationalists. It did not contemplate a world like our own, in which people consider a wide range of options from orthodoxy to nonbelief and then decide which one suits them best.

How could it? The idea of people having the freedom to choose their own way of believing—a little more this week than last, a little bit of Protestantism this month and Catholicism the next—assumes that the individual is in charge of his own destiny. Such an idea was foreign to eighteenth-century conceptions of religious freedom, which assumed that God was in charge of a person's destiny. Indeed the reason to keep the state out of religion was because there was a power higher than the state to which a person owed his obedience. In his *Memorial and Remonstrance* of 1785, James Madison defended the idea that "it is the duty of every man to render to the Creator such homage, and such only, as he believes acceptable to him," but he also wrote that "what is here a right towards men, is a duty toward the Creator."[7] The idea of religious freedom stakes out a position independent of the state's authority only to clear the way for God's authority. Freedom of conscience presumes that we *have* a conscience, that we are already predisposed to say no to our instincts and desire for immediate gratification.

It was not just with respect to religious belief that America's eighteenth-century theorists of freedom assumed the existence of a prior moral world in which freedom would be valued and protected. Students of the classical world, influenced by European writers from Machiavelli to Montesquieu, they were to one degree or another adherents to a conception of republican virtue, which emphasized that freedom was possible only when individuals restrained their self-interest for the sake of the public good. Sober, stern, serious—such virtuous people could hardly be described as morally free. For they did not act by considering all the possible actions they might take before deciding which one to take. Instead they were more likely to consider all the things which could not be done before limiting themselves to those few things which might be permissible.

It would not be surprising to learn that the enemies of freedom over the past two centuries were also opponents of moral freedom: Conservatives since at least Edmund Burke have believed that because "duty and will are . . . contradictory terms," our moral obligations "are such as were never the results of our option."[8] We realize just how radical the idea of moral freedom is when we recognize how little support the idea has received from freedom's greatest friends. To be sure, not all friends of liberty were enemies of moral freedom; John Stuart Mill's *On Liberty* not only defends the idea that people should be free to determine for themselves the plan of their lives but extends the realm of liberty to new terrain. Mill wrote that "over himself, over his own body and mind, the individual is sovereign."[9] Still, if the name we give to the party of freedom is "liberalism," Peter Berkowitz is right to claim that the great liberal thinkers—Hobbes, Locke, Kant, and even Mill in some of his writings—were not opposed to political theories that dealt with virtue and the common good.[10] The one freedom forbidden to us was the freedom to choose all the arenas in which to be free. Some things were simply too important to be left to the whims of caprice and self-interest, and nothing was more important than ensuring that the moral rules that shaped all of society's other rules were secured by something transcendental, impervious to the passions of the moment, and filled with symbolic grandeur.

Despite such long-standing and considerable objections to the principle that people ought to have the freedom to construct their moral rules, it is hard to imagine a situation in which individuals who are free in all other areas of life will stop at the door of morality. For one thing, they may not know where that door is. We often consider abortion or gay rights "moral" issues, but they also involve commercial services provided through the market, a fact that has repeatedly led feminists and gay rights activists to defend *Lochner v. New York* and its laissez-faire principles when bathhouses or abortion clinics are the business firms involved.[11] For another, the crucial importance of morality—its location in what Durkheim would call the "sacred" realm of meaning, as opposed to the "profane" world of commerce and elections—makes unfreedom in that arena particularly poignant to individuals who insist on their liberty. What is striking about moral freedom is not that Americans are insisting that they ought to have it but that they waited so long. The generation now celebrated by writers like Tom Brokaw for its willingness to sacrifice in war and depression was the last generation to live without significant moral freedom in America.[12]

Reviewing the entire history of religion in America since the first Spanish and French settlements, Sidney Ahlstrom concluded that "only in the 1960s would it become apparent that the Great Puritan Epoch in American history had come to an end."[13] Putting aside the hysterical politics and the theatrical demonstrations, something clearly important happened during the 1960s that transformed life in America. The decade began at a time when institutions of moral authority craved obedience: religious leaders were quick to offer unambiguous prescriptions for proper Christian conduct; women were encouraged to stay home and raise their children; government's word was to be trusted; teachers could discipline as well as instruct; and the police enforced laws against what was considered immoral conduct. The 1960s ended at a time when "liberation," once a political slogan with little appeal in the American heartland, had become a way of life for all those Americans determined to rely more on themselves and less on what once would have been called their betters, in the realm of manners and morals. For better or worse, the pollster Daniel Yankelovich is correct to suggest that we have been governed by "new rules" for the last twenty or thirty years.[14] Most prominent among those rules is the idea that people themselves will have a say in determining what the conditions are for good and virtuous lives for themselves and their fellow citizens.

THE CONTROVERSY OVER MORAL FREEDOM

If I am right, then those who set themselves up to counter what they perceive to be the moral decay of the United States are setting themselves up in opposition to moral freedom—a pretty tough-minded, but also probably hopeless, thing to do. To their credit, a number of those who speak in the language of Jonathan Edwards recognize that this is what is required of them. One example is provided by *A Call to Civil Society*, a document issued by the Council on Civil Society, a joint product of the New York–based Institute for American Values and the Divinity School of the University of Chicago.[15] Signed by a number of prominent writers, including John DiIulio, Jean Bethke Elhstain, Glenn C. Loury, Cornel West, and James Q. Wilson, the *Call* filled in many of the moral gaps left behind in the wake of Robert Putnam's now-famous article, "Bowling Alone."[16]

No doubt Putnam thought that he was engaged in a rather clever and important piece of social science research when he reported on a decline in the number of Americans who bowled together in leagues. Little did he know that his article, which would rapidly become one of the most widely cited works of scholarship in the history of American social science, would instead launch a debate about the state of the nation's soul. Putnam described what he called "the strange disappearance of civic America" as an illustration of how America was depleting its social capital. In relying on a concept borrowed from economics, Putnam wrote in the language of efficiency, not the language of morality. Careful in its assessments and scholarly in its tone, "Bowling Alone" was worlds away from the Jonathan Edwards–like sermons of Robert Bork and Paul Weyrich. But despite its social-scientific cast, Putnam's article could not help but become part of the national debate about the state of America's moral health. For unlike industry, which relies on those few individuals with access to significant wealth to replenish its capital, society relies on the propensity of everyone to be at least somewhat active in the world around them for social capital to expand. Even to raise the subject of whether Americans were as willing as they had been in the past to work together to achieve common objectives was to plug into a deep sense of unease about the kind of people Americans had become.

One of the questions raised by Robert Putnam's research was why should we care about declining civic participation in the first place. Writing as a political scientist, Putnam, to the degree that he addressed the question at all, answered it by asserting that low civic participation was bad for democracy. But such an answer was no answer, according to the signers of the *Call*. Participation is a good only to the degree that it serves some higher purpose. We would not admire active civic organizations if their objective were to promote white supremacy. To call for more democracy without raising the question of democracy *for what* is to leave morality out of the picture entirely.

This the Council on Civic Society was unprepared to do. Different writers attach different value to civil society. For the council, that value could be found in the capacity of these organizations "to foster competence and character in individuals, build social trust, and help children become good people and good citizens." Active participation in civic life was necessary not just for the sake of participation itself but because through socially connected activity "we answer together the most important questions: what is our purpose, what is the right way to act, and what is the common good."[17]

In a postmodern age, the council's language was unusual language indeed. For the council was claiming not only that active participation in the institutions of civil society forces us to ask the right questions but also that it *provides* the right answers. As contrary to the times as this way of thinking may be, the authors of the *Call* argued, it was very much along the lines of what the founders believed. In writing a constitution and establishing the framework for a new society, they understood that there were important civic truths to which all Americans ought to be committed, such as the idea that all people were created equal. By themselves, such civic truths "do not tell us how to pursue happiness or how to live a good life." But our founders—as well as those great Americans like Abraham Lincoln and Martin Luther King who followed them—were steeped in biblical and religious sources. When the founders spoke of "laws of nature and of nature's God," or when King made reference to a "higher law," they were expressing the sense that "democracy depends upon moral truths."[18]

Moral truths take on their importance because, timeless and transcendental as they are, they have their origin in forces—such as nature on the one hand or the realm of the supernatural on the other—that are outside the control of human beings. "Our moral truths underwrite our social well being primarily because they teach us to govern our appetites and to transcend selfishness," the council claimed. Those who refused to have their appetites held in check—the children, so to speak, of Herbert Marcuse—thus live under a moral lie. They fail to realize that freedom does not mean "immunity from restraint." Instead freedom must be understood as "an ethical condition," as "the morally defined mean between license and slavery." Human beings, the *Call* concluded, are "not autonomous creatures who are the source of their own meaning and perfection." We are rather "intrinsically social beings" who require "connectedness" in order to "approach authentic self-realization."[19]

One finds the same concern with moral freedom expressed by another high-level effort to combine empirical data about the decline of civil society with moral exhortation, this one initiated by the National Commission on Civil Renewal, chaired by former senator Sam Nunn (D.-GA) and William Bennett. "Compared with previous generations," the commission—or should I say its staff director, William Galston—wrote, "Americans today place less value on what we owe others as a matter of moral obligation and common citizenship; less value on personal sacrifice as a moral good; less value on the social importance of respectability and observing the rules; less value on restraint in matters of pleasure and sexuality; and correspondingly greater value on self-expression, self-realization, and personal choice." The commission further argued that the ultimate cause of America's social decline lies in the emergence of new, and disturbing, conceptions of freedom. "We must ask ourselves some hard questions about this new understanding of individual liberty. Dare we continue to place adult self-gratification above the well being of our children? Can we relentlessly pursue individual choice at the expense of mutual obligation without corroding vital social bonds? Will we remain secure in the enjoyment of our individual rights if we fail to accept and to discharge our responsibilities? Is there a civic invisible hand that will preserve our democratic institutions in the absence of informed and engaged citizens?" The clear answer to all these questions, in the opinion of the National Commission on Civic Renewal, was no.[20]

To illustrate why attacking moral freedom in a free society is such a difficult proposition, we ought to look at the one social institution in the Untied States closest to ordinary people: the family. If one were looking for empirical evidence for the decline of traditional morality in America, trends in family life would certainly seem to offer them. According to the National Marriage Project, led by sociologist David Popenoe and social critic Barbara DaFoe Whitehead, Americans are less likely to marry and more likely to divorce than they were a generation ago. Unmarried cohabitation increased by nearly 1,000 percent between 1960 and 1998.[21] The number of children under eighteen living with a single parent has increased over the same time-period among both blacks and whites, but at especially sharp rates for the former.[22] More and more teenagers endorse the idea of living together before marriage. The effect of these trends, the authors argue, is to undervalue the importance of marriage, its commitments, and its status as the most proper way to raise children.[23] As is often the case with America's moral debate, critics of the National Marriage Project's conclusions tend to focus on problems in its methodology. But no one disputes the fact that if a strong family is defined as one that is formed when people are young and persists until they are very old, that version of the family has clearly weakened in America.

The question is why. The answer has to involve the dawning recognition on the part of women in contemporary America that the family, at least in the version idealized during the 1950s as the best model for family life, did not yield to them autonomy to lead their lives as free individuals. Whether or not the family of the 1950s ever lived up to the moral standard to which it was held—that question calls forth a passionate debate that need not be entered here—these days marriages are undertaken, roles are determined, children are raised, family size is determined, and divorces are influenced by the overwhelming fact that women have achieved a significant degree of moral freedom in contemporary America. The facts that women work and that through both birth control and the availability of abortion they have significant say over how many children they will bear have become symbolic as well as actual realities. For some, they represent a newly won freedom in an arena once governed by traditional morality, a freedom that allows people to lead the best possible lives for themselves. For others, they represent a world in which moral freedom comes at the cost of putting the needs of the self above obligations to others and even above responsibility to the sanctity of life itself.

From the perspective of the latter, the stakes involved are great. "Self-governance begins with governing the self," wrote the authors of the Council on Civil Society's *Call.* "In this sense, the family is the cradle of citizenship, since it is in the family that a child learns, or fails to learn, the essential qualities necessary for governing the self: honesty, trust, loyalty, cooperation, self-restraint, civility, compassion, personal responsibility, and respect for others."[24] In a similar way, the National Commission on Civic Renewal stated that "our civic condition cannot be strong if our families remain weak." In both accounts, the family is not an essentially private institution responsible for the happiness of those who joined together to form it. Each endorses instead an inverted version of the feminist slogan that the personal is the political: we make good families in order to make good citizens. Whether or not the point is true—some of our best citizens (need one again mention Abraham Lincoln and Martin Luther King, Jr.?) lived in less than ideal families—this way of thinking raises the stakes over moral freedom. For if the cause of the family's decline is in any way attributable to the claims women are making for greater autonomy, then moral freedom for women not only threatens the family, it threatens the state as well.

The question of the family illustrates exactly why moral freedom for anyone can be such a difficult topic to address. Clearly, as thinkers concerned with placing limits on unrestricted moral freedom have long recognized, society would be impossible if each person simply decided to follow his/her own inclinations in everything he/she did, including such socially important matters as raising the next generation of adults. It is a basic truth established by modern sociology, one in no way disproved by the popularity of rational choice theory in the social sciences, that institutions must have moral authority if some form of social order is to work well. Yet people struggle to gain—and fight to keep—freedom for a reason. Americans want institutions to justify the authority they presume to exercise. Their skepticism applies most strongly to the institution that Durkheim believed to be a moral institution par excellence: the state. But they have been just as skeptical of preachers, school principals, and physicians when they found them too intrusive, too zealous in lecturing other people on how to live. No institution, including the family, can consider itself immune from this skepticism.

MORALITY AND FREEDOM IN AMERICAN SOCIETY

It is because moral freedom seems to have become so pervasive in American life that Jonathan Edwards's grandchildren have so much to say. At the same time, the world really has changed since the days of Jonathan Edwards. For Edwards, God's power was a truth from which no one could hide. But today it is impossible to establish either the empirical or the moral truths capable of rallying Americans around institutions of moral authority. Despite the entry of so many well-trained social scientists into hotly contested areas of moral debate, reliance on empirical data, as helpful as it can be, rarely settles much of anything. We can generally learn enough about how we behave to rule certain claims out of bounds—no one these days can make a credible case that divorce rates are at historic lows. But the numbers can never command general agreement on the issues so many care most about, such as whether our conduct makes us sinners in the eyes of God.

Against the force of moral freedom, appeals to moral truth seem even weaker than appeals to empirical truth. It is comforting to believe that the American Founders shared conceptions of moral truth shaped by ideas of natural right and by their common Christian faith, but this ignores the fact that some of them were also committed liberals, pretty far along on the road to modernity. If for them moral truths could not be automatically translated into principles that instruct us on what laws to pass or how to behave, one can hardly blame contemporary Americans for modifying their conceptions of moral truth to account for the realities of how they lead their lives. When they do so—when, for example, they shape the institution of the family to take account of the autonomy of its members— they are essentially saying that their institutions are made not by God, and certainly not by nature, but by them. This does not mean that all ways of life are moral equivalents; for all the talk of moral decay, Americans continue to believe, with respect to the family, that two-parent families are the best way to raise children. But it does suggest that those who presume to offer moral advice in the form of unalterable truth will have to listen with as much dedication as they have shown in providing instruction.

For all the fear that society is experiencing moral decline, it would be difficult to imagine a society more obsessed with morality than America at century's end. This became clear in the aftermath of the tragic shootings at Columbine High School in Littleton, Colorado. The locale of this grizzly affair, from a symbolic point of view, could not have been better chosen. Denver, where the Rocky Mountains begin, can, depending on one's point of view, represent either the free air of the West or the costs of uncontrolled planning and ecological arrogance. Littleton, a suburb composed of generally expensive tract homes built around cul-de-sacs, stands for either private property and the benefits of a home of one's own or urban flight and white racism. (In the latter version, the fact that people had fled what they believed to be the violence of the cities only to encounter greater violence in the suburbs seemed especially ironic.) The guns assembled by the two teenagers reflect either constitutional guarantees of freedom, including the right to bear arms, or the freedom of an irresponsible capitalism gone amok, willing to sell any commodity, even one that kills, for the right price. The high school at which the shooting took place suffered from secular America's unwillingness to allow prayer and meaningful moral reflection, or from the failure of Americans to support public education generously with their tax dollars. The gothic images and Nazi regalia that attracted the killers demonstrate for some why censorship is necessary and for others the impossibility of ever controlling people's fantasies. Most dramatic of all, the killings symbolized either unrestrained evil on the one hand or the kind of alienation caused by snobbery and exclusion on the other. No matter what moral point one was trying to make, the events in Littleton seemed to fit the tale.

We were so prepared to leap to moral conclusions about events as important as Littleton because we had already demonstrated a capacity to treat any subject—even such mundane ones as exercise, diet, sports, geography, hobbies, and shopping—as if larger moral implications could be drawn from just about anything we did. It may well be true that conservatives, inspired by what they understood as a moral collapse during the 1960s, began the current wave of moral speculation. But it has not ended there. Even leftists, who tend to be suspicious of the use of moral language for fear that it is designed to impose moral conformity, find themselves talking about good and evil, not only around issues of race but also around issues of the globalization of capital. If talk about morality alone could be taken as a measure of morality, America would be experiencing, not moral decline, but moral renewal.

The talk, of course, exists because of a deep sense among some of America's most respected thinkers that we are not the moral society we once were. What, finally, is one to make of their case? Those who worry that Americans have lost the sense of moral authority embedded in truth, tradition, and time have distinguished pedigrees, for a concern with excess moral freedom has been a consistent theme of Western social and political commentary. Whether or not social trends concerning divorce, single-parent families, crime, civic participation, and trust constitute what Francis Fukuyama has called a "great disruption,"[25] they do justify asking serious questions about the consequences of moral individualism. We ought to be pondering the way we live at any time, especially during those times when social changes seem especially unsettling.

Still, if the period since the 1960s seems disruptive, can we be sure that it has been more disruptive than earlier periods in American history? Conservative moralists, much in the spirit of Jonathan Edwards, write as if America must be worse off the more moral freedom it has. But the situation could prove to be more complicated. Just as there exists a business cycle, there exists a moral cycle. As their religious history attests, Americans love morality. But as their political and economic history attests, they also love freedom. A society committed to morality and freedom at the same time is a society that can expect rapid swings in its moral temperature. Jonathan Edwards, after all, would not have had much of a hearing were it not for the attraction of doctrines that insisted that human beings could play a role in their own redemption. Americans have frequently gone through periods in which excess—say, in how much alcohol we drank—was followed by periods in which regulation—for example, in how zealous we became over Prohibition—took over.

Those worried about moral decline in America do have one strong point propping up their case. Because moral freedom emerged so late in American life, earlier cycles of moral freedom were generally confined to small numbers of intellectuals and bohemians clustered in unrepresentative quarters of American life. The moral freedom that emerged in the 1960s, by contrast, captured the attention of the entire society. Rarely, if ever, has a society had to deal with so many claims, in so many areas of life, and over such intimate and personal matters, as America has faced since the 1960s. It would be surprising indeed if changes of that magnitude did not give rise to serious, thoughtful, and to some degree persuasive explorations of the negative consequences of those trends.

Yet just as America adjusted to the emergence of economic freedom, religious freedom, and freedom of speech—each of which was greeted with warnings from conservatives about great potential damage should it go too far—it may also survive the emergence of moral freedom. There is even the possibility that society might flourish once Americans, as they become more used to the moral freedom they have gained, also become more responsible for managing the moral conditions of their lives. As important as it is to ask questions about moral freedom, it is premature to draw strongly etched answers. All we can say is that the grandchildren of Jonathan Edwards, because of what they got right about America's moral condition as well as what they got wrong, have done their fellow Americans the invaluable service of reminding them why both morality and freedom are goods worth having.

NOTES

1. Wilson H. Kimnach, Kenneth P. Minkema, and Douglas A. Sweeney, eds., *The Sermons of Jonathan Edwards: A Reader* (New Haven, CT: Yale University Press, 1999), 57.

2. Robert Bork, *Slouching towards Gomorrah: Modern Liberalism and American Decline* (New York: Regan Books, 1996), 281.

3. Bork, *Gomorrah,* 277.

4. William J. Bennett, *The Death of Outrage* (New York: Simon and Schuster, 1998).

5. Alan Ehrenhalt, *The Lost City: The Forgotten Virtues of Community in the Chicago of the 1950's* (New York: Basic Books, 1995).

6. Ray Suarez, *The Old Neighborhood: What We Lost in the Great Suburban Migration, 1966–1999* (New York: Free Press, 1999), 13.

7. James Madison, "Memorial and Remonstrance," in *Basic Documents Relating to the Religious Clauses of the First Amendment*, Library Series no. 1 (Washington, DC: Americans United for Separation of Church and State), 7.

8. Edmund Burke, "An Appeal from the New to the Old Whigs," in Issac Kramnic, ed., *The Portable Edmund Burke* (New York: Penguin, 1999), 491.

9. John Stuart Mill, *On Liberty*, in *Utilitarianism and On Liberty*, ed. Mary Warnock (New York: Meridian Books, 1970), 135.

10. Peter Berkowitz, *Virtue and the Making of Modern Liberalism* (Princeton, NJ: Princeton University Press, 1999).

11. *Lochner v. New York*, 198 US 45 (1905), declared unconstitutional a law limiting the number of hours bakers could work each week on the grounds that it interfered with the freedom of contract between employers and employees.

12. See Tom Brokaw, *The Greatest Generation* (New York: Random House, 1998).

13. Sidney Ahlstrom, *A Religious History of the American People* (New Haven, CT: Yale University Press, 1972), 8.

14. Daniel Yankelovich, *New Rules: Searching for Self-Fulfillment in a World Turned Upside Down* (New York : Random House, 1981).

15. Jean Bethke Elshtain, "Symposium: Civil Society and the American Family: A Call to Civil Society" *Society* 36:5 (1999): 11–19.

16. Robert Putnam, "Bowling Alone: America's Declining Social Capital," *Journal of Democracy* 6:1 (1995): 65–78.

17. Elshtain, "A Call to Civil Society," 13.

18. Elshtain, "A Call to Civil Society," 16.

19. Elshtain, "A Call to Civil Society," 18.

20. National Commission on Civic Renewal, Final Report, at www.puaf .umd.edu/.

21. David Popenoe and Barbara Dafoe Whitehead, "The State of Our Unions, 2000: The Social Health of Marriage in America" (New Brunswick, NJ: National Marriage Project at Rutgers University, June 2000), 26.

22. Popenoe and Whitehead, "The State of Our Unions," 31.

23. Popenoe and Whitehead, "The State of Our Unions," 31–34.

24. Elshtain, "A Call to Civil Society," 13.

25. Francis Fukuyama, *The Great Disruption: Human Nature and the Reconstitution of Social Order* (New York: Free Press, 1999).

9

Liberalism, Consumerism, and Citizenship

Michael J. Sandel

Should a democratic society seek to shape the character of its citizens? The answer to this question depends on how we understand citizenship and freedom. According to one conception of freedom prominent in the political discourse of our day, to be free is to choose one's ends for oneself. This might be called the "liberal conception" of freedom. It holds that moral and civic obligations are the products of choice by individuals. According to a rival conception of freedom, a republican conception, to be free is not simply to choose one's ends but to share in self-rule, to participate in shaping the forces that govern the destiny of the community as a whole.[1]

The liberal and republican understandings of freedom lead to different accounts of citizenship and character formation. From the standpoint of the liberal conception, character formation runs the risk of coercion. If the point of politics is to create a framework of rights within which people can choose their own purposes and ends, for the political community to shape the character of its citizens is to interfere with freedom, to be coercive.

On the republican conception, by contrast, character formation is essential to freedom. Why can't people participate in self-government without the political community worrying about their characters? The reason is that in the republican picture, to share in self-rule is not simply to register one's interests and preferences on election day. It is to deliberate about the common good. The republican tradition emphasizes that deliberation about the common good requires citizens who possess certain qualities of character, certain habits and dispositions, qualities that equip them for self-rule. On the republican conception, to share in self-rule, to deliberate about common purposes and ends, requires certain civic virtues; the political community as a whole therefore has a stake in the character of citizens. On the republican account of freedom, politics is a formative project. It aims to cultivate the character, the habits, and the dispositions of citizens.

SOULCRAFT IN THE LIBERAL STATE

Much has been written about the strengths and weaknesses of the liberal and republican conceptions of freedom. However, my purpose here is not to rehearse these debates as they have unfolded in contemporary political philosophy. Instead, I would like to consider the condition of our public life, the shape of our politics now, from the standpoint of these rival theories. I would like to suggest that the liberal conception of freedom that informs our public life does exert a kind of soulcraft, in the sense that it tends to produce citizens of a certain kind. The practice of procedural liberalism perpetrates a de facto soulcraft that the theory of liberal freedom does not fully acknowledge.

What kind of citizens does procedural liberalism produce? What does its de facto soulcraft consist in? I would like to suggest (this cannot, of course, be a proof or a definitive argument) that the ideal of the freely choosing, individual self, unencumbered by antecedent moral ties, though in many ways a noble and high-minded ideal, slides into a practice and set of self-understandings that caricature, degrade, and even mock the nobler versions of the ideal. In the consumer society that we inhabit, the practice of procedural liberalism mocks—but in an eerie way also tracks and reflects—the more high-minded version of the ideal. In our contemporary social life, the ideal of the freely choosing, individual self is hijacked, absorbed, and appropriated by a commercial culture in ways that make manifest the disempowering tendencies to which it is prone.

Contemporary political argument is awash with worries about a neutral, proceduralist understanding of citizenship and freedom. However, a certain kind of politics of virtue has become familiar in our political discourse over the last twenty years. Talk of family, community, virtue, and civil society— themes long neglected by liberalism—has become a pervasive feature of American political discourse, though often in a hortatory way.

In the last two decades, these themes have been associated with conservatives, such as Jerry Falwell and Pat Robertson, Robert Bork and William Bennett. Liberals, at least until recently, have largely resisted these themes, fearing that the politics of virtue amounts to a politics of intolerance and coercion. But the cultural conservatives have struck a resonant chord. Their concern with character formation is well taken, even if their account of the source of civic virtue is partial and misleading. Conservatives like Bennett locate the threat to virtue-sustaining institutions in two places—the popular culture and big government. Rap music and vulgar movies corrupt the youth, they argue, while big government and the welfare state sap individual initiative, enervate the impulse for local self help, and preempt the role of mediating institutions. Prune the shade tree of big government, they argue, and families, neighborhoods, and church-based charities will flourish in the sun and space, not crowded out by the overgrown tree.

The cultural conservatives are right to worry, it seems to me, about the coarsening effects of popular entertainment, which, taken together with the advertising that drives it, induces a passion for consumption and a passivity toward politics at odds with civic virtue. But they are mostly concerned with sex and violence in television and movies. Where they are wrong is to ignore the most potent force of all, the corrosive power of an unfettered market economy. What they overlook, or at least underemphasize, is the way in which the operation of the market, especially in an increasingly consumerist and commercialized society, does the work of de facto soulcraft in the image of the voluntarist ideal of freedom.

Let me suggest a few examples of the way economic forces contribute to the de facto soulcraft of the procedural republic. Consider the growing gap between rich and poor. Today 1 percent of the American population owns about 45 percent of the total private wealth, more than twice the concentration of wealth in Britain. In fact, the net worth of Bill Gates is equal to the total net worth of the bottom 35 percent of the American population. The top 1 percent of Americans has a net worth that is greater than the gross domestic product of China.[2] Why worry about facts such as these? One reason to worry about the gap between rich and poor is that it is unfair to those on the bottom. They are cut out of the opportunity to share in the bounty of American prosperity. They do not have a fair opportunity to choose their own way of life, to choose their own ends.

But that is not the only reason to worry about the growing inequality of American society. The republican conception of freedom draws our attention to the way in which the character, the civic character, of both rich and poor are corrupted by this condition, in a way that destroys, or at least calls into question, the commonality necessary to self-government. The republican worry about too great a gap between rich and poor goes back to Aristotle, who said that both rich and poor are corrupted—in one case by luxury, in the other case by necessity.[3] In our time, the new inequality does more than prevent the poor from sharing in the bounty of an affluent society. It leads rich and poor to live completely separate ways of life. We can see how the worry of Aristotle is actually played out in our practice. Affluent professionals gradually secede from public life into homogenous enclaves. They buy their way out of public facilities and public institutions. The children of the prosperous enroll in private schools or in relatively homogenous suburban schools, leaving urban public schools to the poor. Over time, public institutions cease to be places that gather people together across class and race. Instead, they become the place for those left behind, for the poor who have no alternative, who cannot buy their way out.

Something similar happens with municipal services. They decline in urban areas. Meanwhile, residents and businesses in upscale districts are able to insulate themselves from those effects. They hire private garbage collectors, private street cleaners, and private police protection, unavailable to the city as a whole. What we find is a privatization and a commodification of policing and the police function. By 1990, the labor department found that for the first time, there were more Americans employed as private security officers than as public police officers. Americans now spend forty billion dollars a year on public police and ninety billion dollars a year on private security services in shopping malls, in airports, in condominium complexes, in private residential communities, and the like. Similar things are happening in Britain, Australia, and Canada.[4]

The republican conception of citizenship gives us a reason to worry about the fate of the public realm. The public realm is not just a place, the republican tradition reminds us, for common provision of goods. It is also a setting for civic education. Here is where the formative project comes in. The most damaging effect can be seen in the public schools. Ideally, at least, the public school is not just a place where the poor can get a free education. It is also a place where children of different classes can mix and learn the habits of democratic citizenship. This was the idea of Horace Mann and those who began the common school movement. Even municipal parks and playgrounds, the product of the progressive movement around the turn of the century, were seen not just as places of recreation but also as sites for the promotion of civic identity and community.

A more mundane example of the erosion of public spaces can be seen in the proliferation of luxury skyboxes at sports stadiums around the country. There was always a difference between the box seats and the bleachers. But sports stadiums, until recently, were among the last outposts of class-mixing public spaces. CEO's found themselves sitting side by side with mailroom clerks. Everyone had to eat the same soggy hotdogs. Rich and poor alike got wet when it rained, and everyone's hearts would sink and soar with the fate of the home team. But all that has changed. Now, every new stadium that is built has luxury skyboxes. This has transformed sports events in ways that destroy the class-mixing habits and shared sense of place on which sports and democracy thrive. I don't mean to suggest that fans once went to the ballpark for the sake of a civic experience; they went to see Ken Griffey, Jr., hit the ball a very long way. But the effect was an effect on soulcraft. The formative project was being carried out willy-nilly by the class-mixing aspect of the experience. Today, however, sports events exert a different kind of soulcraft, as luxury skyboxes segregate the upper crust from the common folk in the stands below.[5]

The trend began when the Dallas Cowboys installed luxury suites at Texas Stadium in the early eighties. It has now spread to almost every team in professional sports. I have seen it in Boston. The Celtics used to play in the Boston Garden, an old rattletrap of a place underneath North Station. In the glory days of Larry Bird, there was a sweaty, egalitarian intensity in the Boston Garden. There was no air conditioning, the sight lines were poor, but everyone was drawn together in the discomfort and the intensity of watching the Celtics defeat the Lakers in the playoffs. Today, the Boston Garden has been demolished. The Celtics now play in the sterile, air-conditioned, class-stratified Fleet Center (which bears the name of the bank that paid for the naming rights). Patrons of the Fleet Center dine in different restaurants on different levels, corresponding to ticket price. At the very top, there is a restaurant that is so exclusive that while the game is going on down below, patrons dine on pistachio-encrusted salmon. Unable even to see the court below, they watch the game on video monitors. In the new Staples Center in Los Angeles, a courtside seat—never mind a skybox seat—costs $350. And that is when the lowly Clippers are playing. When the Lakers are playing, that seat goes for $1,150. And then there are the skyboxes. They so dominate the Staples Center that when Bruce Springstein came to give a concert, he came out on stage, looked at these mammoth skyboxes, and called out "Come on out, now. The show is starting!"[6]

The advent of skyboxes has changed the character of sports stadiums as public spaces. A more egregious example of the commercialization of public spaces is the intrusion of marketing in public schools. Consider the case of Channel One, which brings advertising into the nation's classrooms. The business, founded by entrepreneur Chris Whittle, operates as follows. The company offers public schools free television monitors, VCRs, and a satellite link, in exchange for their agreeing, by contract, to show a twelve-minute television news program every morning and to require the kids to watch it. The news program includes two minutes of commercials.[7]

Eight million students in twelve thousand schools now see Channel One across the country. Since it reaches over 40 percent of the nation's teenagers, it is able to charge advertisers two hundred thousand dollars per thirty-second spot. As the company explains in its marketing literature, it is able to offer commercial sponsors access to the largest teen audience in history, in a setting "free of the usual distractions of telephones, stereos, and remote controls." The success of Channel One reflects the erosion of taxpayer support for public institutions and the commercial invasion that follows. Rather than raise the public funds that would be necessary to support the public schools that educate our children, we sell their time and rent their minds to advertisers such as Reebok, Pepsi, and Snickers.[8]

The commercialization of the public schools is an example of the growing tendency to fund government functions in ways that do not require higher taxes or civic sacrifice. As civic spirit wanes, commercialization fills the void. Another example is the trend over the last twenty-five years towards reliance on state lotteries to fund public services. Lotteries have the appeal of seeming to be a wholly voluntary tax. You do not have to pay if you do not want to. Nobody forces you to play.

The argument from state lotteries draws upon the voluntarist conception of freedom. Here is a way of funding government that, though corrupting in important ways, can be presented as a matter of choice. Of course, the system is not always as voluntary as it seems. Once states come to depend on lottery revenue, they have to promote the lottery and encourage people to play. Over four hundred million dollars are spent on lottery advertising by states each year, placing the lottery industry among the biggest advertisers in the country.[9]

Here is another instance of market-driven, de facto soulcraft. Though some object that government should not benefit from the morally dubious activity of gambling, lottery advocates point out that government benefits from other "sin taxes," such as taxes on cigarettes and alcohol. But lotteries are the only kind of sin tax where the state spends huge sums of money to encourage its citizens to commit the sin. Not surprisingly, lotteries direct their most aggressive advertising at their best customers—the working class, minorities, and the poor. A billboard in a Chicago ghetto advertised the Illinois lottery with the message, "This could be your ticket out."[10]

Think about the soulcraft, the moral teaching, that such advertising represents. In order to boost state revenues, government-sponsored billboards and commercials evoke the fantasy of winning a big jackpot and never having to work again. Not surprisingly, lottery ticket outlets and ticket sellers represent one of the few agencies of government that provide more service to poor and blue-collar neighborhoods than to affluent ones. Massachusetts has a state lottery that accounts for 13 percent of state revenue. According to a study by the *Boston Globe,* Chelsea, one of the poorest towns in the state, has one lottery agent for every 362 residents. Wellesley, an affluent suburb, has one lottery agent for every 3,063 residents. Residents in Chelsea spent over $900 per capita on lottery tickets each year, 8 percent of their income.[11]

The moral and civic cost of state lotteries goes beyond the regressive character of the tax and the number of gamblers who become addicted. These are grave social ills, but the greatest civic corruption is that the educative function of the political community is degraded as government is cast as the purveyor of a perverse civic education. To keep the money flowing, state governments across American now have to use their authority and influence not to cultivate civic virtue but to peddle false hope, to hold out the promise that a few lucky citizens may one day escape the veil of tears represented by the world of work.

THE SOVEREIGN SELF IN THE GLOBAL MARKETPLACE

The alternative to an explicitly public formative project is not a neutral arena of choice but a kind of soulcraft by default, exerted by the commercializing tendencies of market societies. These tendencies fit easily with the voluntarist conception of freedom that informs procedural liberalism. The high-minded picture of the freely choosing, sovereign self can be glimpsed in degraded form in the practices of an increasingly commercialized, privatized society. One striking illustration can be seen in the way the internet allows marketers to target children. One of the problems marketers have had is that though the internet enables them to reach children directly, children do not have credit cards of their own. A new website, "iCanBuy.com," offers a solution to this problem. It allows a parent to give his or her child a digital allowance, an e-allowance, by designating a fixed amount of money on the website. The child can click away, spending down the allowance from the digital account.[12]

Mattel has a Barbie website that makes explicit the link between consumerism and an ideal of freedom that emphasizes the capacity to choose, even to design, the things we want. According to a story in the *Washington Post*, experts in children's marketing view kids today as the "clickerati" generation. They are used to clicking on a mouse and do not want products that are prefabricated for them. On the Barbie site, called "My Design," you can design your very own "friend of Barbie" (FOB). "Pretend you were born after 1990," a Mattel marketer explains. "You want toys and games that are meant for you, not for who someone thinks you should be. You want to play your own way." Here we have the ultimate expression of the voluntarist conception of freedom. "You get to choose all kinds of stuff about her," the marketer continues. "You get to decide what her face or her skin color is, her eye color, her hairstyle, her hair color. And you get to choose what she is wearing and her accessories—because, of course, without accessories we're nothing. And you get to make up a story about her." When the customized doll is done, it can be ordered for $39.95 plus shipping and handling. Then, the marketer says, "We are counting on a conversion experience of them playing with it and saying 'Mom, look what I made!' and, eventually getting to the point where Mom says, 'Well, I guess I'll buy it for you.'"[13]

Here is the Promethean vision of the freely choosing, sovereign self. You make your own Barbie doll, to your specifications. Then you buy it with your digital allowance. Another advertising executive quoted in the *Washington Post* describes children's marketing in ecstatic terms, as if it were a source of liberation and empowerment. Part of what makes today's kids different, she argues, is that "they are one of the first generations to have been embraced at this young age as a marketing target." This "validates" them. "These kids are growing up feeling like, you know, 'I can make choices!' They are marketed to; they are being given reasons to think they are important. They get a say in decisions in the home." When you add access to computer technology, "you get a generation with a sense of power and optimism and capability that is quite magnificent."[14]

In the advertising jargon of the day, the new buyers are simultaneously producers and consumers, or "prosumers." Today, the marketer says, children "are accustomed to creating what they want. Not being given, 'Here are your choices. Do you want A, B, or C?' but saying, 'You know, I would really like B, G, and F somehow combined, and here is what it would look like.' So that is what prosumer really means. It is producer and consumer. The idea that they act as a consumer, but in the way that they produce something wholly new that they want."[15] Here, through a glass darkly, we see an ultimate expression of the voluntarist self—freely choosing, self-creating, seemingly sovereign, and yet, from the standpoint of civic life, ultimately disempowered.

Consider another website—this one for adults—that offers an eerily similar Promethean promise. "Ron's Angels" auctions the eggs of models whose photos are displayed on the site. The bidding begins at $15,000 and goes up to $150,000. *USA Today* interviewed two of the models, one of them a struggling actress in Southern California: "I'd rather do this than do *Playboy* or *Penthouse.*" She is asking $50,000 for her eggs. Another model is asking more; she wants to fund her tuition at USC. Ron Harris, the sponsor of the site, expects to sell $2 million worth of eggs a year. He gets a 20 percent commission. His background is well suited to his new venture; he has been a photographer for fashion magazines like *Vogue* and *Elle* and *Cosmopolitan,* and has also bred Arabian horses that sold for $200,000 each.[16]

Subsequent news accounts have suggested a fraudulent aspect to the site, and it is unclear whether it is a cover for a pornographic site or whether Ron Harris is really auctioning the eggs. In some ways, however, the ambiguity is beside the point. Buying and selling eggs for the sake of creating the right kind of offspring does not occupy only the netherworld of the internet. Recently, a large ad appeared in the *Harvard Crimson,* the student newspaper, offering $50,000 for an ovarian egg. The buyer was not interested in just any old egg. The ad specified that the donor had to be at least 5'9", athletic, attractive, and with SAT scores of 1,400 or above.[17]

The website that sells designer Barbie dolls and the ads for eggs to produce designer children express a certain aspiration to mastery. This aspiration reflects, even as it degrades, the ideal of persons as freely choosing, sovereign selves. In this respect, the ideal of freedom that animates the procedural republic, whatever its philosophical flaws, informs the self-understandings of contemporary consumer culture. This culture does not reject soulcraft but exerts an implicit, de facto soulcraft. In the name of the voluntarist conception of freedom, it shapes persons who think of themselves more as consumers with choices and less as citizens with duties and obligations.

THE CHALLENGE OF CITIZENSHIP FOR CONTEMPORARY DEMOCRACY

What can the republican tradition possibly have to offer under these conditions? Is it possible to reconstitute public debate about the formative project, about the qualities of character that modern democracies should seek to cultivate?[18] The global media and markets that shape our lives beckon us to a world beyond boundaries and belonging. But the civic resources we need to master these forces, or at least to contend with them, are still to be found in the places and stories, memories and meanings, incidents and identities, that situate us in the world. The public philosophy by which we live bids us to bracket these attachments, to set them aside for political purposes. But a procedural republic that banishes moral and religious argument from political discourse makes for an impoverished civic life. It also fails to answer the aspiration for self-government. Its image of citizens as free and independent selves cannot sustain the public spirit that equips us for self-rule.

Since the days of Aristotle's polis, the republican tradition has viewed self-government as an activity rooted in a particular place, carried out by citizens loyal to that place and to the way of life it embodies. Self-government today, however, requires a politics that plays itself out in a multiplicity of settings, from neighborhoods to nations to the world as a whole. Such a politics requires citizens who can think and act as multiply situated selves. The civic virtue distinctive to our time is the capacity to negotiate our way among the sometimes overlapping and sometimes conflicting obligations that claim us, and to live with the tension to which multiple loyalties give rise.

This capacity is not so easy to sustain, and any attempt to revitalize the project of soulcraft under modern conditions has to acknowledge the characteristic corruption to which civic virtue of this kind is prone. I have focused here on the corruption of the liberal ideal, of the voluntarist conception of the self. But where civic virtue depends on holding together complex identities, as it does today, it is vulnerable to two kinds of corruption. The first is the tendency to fundamentalism. This is the response of those who cannot abide the ambiguity associated with divided sovereignty and multiply encumbered selves. We live in a world that puts sovereign states and sovereign selves in question. It is therefore not surprising that this condition provokes reactions from those who would banish ambiguity, shore up borders, and harden the distinction between insiders and outsiders. We see a lot of that in our politics, including from some of those who preach the politics of virtue.

The second corruption to which multiply encumbered citizens are prone is the drift to formless, protean, storyless selves, unable to weave the various strands of their identity into a coherent whole. This is the drift toward a postmodern picture of the self. But political community depends on the narratives by which people make sense of their condition and interpret the common life they share. At its best, political deliberation is not just about competing policies; it is about competing interpretations of the character of a community, of its purposes and ends. A politics that proliferates the sources and sites of citizenship complicates the interpretative project. At a time when the narrative resources of civic life are already strained—as the sound bites, factoids, and disconnected images of our media-saturated culture attest—it becomes increasingly difficult to tell the tales that order our lives. There is a growing danger that, individually and collectively, we will find ourselves slipping into a fragmented, storyless condition. The loss of the capacity for narrative amounts to the ultimate disempowering of the human subject, for without narrative there is no continuity between present and past, and therefore no responsibility, and therefore no possibility of acting together to govern ourselves.

There is no guarantee that a renewed attention to character formation and civic virtue will lead to a revitalization of self-government. But the project of character formation cannot be avoided. If we do not attend to it explicitly, through active deliberation about the kind of citizens our public life should shape, the forces of the consumer culture and global economy will craft our souls instead. The challenge for politics now is to shore up the spheres of life that lie beyond commerce and consent, in the moral and civic goods that markets do not honor and money cannot buy.

NOTES

This essay is an edited version of a lecture delivered at the 1999 Pruit Memorial Symposium at Baylor University. I would like to express deep appreciation to Professors Michael Beaty and Dwight Allman, the organizers of the symposium, for their warm hospitality and thoughtful comments on my paper.

1. I develop this distinction more fully in Michael Sandel, *Democracy's Discontent: America in Search of a Public Philosophy* (Cambridge, MA: Harvard University Press, 1996), 4–28.

2. See Richard Newcomb, "The Richest People in America: The Forbes 400," *Forbes Magazine,* October 11, 1999, 169. See also, Edward Wolff, "Recent Trends in the Size Distribution of Household Wealth," *The Journal of Economic Perspectives* 12 (3): 131–50.

3. Cf. Aristotle, *The Politics,* 1295b.1–35.

4. "Welcome to the New World of Private Security," *Economist,* April 19, 1997, 21.

5. See Michael Sandel, "Spoiled Sports," *New Republic,* May 25, 1998, 14. Also, "Ad Nauseum," *New Republic,* September 1, 1997, 23.

6. Bob Ryan, "Usual Excessive Staples Aside," *Boston Globe,* October 29, 1999, E7.

7. Mark Francis Cohen, "Channel One Is Now Required Viewing in Many Schools," *Washington Post,* April 9, 2000, W20.

8. Cohen, "Channel One," W20. See also, Sandel, "Ad Nauseum," 23.

9. Michael Sandel, "Bad Bet," *New Republic,* March 10, 1997, 27.

10. Sandel, "Bad Bet," 27.

11. Sandel, "Bad Bet," 27. See also, David Halbinger and Daniel Golden, "The Lottery's Poor Choice of Locations," *Boston Globe,* February 12, 1997, A1.

12. Bob Thompson, "The Selling of the Clickerati," *Washington Post Magazine,* October 1999, W11.

13. Thompson, "Clickerati," W11.

14. Thompson, "Clickerati," W11.

15. Thompson, "Clickerati," W11.

16. Bruce Horovitz, "Selling Beautiful Babies," *USA Today*, October 25, 1999, 1A.

17. Cf. Rachel P. Kovner, "Egg-Seeking Ad Attracts Nearly 30 Harvard Applicants," *Harvard Crimson*, July 2, 1999.

18. In this and the following paragraphs, I draw from Sandel, *Democracy's Discontent*, 349–51.

Suggested Readings

BOOKS

Ackerman, Bruce, and Anne Alstott. *The Stakeholder Society*. New Haven, CT: Yale University Press, 1999.

Andrews, Geoff, ed. *Citizenship*. London: Lawrence and Wishart, 1991.

Audi, Robert. *Religious Commitment and Secular Reason*. New York: Cambridge University Press, 2000.

Bader, Veit, ed. *Citizenship and Exclusion*. New York: St. Martin's Press, 1997.

Barbalet, J. M. *Citizenship: Rights, Struggle and Class Inequality*. St. Paul: University of Minnesota Press, 1988.

Barber, Benjamin. *Strong Democracy: Participatory Politics for a New Age*. Berkeley: University of California Press, 1984.

Batstone, David, and Eduardo Mendieta, eds. *The Good Citizen*. New York: Routledge, 1999.

Battistoni, Richard M. *Public Schooling and the Education of Democratic Citizens*. Jackson: University Press of Mississippi, 1985.

Beiner, Ronald. *Philosophy in a Time of Lost Spirit: Essays on Contemporary Theory*. Toronto: University of Toronto Press, 1997.

———, ed. *Theorizing Citizenship*. Albany: State University of New York Press, 1995.

———. *What's the Matter with Liberalism?* Berkeley: University of California Press, 1992.

Bellah, Robert N., Richard Madsen, William M. Sullivan, Ann Swidler, and Steven M. Tipton. *Habits of the Heart: Individualism and Commitment in American Life*. Berkeley: University of California Press, 1996.

Berkowitz, Peter. *Virtue and the Making of Modern Liberalism*. Princeton, NJ: Princeton University Press, 1999.

Bohman, James. *Public Deliberation: Pluralism, Complexity and Democracy*. Cambridge, MA: MIT Press, 1996.

151

Bridges, David, ed. *Education, Autonomy and Democratic Citizenship: Philosophy in a Changing World.* New York: Routledge, 1997.

Brighouse, Harry. *School Choice and Social Justice.* New York: Oxford University Press, 2000.

Bubeck, Diemut. *Care, Gender and Justice.* New York: Oxford University Press, 1995.

Callan, Eamonn. *Creating Citizens: Political Education and Liberal Democracy.* New York: Oxford University Press, 1997.

Christodoulis, Emilios, ed. *Communitarianism and Citizenship.* Aldershot, UK: Ashgate, 1998.

Clarke, Paul Barry, ed. *Citizenship.* Sydney, Australia: Pluto Press, 1994.

Dagger, Richard. *Civic Virtues: Rights, Citizenship and Republican Liberalism.* New York: Oxford University Press, 1997.

Elkin, Stephen, and Karol Soltan, eds. *Citizen Competence and Democratic Institutions.* University Park: Pennsylvania State University Press, 1999.

Elshtain, Jean Bethke. *Democracy on Trial.* New York: Basic Books, 1995.

———. *Public Man, Private Woman: Women in Social and Political Thought.* Princeton, NJ: Princeton University Press, 1981.

Elster, Jon, ed. *Deliberative Democracy.* New York: Cambridge University Press, 1998.

Fullinwider, Robert, ed. *Civil Society, Democracy and Civic Renewal.* Lanham, MD: Rowman & Littlefield, 1999.

———, ed. *Public Education in a Multicultural Society.* New York: Cambridge University Press, 1995.

Galston, William. *Liberal Purposes: Goods, Virtues and Duties in the Liberal State.* New York: Cambridge University Press, 1991.

Glendon, Mary-Ann. *Rights Talk: The Impoverishment of Political Discourse.* New York: Free Press, 1991.

Glendon, Mary-Ann, and David Blankenhorn, eds. *Seedbeds of Virtue: Sources of Competence, Character and Citizenship in American Society.* New York and Lanham, MD: Madison Books, 1995.

Gutmann, Amy. *Democratic Education.* Princeton, NJ: Princeton University Press, 1999.

Gutmann, Amy, and Dennis Thompson. *Democracy and Disagreement.* Cambridge, MA: Harvard University Press, 1996.

Habermas, Jürgen. *Between Facts and Norms: Contributions to a Discourse Theory of Law and Democracy.* Cambridge, MA: MIT Press, 1996.

Hauerwas, Stanley. *In Good Company: The Church as Polis.* Notre Dame, IN: University of Notre Dame Press, 1995.

———. *The Wisdom of the Cross: Essays in Honor of John Howard Yoder.* Grand Rapids, MI: Wm. B. Eerdmans, 1999.

Hauerwas, Stanley, and William H. Willimon. *Resident Aliens: Life in the Christian Colony.* Nashville, TN: Abingdon Press, 1989.

———. *Where Resident Aliens Live: Exercises for Christian Practice.* Nashville, TN: Abingdon Press, 1996.

Heater, Derek. *Citizenship: The Civic Ideal in World History, Politics, and Education.* New York: Longman Press, 1990.

————. *What Is Citizenship?* Oxford: Blackwell, 2000.

————. *World Citizenship and Government: Cosmopolitan Ideas in the History of Western Political Thought.* New York: St. Martin's Press, 1996.

Held, David. *Democracy and the Global Order: From the Modern State to Cosmopolitan Governance.* Cambridge: Polity Press, 1995.

Holmes, Stephen. *Passions and Constraint: On the Theory of Liberal Democracy.* Chicago: University of Chicago Press, 1995.

Isin, Engin, and Patricia Wood. *Citizenship and Identity.* Thousand Oaks, CA: Sage, 1999.

Janoski, Thomas. *Citizenship and Civil Society: Obligations in Liberal, Traditional and Social Democratic Regimes.* New York: Cambridge University Press, 1998.

Kymlicka, Will. *Contemporary Political Philosophy: An Introduction.* 2nd ed. New York: Oxford University Press, 2002.

————. *Liberalism, Community, and Culture.* Oxford: Clarendon Press, 1989.

Kymlicka, Will, and Wayne Norman. *Citizenship in Diverse Societies.* New York: Oxford University Press, 2000.

Lehning, Percy, and Albert Weale, eds. *Citizenship, Democracy and Justice in the New Europe.* New York: Routledge, 1997.

Levinson, Meira. *The Demands of Liberal Education.* New York: Oxford University Press, 1999.

Lister, Ruth, ed. *Citizenship: Feminist Perspectives.* New York: New York University Press, 1998.

Lomasky, Loren. *Persons, Rights and the Moral Community.* New York: Oxford University Press, 1987.

Macedo, Stephen, ed. *Deliberative Politics: Essays on Democracy and Disagreement.* New York: Oxford University Press, 1999.

————. *Diversity and Distrust: Civic Education in Multicultural Democracy.* Cambridge, MA: Harvard University Press, 2000.

————. *Liberal Virtues: Citizenship, Virtue and Community.* New York: Oxford University Press, 1990.

MacIntyre, Alasdair. *After Virtue.* Notre Dame, IN: University of Notre Dame Press, 1981.

————. *Whose Justice? Which Rationality?* Notre Dame, IN: University of Notre Dame Press, 1988.

Marshall, T. H. *Class, Citizenship and Social Development.* New York: Anchor Books, 1965.

Marty, Martin E. *Education, Religion, and the Common Good: Advancing a Distinctly American Conversation about Religion's Role in Our Shared Life.* San Francisco: Jossey-Bass, 2000.

Mead, Lawrence. *Beyond Entitlement: The Social Obligations of Citizenship.* New York: Free Press, 1986.

Mouffe, Chantal, ed. *Dimensions of Radical Democracy: Pluralism, Citizenship and Community.* New York: Routledge, 1992.

Oldfield, Adrian. *Citizenship and Community: Civic Republicanism and the Modern World.* New York: Routledge, 1990.

Pangle, Thomas L. *The Spirit of Modern Republicanism.* Chicago: University of Chicago Press, 1988.

Putnam, Robert D. *Bowling Alone: The Collapse and Retrieval of American Community*. New York: Simon and Schuster, 2000.

———. *Making Democracy Work: Civic Traditions in Modern Italy*. Princeton, NJ: Princeton University Press, 1993.

Robbins, Bruce, ed. *Cosmopolitics: Thinking and Feeling beyond the Nation*. St. Paul: University of Minnesota Press, 1998.

Rosenblum, Nancy. *Another Liberalism: Romanticism and the Reconstruction of Liberal Thought*. Cambridge, MA: Harvard University Press, 1987.

———. *Membership and Morals: The Personal Uses of Pluralism in America*. Princeton, NJ: Princeton University Press, 1998.

———. *Obligations of Citizenship and Demands of Faith: Religious Accommodation in Pluralist Democracies*. Princeton: Princeton University Press, 2000.

Sandel, Michael. *Democracy's Discontent: America in Search of a Public Philosophy*. Cambridge, MA: Harvard University Press, 1996.

———. *Liberalism and the Limits of Justice*. New York: Cambridge University Press, 1982.

Sevenhuijsen, Selma. *Citizenship and the Ethics of Care: Feminist Considerations on Justice, Morality and Politics*. New York: Routledge, 1998.

Shafir, Gershon, ed. *The Citizenship Debates: A Reader*. St. Paul: University of Minnesota Press, 1998.

Sinopoli, Richard. *The Foundations of American Citizenship: Liberalism, the Constitution, and Civic Virtue*. New York: Oxford University Press, 1992.

Smith, Rogers. *Civic Ideals: Conflicting Visions of Citizenship in American History*. New Haven, CT: Yale University Press, 1997.

Spinner, Jeff. *The Boundaries of Citizenship: Race, Ethnicity and Nationality in the Liberal State*. Baltimore: Johns Hopkins University Press, 1994.

Spragens, Thomas. *Civic Liberalism: Reflections on Our Democratic Ideals*. Lanham, MD: Rowman & Littlefield, 1999.

Stassen, Glen H., D. M. Yeager, and John Howard Yoder. *Authentic Transformation: A New Vision of Christ and Culture*. Nashville, TN: Abingdon Press, 1996.

Tam, Henry. *Communitarianism: A New Agenda for Politics and Citizenship*. New York: New York University Press, 1998.

Taylor, Charles. *Sources of the Self: The Making of the Modern Identity*. New York: Cambridge University Press, 1989.

Van Gunsteren, Herman. *A Theory of Citizenship: Organizing Plurality in Contemporary Democracies*. Boulder, CO: Westview Press, 1998.

Vogel, Ursula, and Michael Moran. *The Frontiers of Citizenship*. New York: St. Martin's Press, 1991.

Walzer, Michael, ed. *Toward a Global Civil Society*. New York and Oxford: Berghahn Books, 1995.

Yoder, John Howard. *Body Politics: Five Practices of the Christian Community before the Watching World*. Nashville, TN: Discipleship Resources, 1992.

———. *The Christian Witness to the State*. Newton, KS: Faith and Life Press, 1964.

———. *The Royal Priesthood: Essays Ecclesiological and Ecumenical*. Grand Rapids, MI: Wm. B. Eerdmans, 1994.

Young, Iris Marion. *Inclusion and Democracy*. New York: Oxford University Press, 2000.

ARTICLES

Banting, Keith. "Social Citizenship and the Multicultural Welfare State." In *Citizenship, Diversity, and Pluralism*, edited by Alan Cairns. Montreal: McGill-Queens University Press, 2000.

Beiner, Ronald. "Citizenship." In *What's the Matter with Liberalism?* edited by Ronald Beiner. Berkeley: University of California Press, 1992.

Christiano, Thomas. "Is There Any Basis for Rawls's Duty of Civility (A Commentary on Weithman)." *Modern Schoolman* 78, no. 2–3 (2001): 151–61.

Dietz, Mary. "Citizenship with a Feminist Face: The Problem with Maternal Thinking." *Political Theory* 13 (1985): 19–35.

Enslin, Penny, Shirley Pendlebury, and Mary Tjiattas. "Deliberative Democracy, Diversity and the Challenges of Citizenship Education." *Journal of Philosophy of Education* 35, no.1 (2001): 115–30.

Fullinwider, Robert. "Citizenship and Welfare." In *Democracy and the Welfare State*, edited by Amy Gutmann. Princeton, NJ: Princeton University Press, 1988.

Gimmler, Antje. "Deliberative Democracy, the Public Sphere and the Internet." *Philosophy and Social Criticism* 27, no. 4 (2001): 21–39.

Habermas, Jürgen. "Citizenship and National Identity: Some Reflections on the Future of Europe." *Praxis International* 12, no. 1 (1992): 1–19.

Held, David. "Between State and Civil Society: Citizenship." In *Citizenship*, edited by Geoff Andrews. London: Lawrence and Wishart, 1991.

———. "Citizenship and Autonomy." In *Political Theory and the Modern State*. Stanford, CA: Stanford University Press, 1989.

Hill, Greg. "Citizenship and Ontology in the Liberal State." *Review of Politics* 55 (1993): 67–84.

Ignatieff, Michael. "Citizenship and Moral Narcissism." *Political Quarterly* 60 (1989): 63–74.

James, Susan. "The Good-Enough Citizen: Citizenship and Independence." In *Beyond Equality and Difference: Citizenship, Feminist Politics, and Female Subjectivity*, edited by Gisela Bock and Susan James. New York: Routledge, 1992.

Janara, L. "Commercial Capitalism and the Democratic Psyche: The Threat to Tocquevillean Citizenship." *History of Political Thought* 22, no. 2 (2001): 317–50.

Kymlicka, Will, and Wayne Norman. "Return of the Citizen." *Ethics* 104, no. 2 (1994): 352–81.

Macedo, Stephen. "Capitalism Citizenship and Community." *Social Philosophy and Policy* 6, no. 1 (1988): 113–39.

———. "Liberal Civic Education and Religious Fundamentalism." *Ethics* 105, no. 3 (1995): 468–96.

Mulgan, Geoff. "Citizens and Responsibilities." In *Citizenship*, edited by Geoff Andrews. London: Lawrence and Wishart, 1991.

Nauta, Lolle. "Changing Conceptions of Citizenship." *Praxis International* 12, no. 1 (1992): 20–34.

Nussbaum, Martha. "Patriotism and Cosmopolitanism." In *For Love of Country: Debating the Limits of Cosmopolitanism*, edited by Joshua Cohen. Boston: Beacon Press, 1996.

Okin, Susan. "Women, Equality and Citizenship." *Queen's Quarterly* 99 (1992): 56–71.

Oldfied, Adrian. "Citizenship: An Unnatural Practice?" *Political Quarterly* 61 (1990): 177–87.

Olson, Joel. "The Democratic Problem of the White Citizen." *Constellations* 8, no. 2 (2001): 163–83.

Pateman, Carole. "Equality, Difference and Subordination: The Politics of Motherhood and Women's Citizenship." In *Beyond Equality and Difference: Citizenship, Feminist Politics, and Female Subjectivity,* edited by Gisela Bock and Susan James. New York: Routledge, 1992.

Phillips, Anne. *Citizenship and Feminist Theory.* In *Citizenship,* edited by Geoff Andrews. London: Lawrence and Wishart, 1991.

Pocock, J. G. A. "The Ideal of Citizenship since Classical Times." *Queens Quarterly* 99 (1992): 33–55.

Pring, Richard. "Education as a Moral Practice." *Journal of Moral Education* 30, no. 2 (2001): 101–12.

Putnam, Robert. "Bowling Alone: America's Declining Social Capital." *Journal of Democracy* 6, no. 1 (1995): 65–78.

———. "The Prosperous Community: Social Capital and Public Life." *American Prospect* (Spring 1993).

Rorty, Richard. "Postmodernist Bourgeois Liberalism." In *Hermeneutics and Praxis,* edited by R. Hollinger. Notre Dame, IN: University of Notre Dame Press, 1985.

Shklar, Judith. "American Citizenship: The Quest for Inclusion." In *The Tanner Lectures on Human Values,* vol. 10. Salt Lake City: University of Utah Press, 1991.

Turner, Bryan. "Outline of a Theory of Citizenship." *Sociology* 24 (1989): 189–217.

Walzer, Michael. "Citizenship." In *Political Innovation and Conceptual Change,* edited by T. Ball and J. Farr. New York: Cambridge University Press, 1989.

Ward, Cynthia. "The Limits of 'Liberal Republicanism': Why Group-Based Remedies and Republican Citizenship Don't Mix." *Columbia Law Review* 91, no. 3 (1991): 581–607.

Weinstock, Daniel. "Citizenship and Pluralism." In *Blackwell Guide to Social and Political Philosophy,* edited by Robert L. Simon. Oxford: Blackwell, 2001.

Weithman, Paul J. "Reflective Endorsement and Political Autonomy." *Modern Schoolman* 78, no. 2–3 (2001): 135–49.

White, Patricia. "Decency and Education for Citizenship." *Journal of Moral Education* 21, no. 3 (1992): 207–16.

Wolff, Robert Paul. *The Ideal of the University.* Boston: Beacon Press, 1969.

Young, Iris Marion. "Mothers, Citizenship and Independence: A Critique of Pure Family Values." *Ethics* 105, no. 3 (1995): 535–56.

Young, Iris Marion. "Polity and Group Difference: A Critique of the Ideal of Universal Citizenship." *Ethics* 99, no. 2 (1989): 250–74.

Index

About the Contributors

Dwight D. Allman is an associate professor of political science and coordinator of the Oxford program at Baylor University. In 1999, he was co-organizer and director of Baylor's Pruit Memorial Symposium, at which the essays for this volume were originally presented. His publications include articles on Plato, Nietzsche, and contemporary citizenship. He is currently at work on a book entitled *The Citizen and the Soul: Philosophy: Religion and the Construction of Civic Life*.

Alexander Astin is the Allan M. Cartter Professor of Higher Education and director of the Higher Education Research Institute at UCLA. He has served as director of research for both the American Council on Higher Education and the National Merit Scholarship Corporation. He is also the founding director of the Cooperative Institutional Research Program. He has authored many publications concerned with outcomes of higher education, values in higher education, institutional quality, institutional leadership, citizenship, and the interface between research and policy. His most recent book is entitled *What Matters in College? Four Critical Years Revisited* (1993).

Michael D. Beaty is professor of philosophy and director of the Institute for Faith and Learning at Baylor University. In 1999, he was co-organizer and director of Baylor's Pruit Memorial Symposium, at which the essays for this volume were originally presented. His publications include books and articles on moral philosophy, philosophy of religion, and religious higher education. His most recent publication is "Identity and Relationships: Baptist Models—Past, Present, and Future," in an edited volume entitled *The Future of Religious Colleges: An Analysis of Christian Higher Education* (2002).

Jean Bethke Elshtain is the Laura Spelman Rockefeller Professor of Social and Political Ethics at the University of Chicago, where she also has appointments in the Divinity School, the Department of Political Science, and the Committee on International Relations. She is the author of numerous books and articles, including *Public Man, Private Woman: Women in Social Thought* (1981); *Democracy on Trial* (1995); *Augustine and the Limits of Politics* (1996); *Political Mothers* (2000); *Real Politics: At the Center of Everyday Life* (1997); and *New Wine in Old Bottles: International Politics and Ethical Discourse* (1998). Her most recent book is entitled *Jane Addams and the Dream of American Democracy* (2001).

Cary J. Nederman is professor and director of the graduate program in the Department of Political Science at Texas A&M University. His has many publications concerned with the history of medieval political thought and philosophy, which include *Community and Consent: The Secular Political Theory of Marsiglio of Padua's* Defensor Pacis (1995); *Medieval Aristotelianism and Its Limits: Classical Traditions in Moral and Political Philosophy, 12th–15th Centuries* (1997); and *Worlds of Difference: European Discourses of Toleration, c. 1100–c. 1550* (2000). His most recent book is entitled *John of Salisbury* (2002).

Walter Nicgorski is professor in the Program of Liberal Studies and concurrent professor of government and international studies at the University of Notre Dame. He is also the chief editor of *The Review of Politics*. His publications include essays on Cicero, liberal and character education, the American founding, Leo Strauss, and Allan Bloom. He is coeditor with Ronald Weber of *An Almost Chosen People: The Moral Aspirations of Americans* (1977); and with Kenneth Deutsch of *Leo Strauss: Political Philosopher and Jewish Thinker* (1994). He is currently at work on a book-length study of Cicero's political philosophy.

Michael J. Sandel is professor of government at Harvard University, where in 1999 he was named a Harvard College Professor in recognition of his contributions to undergraduate teaching. He is a former Rhodes Scholar to Oxford University, where in 1998 he delivered the Tanner Lectures on Human Values. His many publications include *Liberalism and the Limits of Justice* (1982); *Liberalism and Its Critics* (1984); and *Democracy's Discontent: America in Search of a Public Philosophy* (1996). He is currently at work on a book-length study of economic and civic life.

Nathan Tarcov is professor in the Committee on Social Thought, the Department of Political Science, and the College at the University of Chicago, where he is also director of the John M. Olin Center for Inquiry into the Theory and Practice of Democracy. His many publications include *Locke's Education for Liberty* (1984); an edition of John Locke's *Some Thoughts Concerning Education* and *On the Conduct of the Understanding* (1996); and "John Locke and the Foundations of Toleration" (1999). He is currently at work on a book-length study of Machiavelli's *Prince*.

John von Heyking is assistant professor in political science at the University of Lethbridge in Lethbridge, Alberta, Canada. He is the author of several articles on Augustine's political thought and of recent book entitled *Augustine and Politics as Longing in the World* (2001).

Alan Wolfe is professor of political science and director of the Boisi Center for Religion and American Public Life at Boston College. He is a contributing editor to *The New Republic* and *The Wilson Quarterly*. His many publications include *The Human Difference: Animals, Computers and the Necessity of Social Science* (1993); *Marginalized in the Middle* (1996); and *One Nation after All: What Middle-Class Americans Really Think about God, Country, Family, Racism, Welfare, Immigration, Homosexuality, Work, the Right, the Left, and Each Other* (1998). His most recent book is entitled *Moral Freedom: The Search for Virtue in a World of Choice* (2001).